Orange County, N.C.

Abstracts of the Minutes
of the
Court of Pleas and Quarter Sessions
of:
Sept. 1752 - Aug. 1766

By
Ruth Herndon Shields

Southern Historical Press, Inc.
Greenville, South Carolina

This volume was repropuced from
a 1963 edition located in the
Publisher's private library
Greenville, South Carolina

Please direct ALL correspondence and book orders to:
www.southernhistoricalpress.com
or
Southern Historical Press, Inc.
PO Box 1267
Greenville, SC 29602-1267
southernhistoricalpress@gmail.com

Originally published: Chapel Hill, NC 1963
ISBN #0-89308-456-5

Printed in the United States of America

FOREWORD

A FEW FACTS ABOUT ORANGE COUNTY, N.C. Orange County was formed in 1752, largely from Granville County, partly from Bladen and Johnston. (Granville was formed from Edgecombe in 1746.) The western boundary of Orange was indefinite until Rowan County was formed about a year later. Then Rowan became the western boundary.

FROM ORANGE COUNTY WERE TAKEN -
all of Chatham and Wake in 1771, part of Guilford in 1771,
all of Caswell in 1777 (Person formed from Caswell in 1792),
all of Alamance in 1849, part of Durham in 1881 (the other part of Durham County was taken from Wake, which was formerly Orange).
SEE THE MAP.

During the fourteen years covered by the MINUTES abstracted in this book, Orange was a very large county, containing all its orig - inal territory except the westernmost portion which had been cut off into Rowan. North Carolina was still the Province of Great Britain, and all county officers were Officers of the Crown, and owed allegi- ance to His Majesty King George the Third.

The Clerk of Orange County used several phrases to describe the nature of the quarterly court at which all legal business of the whole county was handled, with the exception of murder cases, trials for passing counterfiet money, appeals, etc., which were tried at the Superior Court at Halifax or Salisbury. This local quarterly court was presided over by four or more magistrates (Justices of the Peace) appointed by the Governor of the Province of North Carolina. Later three or more Justices presided.

In September and December 1752, in March, June, September and December 1753, in March and July 1754, and in January 1755, it was called " A Court of Common Pleas and Quarter Sessions ". In October 1754, the word " Common " was omitted. In March 1755 it was " An Inferior Court of Pleas and Quarter Sessions ". In June and September 1755 it was " A Court of Pleas and Quarter Sessions ", and in Sept - ember 1756, " An Inferior Court of Pleas and Quarter Sessions ".

In these MINUTES will be found registration of " Marks " for the ears of hogs and cattle (which roamed the woods), lists of Justices of the Peace, Constables, Commissioners of the Roads, Overseers of the Roads, " Road Juries " which were appointed to " lay out " new roads, all the county officers, both civil and military, all lists of jurors, all probates of wills, all appointments of admin - istrators for persons who died intestate, all references to orphans, all licenses for Taverns or " Ordinaries ", permits for ferries and for building grist mills, all suits, plus many other items. These have either been copied word for word, or abstracted. Everything which proves age, family relationships or place of residence has been copied.

SUITS. A large part of these MINUTES consists of short notices of hundreds of small suits. There was very little information given beyond the names of the parties involved, and the verdict. Many are for debt. Those listed " Or.Attch." (Original Attachment) mean that the Sheriff was authorized to take the property from the defendant and sell it for the benefit of the plaintiff. Many persons were imprisoned for debt. Many declared themselves insolvent.

Those suits marked " T.A.B. " seem to be personal quarrels. In many of them women are involved. The abbreviation " & Ux'r " is for " et Uxor " (and wife). In some of these cases the verdict was "False Clamor ", but in most of them the plaintiff was awarded a few pennies damages and the defendant had to pay the costs. " Sciere Facias " was an action to keep the case alive.

DEEDS. There are hundreds of short items about deeds. These were proved by a witness to the deed or otherwise, and then " ordered to be registered ". The old book in which these deeds were registered (one line for each registration) is now in the Archives of the N.C. Historical Commission in Raleigh, N.C., so I have not copied the names involved. The deeds themselves were recorded in Hillsborough. The deeds (grants) from the Earl of Granville are in the Secretary of State's files in Raleigh. A few deeds were proved by the affirmation of Quakers. A few were for lots in the county seat, and a few mentioned wives. These have been copied.

THE COUNTY SEAT. The courthouse was not built at the first site chosen (see page 1-2). This was on Haw River. The courthouse was built in the " Town laid out on the Enoe " (page 24-47). This " Town " was first called Orange Courthouse, then Corbintown, Childsburg, and lastly, Hillsborough. The name was officially fixed as Hillsborough in November 1766.

OMISSIONS. A few items were not abstracted, such as payment for serving as a juror at Superior Court, since the jury lists are given. The Justices presiding at each session have not always been copied; many times they were not listed. Repetitive items about extra pay, etc., for county officers have not been copied.

I am much indebted to Mrs. Alma Cheek Redden, of Hillsborough, N.C. She made it possible for me to complete this book by taking me along to Raleigh so many times, as she worked on her own volume of abstracts of the Minutes. Her book is a companion to, and a continuation of this one. See the last page of this book for a description of her book, and for two books of Orange County Wills which I published a few years ago.

It is my sincere wish that these MINUTES will be useful to students of local history, as well as to persons interested in family history. If they understand the significance of one group of items - the " Road Juries "- they will grasp the fact that these men were pioneers, who had recently moved into what was practically a pathless forest a very few years earlier.

Ruth Herndon Shields

Chapel Hill, N. C.
December 1965

O R A N G E   C O U N T Y,   N.   C.
1 7 5 2

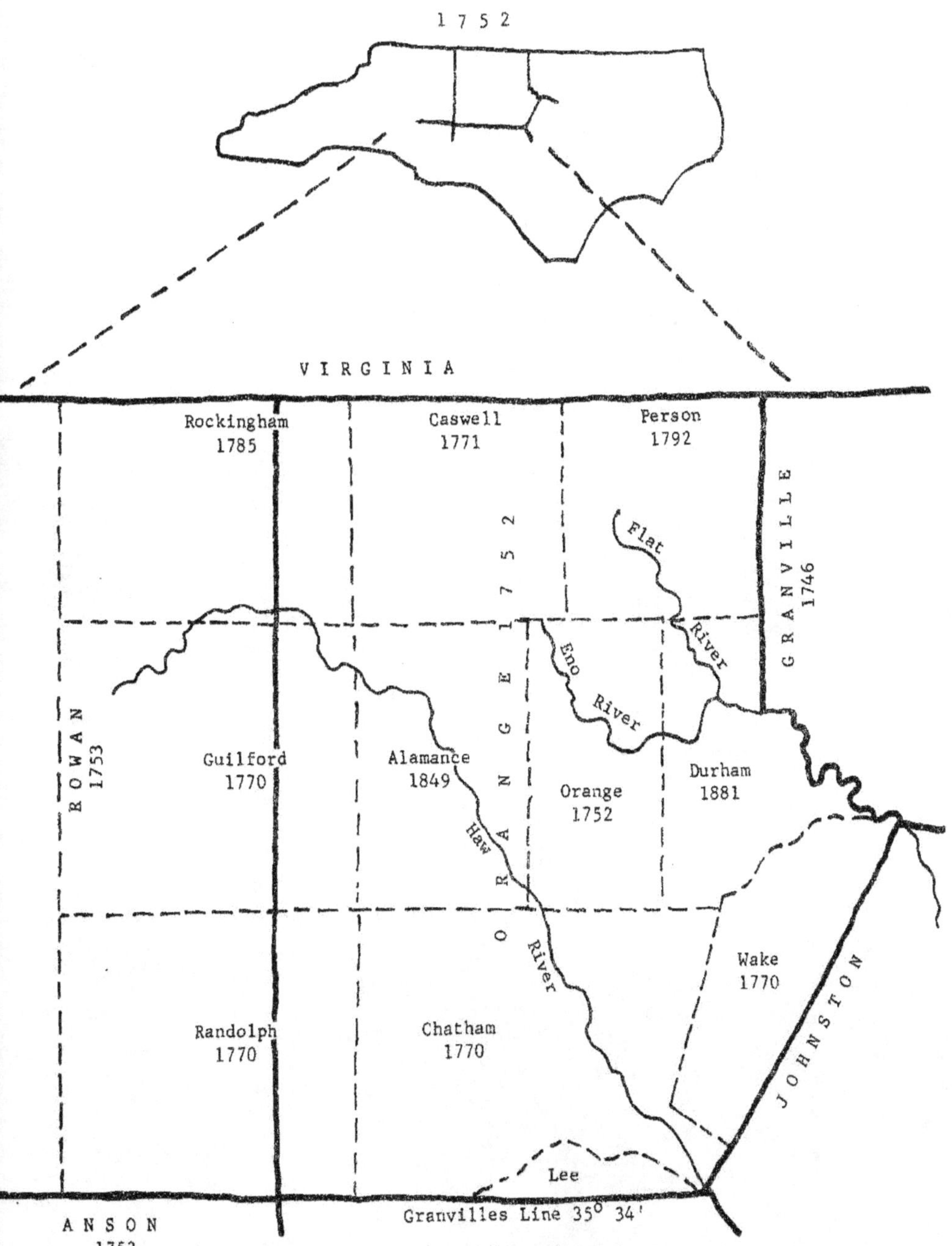

ABSTRACTS OF THE MINUTES OF THE COURT OF PLEAS & QUARTER SESSIONS OF ORANGE COUNTY, N. C.

September 1752 through August 1766

Folio and page# 1-1 The first court of the newly-formed county was held at the home of Mr. John Gray on Eno River. It began the 2nd Tuesday of September 1752, which was the 9th day. Gabriel Johnston was Governor of North Carolina at this time.

The eight Justices present were:

Lawrence Bansom (Bankston)	John Patterson
Andrew Mitchel	John Pittman
James Dickey	Marmaduke Kimbrough
Mark Morgan	Joseph Tate

The first items in the minutes are the Cattle marks registered by Henry Bedingfield, Lawrence Bankson & William Serjant.

The Grand Jury called & Impanelled - to wit-

William Chambers	1	John Pike	6	John Tinnen	11
William Coupling	2	John Sidwel	7	William Miers	12
James Hendricks	3	David Staptoe	8	Lawrence Rambo	13
John Hurley	4	William Serjant	9	Robert Taylor	14
Anthony Chamney	5	James McAlister	10	Cairnes Tinnen	15

Deed of Gift from John Douglas to his son George Douglas, for chattels. Proved by oath of Andrew Mitchel & James Dickey.

1-1' Deed of Gift from Joseph Wells to his son Joseph Wells, for 269 acres, proved by oath of John Pike.

A Courthouse for the new county to "be built near the Piney ford on haw river & on the north side of said River" - 32 feet long - 22 ft wide - & 11 ft pitch. etc. - prison & stocks. etc. - (specifications given). Marmaduke Kimbrough to build them - his securities were William Miers & John Sidwell. James Allison, James Dickey & John Pittman to select a site within two miles of Piney Ford on Haw River. (This item is over half a page long).

Edward Ball, an orphan, 16 years old bound to James Lea until he is 21 yrs. old.

The Quaker, John Sidwell, was granted Administration on the Estate of his brother Joseph Sidwell, dec'd. Bond 80 pounds. Bondsmen: Joseph Wells, David Miers.

1-2' "In pursuance of the act of the General Assembly etc, the Court do appoint the following persons Commissioners of the Roads, to wit-
James Dickey, John Pittman & James Allison from the County line to the Haw River -

Court of September 1752, Continued.

Mark Morgan, John Patterson & William Rhodes from the lower line of the County up between Nuse & Haw River to the Trading Path -
Timothy Terrell, David Miers & William Miers from the lower line up the S side of Haw River to the Western path -
Marmaduke Kimbrough, Henry Bedingfield & Joseph Boggs above the Western path on the S side of Haw River -
Lawrence Banckson, Josias Dixon & James Hendricks from Hico upwards-"

The county tax to be one shilling on each Tythable.

"Ordered that John Williams be appointed Constable from the trading path down the Eno to new hope".

The next court "to be held where the Courthouse is to be built".

2-3 Court of December 1752 began. Held at the home of Marmaduke Kimbrough. Justices present:

Lawrence Banckson	James Dickey
James Allison	Andrew Mitchel
Joseph Tate	Thomas Lovelatty, Esquires.

"Mr. Underhill presented a commission from Gabriel Johnson, Esq. late Governor, to William Churton, gent., constituting him public Register of Orange County" - Mr. Churton is unable to attend at present.

Mr. William Reed was appointed Deputy to Mr. Churton.

"The Grand Inquest called & Impanelled to wit -

Hosea Tapley	1	Robert Nelson	5	Cairnes Tinnen	9
James Watkins	2	William Coupland	6	John Tinnen	10
William Reves	3	John McFarland	7	David Mitchel	11
James Forrest	4	Robert Thompson	8	James Swafort	12
				Robert Harper	13"

Cattle marks recorded by Wm. Pitman, Jr., Wm. Pitman, Sr, John Pitman, Miles Parker, James Watkins.

2-3' John Boyd granted license to keep an Ordinary. Securities were James Dickey, Esq., & Robert Tate.

Joseph Pinson granted license to keep an Ordinary.
John Pitman, Esq., " " " " " " .

Power of Att'y from Zachariah Martin to his son Zach. Martin, Jr. recorded.

2-4 Henry Shaddock's petition to keep a Ferry on Haw River & Deep River was rejected.

"Court adjourned til tomorrow at 8 o'clock".

Court of December 1752, continued -

Present: James Dickey, John Pittman, James Allison, Andrew Mitchel, Esqs.

Marmaduke Kimbrough Esq. granted license to keep an Ordinary.

"Following Jurors were sworn to wit -
William Blackwood, James McGowan, David Steel, John McDaniel, William Nelson, Samuel Nelson, William Meand (?), Robert Eusen (?)(Huston?), William Mebane, Henry Shaddock, Miles Parker, Robert Tate."

Richard Cronk granted letters of Administration on the Estate of Jacob Pratt, dec'd, he being the greatest creditor.

John May appointed a Constable on the S side of Rocky River.

2-4' The King against John Chapman - Issue of Traverse - not guilty.
Deed from Hosea Tapley & Sarah his wife to William Taylor - 64 acres.

3-5 Henry Shaddock proves an account of £ 2.0.2. against Ruth Creel (?).

Mr. Underhill says Thomas Combast (?) is not liable for taxes in Orange County.

3-5' Alex. Mebane, Esq petitions "to build a Grist Mill on Haw River near the trading path"... granted.

... "following persons chosen to serve as Jurors at the next General Court - to wit -

James Watkins Joseph Seals (?) Richard Cronk	Grand Jurors	Michael Dixon David Stapler Timothy Terrell	Petty Jurors"

"Court adjourned till Court in Course"

3-5' Court of March began on the 13th day, at the Courthouse.

Justices presiding: James Dickey, John Patterson, James Allison, Joseph Tate

Mr. Reed presented his Commission from Richard Caswell, Clerk of the County, appointing him Deputy Clerk -

Deed from John Sidwell to Thomas Matthews for 240 acres proved by the affirmation of Joseph Wells, a Quaker.

3-6 "Grand Jury called & Impanelled to wit" -
Henry Bedingfield, Benjamin Martin, James McAlester, John Devon (?), Lodowick Clap, John McFarland, Zachariah Martin, William Miers, Abraham Whithersworth, Lawrence Rambo, Robert Patterson, David Stapler, & Thos Mathews.

Court of March 1753, Continued.

Robert Harris' cattle mark recorded. Also Zach. Headle & Thomas Saxton or Laxton.

William Morrow granted leave to keep an Ordinary at his dwelling house in the Haw fields. Security: Alex Mebane, Esq.

"John West, Sr appointed Constable in the room of James Owen."

3-6' Cattle marks recorded by Daniel Stilwel & John Pryor.

"James McGee appointed Constable in the room of John McAdow."

George Hut (?) was charged 2 Tythables for 1752, had only 1.
Richard Hasell (?) was not a Tythable in 1752.
William Reynolds was charged an extra Tythable in 1752.

4-7 Abraham Whitworth was appointed Adm. of Jacob Prat, dec'd, he being the principal creditor, instead of Richard Cronk.

A deed of marriage settlement between Elizabeth Douglas and William Reed was exhibited in open court and ordered to be registered. (They were married in Pennsylvania ? See Court of July 1754.)

John Cargdel came & swore that "Henry Davenport was reputed a Tattler, & Disturber where he lived in Virginia."

"Ordered that Marmaduke Kimbrough Esq, Henry Bidings & Joseph Boggs be appointed Commissioners of the Roads from the Lower line up the South side of haw River to the western path in the room of Timothy Terrell, David Miers & William Miers."

4-7' John Williams, John McGee & John West, Constables to attend next Court -

"Court adjourned till Court in Course."

List of 16 men who were appointed as Justices of the Peace the 2nd Tuesday in June (12th day) 1752.
James Watson, Alexander Mebane, James Dickey, John Gray, Lawrence Bankson, Mark Morgan, John Patterson, Andrew Mitchel, John Pitman, James Allison, Marmaduke Kimbrough, Josias Dixon, Joseph Boggs, John Pryor, John Gordon, & Lawrence Thompson, Esquires.

All have qualified and taken the oaths.

4-7' Court of June 1753 began on 2nd Tuesday, 12th day.

4-8 Richard Caswell was qualified as Clerk of Court of Orange County.

William Reed was appointed Standard Keeper for the County.

Court of June 1753 continued -

4-8 Commissioners for running the dividing line between Orange, Granville, & Johnston counties are to get 10 shillings per day.
William Churton to get 10 shillings per day as Surveyor.

4-8' "The following Military officers of this county"... qualified:
"Josias Dixon Lieutenant Colonel Mebane Major Mark Morgan John Gray
James Watson James Dickey John Gordon -
Lawrence Thompson Robert Harper & Joseph Boggs Captains."
(If there was ever any punctuation it has faded away.)

William Churton produced his commission as Public Register for Orange County, and qualified. Securities: Michael Synnot & John Gray Esq.

Cattle marks recorded by James Watson, Zachariah Martin, William Johnson, John Hunter.

5-9 "Grand Inquest"... Impanelled & sworn -
Henry Bedingfield, Abraham Whitworth, John Dunnagan, John White, John Rhodes, William Copeland, William Rhodes, William Reaves, William Miers, James Swafort, Lodowick Clap, Robert Patterson, Thomas Mathews, Hosea Tapley, James Hendricks.

3 Deeds from James Taylor proved & registered.
Deed - James Taylor to Judith Coates for 320 acres.
" " " " Thomas Utley " 381 acres.
" " " " John Taylor " 320 acres.
All proved in open Court by James Taylor, and registered.

5-9' "The following persons appointed Constables to wit -
Thomas Prestwood app. Constable in the room of Richard Parker.
James Currie Constable at Hico (?)
Jsoeph Duncanson Constable at Enoe.
Samuel Sowel (or Sorrel or Lowel) in the room of Hugh Dobbin.
James Williams in the room of Daniel McDaniel.
Peter Helton in the room of Gabriel Johnson.
William Johnson in the room of James Collins."

Cattle marks recorded by David Stapler (?) & John White.

5-10 Wm. Vanal (?) proved his attendance at court in behalf of Wm. Miers in the suit of Patrick Boggan.

	Thomas Smith	vs	William Williams	In Case
5-10'	" "	"	Thomas Coates	" "
	Michael Synnot	"	Charles Fogerson	Debt
5-11	" "	"	Benjamin Boling	In Case
5-11'	Joseph Bridger, Assignee	"	Elisha Fowler	" "
	Benton, Assignee of Goss	"	William Cox	" "
6-12	Samuel Benton	"	Benjamin Boling	" "
6-12'	Patrick Boggan	"	William Miers	" "
	Josias Dixon	"	James Satterfield	Slander

Court of June 1753 continued -

7-13	Anthony Metcalf	vs	Robert Cate	In Debt
	William Eaton	"	Thomas Priesthood	In Case
	Richard Knight	"	Charles Dodson	" "
7-13'	John Ford, Ex. &	"	James Lanceford (?)	" "
	Peter Wilson	"	Richard Robins	" "

7-14 Inventory of Joseph Sidwel, filed by Joseph Sidwel, Quaker, Adm.

Samuel Nelson prayed that Timothy Tyrrell be bound to good behavior. Tyrrell's Securities: Josias Dixon & James Dickey.

The King vs Henry Reynolds - Issue of Traverse.
" " " Benjamin Merrit - " " "
7-14' " " " Joseph Dolittle - " " "

8-15 "The following Jurors impanelled & sworn to wit - Giles Tillet, David Steel, John West, Alexander West, Thomas Saxton, Daniel Stilwel, Joseph Boring, Robert Tate, William Wilson, Joseph Pinson, Braswell Brashear, William Kilgore."

	Samuel Benton	vs	Thomas Mathews	In Case
	Dolittle	"	Hughes	" "
8-15'	Maccadow	"	Merret	" "
8-16	Johnson	"	Davis	" "
	Synnot, Assignee	"	Owen	" "
8-16'	Pittman	"	Headle	" "
	Johnson	"	Combast	" "
9-17	"	"	McAdow	" "
9-17'	McAdow	"	Chapman	" "
	Allison	"	Brown	" "

9-18 "Ordered that Thomas Prestwood, Joseph Duncan & John McGee, Constables, be appointed to attend the next Inferior Court."

"Court adjourned till Court in Course."

Court of September began 2nd Tuesday, 11th day, 1753.

9-18' Cattle marks recorded by John Wade, John Douglas, Joseph Sharp, & Elizabeth Reed.

Deed from Anthony Chamness & Sarah his wife, to Richard Kemp, for 90 acres, proved by the affirmation of William Cox, Quaker.

Deed from Anthony Chamness & Sarah his wife, to William Cox, for 100 acres, proved by affirmation of Richard Kemp, Quaker.

Court of September 1753 continued -

9-18' "On motion of the Commissioners for running the dividing lines of this county ... the following attendance be allowed ...

To Mr. James Paine	22 days attendance @ 10 sh.	£ 11.__ -
" Mr. James Taylor	21 days "	10.10. -
" Mr. Josias Dixon, Esq	21 " "	10.10. -
" Mr. William Churton, Surveyor	21 days @ 10 sh.	10.10 -
" Mr. John Rhodes, Laborer	21 days @ 3 sh each	3. 3. -
" Mr. Joseph Barnett, Laborer	21 " " " " "	3. 3. -
" Mr. Mathew McMillen	20 "	3. _. -"

10-19' A negro boy belonging to Henry Webb is judged to be 10 years old.

"Thomas Mathews to be set in the stocks one-quarter-hour for his contempt, offered to this court."

10-20 "Mary Torrington petition this Court praying that an orphan female child, called Sarah Torrington taken from her in a forcible manner by a certain Ephriam Sizemore a mulatto & be bound to Miles Parker..."

Deed from Frances John(t)on, Exec'x of Gabriel Johnston, dec'd, was proved by James Taylor, Quaker.

11-21 John & Henry Pinsons, Execs. against Hosea Tapley. CASE

Deed of Gift from James Muse, Sr. to James Muse, Jr. for negroes, hogs, horses, cattle, beds & furniture, etc.
Witnesses: Giles Tillet, Charles Steel, Alex. Going ? or Young?.

11-21' Deed of Sale from James Swafort to James Dixon, 159 acres.
Deed of Gift Thomas Wilkinson to Francis Wilkinson, land.

11-22 Petition of Joseph Davis concerning two orphan children (their names not stated) to be considered later.

Marks recorded by James Forrest, Sr and Mathew Couch.

11-22' Michael Synnot granted license to keep an Ordinary at his dwelling house at Little River.

Patrick Boggan granted license to keep an Ordinary at his dwelling house at Little River.

..."following persons appointed to serve as grand jurors - Jno Gray, John Hendricks, John Pryor, John Wade, John White, Zachariah Martin, Jr., Jno. Gordon, Hosea Tapley, Lodowick Clap, Hugh Wood, Miles Parker, Michael Dixon, as Petit Jurors".

12-23 The King against Joseph Frazier

Peter Gold, an Insolvent.

Court of September 1753 continued -

12-23 Jacob Brooks app. Overseer of Road in room of Henry Bedingfield.

Peter Hilton, Sr. app. Overseer of Road in room of Marmaduke Kimbrough.

"On motion of Daniel Weldon in behalf of Peter Youngblood - Ordered that a Capias Issue to take Benjamin Williams & Sarah Youngblood to appear before the Justices of next Court to be delt with as the law decrees."

"Ordered that John McGee, Thomas Prestwood & James Williams attend next Court as Constables & that they do not depart without leave."

12-23' Michael Sinnot against Stephen Merret In Debt.

"Court adjourned till Court in Course."

12-24 Court of December 1753 began 2nd Tuesday, 11th day.

Juctices present: James Allison, Marmaduke Kimbrough, Lawrence Thompson, John Pitman, Esquires.

Marks recorded by Hugh Wood, William Creeg (Craig), John Rhodes, & Henry Webb.

Two deeds of Sale for land proved.

12-24' Marks recorded by James Denny & William Rhodes.

"On motion of Mr. Parker in behalf of Joseph Davis, ordered that Elizabeth Aiken an orphan 9 years old be bound to said Davis" (until she is 18).

James Denny's mark recorded. Two deeds proved.

13-25 Bill of Sale from John McCarver to James McAllister for "sundry horses and colts" - dated 13 Dec 1753. Witnesses: Thomas Parker, James Allison

13-25' John Boyd's Ordinary license renewed.

Deed of Sale from John Wood to Robert Little, 320 acres.

John Wood fined 20 shillings for "profanely swearing two oaths in Court."

Hayes sues Cate "In Traver."

Court of December 1753 continued -

13-26	William Armstrong	vs	Edward Thompson	In Case
	Patrick Boggan	"	Giles Tillett	" "
13-26'	Peter Wilson	"	Abraham Whitworth	" "
	John McGee	"	William Miers	" "
14-27	Cairns Tinnen	"	Thomas Wilkinson	" "

14-27' James Dickey, Esq granted license to keep in Ordinary at his dwelling house.

"Francis Day, Alexander Mebane & Robert Erwin appointed Commissioners for the old trading path from the County line to Haw River and thence to the great Alamanze."

	The King	vs	Gabriel Crocket	Issue of Traverse
14-28	" "	"	..... London	" " "
	" "	"	John Ward	" " "
	.... Dickey	"	..... Mathews	In Case
14-28'	Adam Caruth	"	William Travis	" "

Brasel Brashear granted license to keep an Ordinary at the Courthouse.

William Johnson, Under Sheriff, to be paid 17 shillings for boarding John Aaron 17 days.

15-29 Moses Hollis app. Constable "about Dan River and the County line."

Grace Crockett to give security for her good behavior.

"Court adjourned till Court in Course."

Court of March 1754 began on 2nd Tuesday, 12th day.

Justices present: John Patterson, Lawrence Thompson, James Dickey, Mark Morgan, Esquires.

15-29' Five deeds proved & registered. James Clark's mark recorded.

James Allison, Esq. granted license to keep Ordinary at his dwelling house.

John McGee granted license to keep an Ordinary at his dwelling house in the hawfields.

William Craig appointed Constable in room of John McGee.
Thomas Cate " " " " " John Williams.

15-30 Thomas King appointed Constable "for Flatt river Little River and parts adjacent."

Court of March 1754 continued -

15-30 Cattle marks recorded by David Miers, Robert Reed, Thomas Whitehead, David Bradford, William Reed Jr, John Johnson & William Martin.

Deed from Robert Cate & Elizabeth his wife to Andrew Mitchel, Esq proved by James Dickey, Esq.

"Ordered that a Capias be issued against Grace Crockett to appear at next Court."

Deposition of Thomas Shiles - "He was drunk at the time of his having uttered certain Slanderous & Defamous words touching the character and reputation of Samuel Nelson & that he acknowledges them to be false & without grounds of truth & further that it was by the instigation of Timothy Terrell, that the said faulse & slanderous words were spoken --" Dated 5 January 1754 -
(Samuel Nelson was sueing Timothy Terrell, see 18-35).

15-30' Appointed to attend next general court, as Grand Jurors, William Reaves, James Rainey, John Wade, Mark Morgan, Joseph Boggs, & James Dickey.

As Petty Jurors, William Horton, George Laws, Lawrence Barbe, William Barbee, William Rhodes, James Wilkinson.

John Gray (10 votes), Lawrence Thompson (8) James Dickey (6), recommended as candidates for Sheriff.

"Thomas Hodge appointed Constable for the lower part of the County."

16-31	Liarges (?)	Administrators	against .... Cate	In Case
	James Boyd	vs	Thomas Lovelatty	" "
16-31'	John Dawson	"	Joseph Sooten (?)	" "
	Thomas Davis	"	William Bobbit, jr	" "
16-32	John Wade	"	Giles Tillet	Case
	John Dawson	"	William Wilson	In Case
16-32'	Michael Synnot	"	Andrew Banckson	" "
	" "	"	James Webb	In Debt
17-33	" "	"	Lawrence Bankson	In Case
	John Boyd	"	Baz'l Brashear	" "
17-33'	Hosea Tapley	"	Thomas Prestwood	" "
	Robert Harper	"	Dudley Reynolds	" "
18-34	Michael Synnot	"	Thomas Gibson	" "
	Joseph Montfort	"	William Reed	" "

18-34' "Ordered that the old road leading from the Haw old fields toward Cape fare be repaired and kept in order, and that the Inhabitants on the north east side of the said road & those adjoining .... work on the same ... that Zachariah Martin, Sr, William Copeland & James Collins be appointed Commissioners."

"Ordered that Robert Cate be app. Commissioner of Road in the room of Jo Patterson, Esq ... and Thomas Lloyd in the room of Mark Morgan, Esq.

Court of March 1754 continued -

18-35 "McAdow against Best - In Case on a Writ of Inquiry"
"Samuel Nelson against Timothy Terrel - Arbitrariment"

18-35' William Morrow's Ordinary license renewed.

A long item about the complaint made by "John Scott, a freeborn negro" in Berkley County, S. C., - that Joseph Dewit (?), Wm. Dewit & Zachariah Martin, entered by force, the house of his daughter Amy Hawley and carried her off, by force, with her six children, and he thinks they are taking them north to sell as slaves. The affidavit was made 17 Jan 1754.
Registered in Anson County, N. C. 20 Feb. 1754.
" " Orange County, N. C. 8 March 1754.

18-36 "Upon reading the above hue and cry, the court is of opinion that the mulatto boy called Busby is the reputed son of Amy Hawley as of oath of John Wade and found in the possession and custody of William Johnson".

"John Wade, having entered himself security that Thomas Chavis will deliver a mulatto boy Busby, alias John Scott to his reputed mother Amy Hawley. Ordered that he be delivered."

18-36' "Court adjourned till Court in Course."

19-37 Court of July 1754 began Tuesday, 2nd day, at the house of James Watson, Esq.

List of Justices appointed: James Watson, Alexander Mebane, James Dickey, John Gray, Lawrence Banckson, Mark Morgan, John Patterson, Andrew Mitchel, John Pitman, James Allison, Marmaduke Kimbrough, James Dickey, Josias Dixon, Joseph Boggs, John Pryor, John Gordon & Lawrence Thompson, Esquires. (Same list as that of June 1752.)

Court to be held on first Tuesdays in July, October, January & April.

John Gray Gentleman, qualified as High Sheriff for Orange County.

19-37' Five deeds proved.

"William Morrowmore app. Constable in the room of James Williams."

"On motion of Mr. Parker the last will & Testament of Samuel Harlan & the codicil thereto annexed was proved in open Court by the oath of James Vassey (?), & affirmation of Valentine Hollingsworth, being one of the people called Quakers...."

19-38 "Elizabeth Harlan, widow of the deceased, & Aaron Harlan, Executors thereof & qualified as such ..." See October 1754 Court, page 23. (This will is not now on record in Hillsborough, and is not recorded in Grimes ABSTRACTS,).

Court of July 1754 continued -

19-38 George Allen granted license to keep an Ordinary.

"Gabriel Davis appointed Constable in the room of James Currie."
"William Chambers appointed Constable in the lower settlement of Hico.
"William Barbee appointed Constable in the lower part of Enoe and part adjacent "in the room of Thomas Prestwood.

"Grand Jury called & impanelled to wit -
James Bowie, George Williams, John Dunnagan, Zachariah Martin, William Hellems, Lawrence Rambo, William Horton, William Rhodes, David Mitchel Hugh Wood, William Reaves, William Barbee."

19-38' Will of Joseph Hardin dec'd proved by oath of Benjamin Martin. Elizabeth Harlan, widow of the said deceased, appeared and qualified as Executrix. (This will is not now on record in Hillsborough, and is not in Grimes' ABSTRACTS.)

Thomas Burchfield asks to be struck off the list of Tythables.

20-39 James Crow has taken up "a parcel of swine"... they were appraised 30 March 1754 by William Barbee, Isaac Collins & Joseph Walker.

"Joseph and Mary Douglas, two orphan children of Jeremiah Douglas, late of Pennsylvania, dec'd." Josias Dixon and Lawrence Thompson are appointed Guardians to them. Elizabeth Reed, wife of William Reed, is the late wife of Jeremiah Douglas....
"Legacies left said orphan children in the hands of Thomas Brian of London Grove in the County of Chester in Pennsylvania aforesaid as left them in the .... will .... of their grandfather Joseph Sharp, late of Chester County ......"

20-39' Samuel Sorrell records his mark. Two deeds from Earl of Granville.

John Patterson, Esq granted license to keep an Ordinary at his dwelling house.

Tavern rates listed.

20-40	The King	against	John Dunnagan.	Recognizance
20-40'	Synnot	"	Forrest, Jun.	In Case
	"	"	" Sr.	In Case of a Suit of Inquiry

William Travis "a poor prisoner under Execution", declared insolvent. Adam Curuth is the plaintiff in the case.

James Watson granted license to keep an Ordinary at his dwelling.

21-41 "Ordered that the Tythables between the Orange New Road and the trading path be equally divided on the said roads as first delivered to the Clerk." (See page 37-73 for this list.)

Court of July 1754 continued -

21-41 "Ordered that Henry Reynolds, William Armstrong & Benjamin King be appointed Commissioners of the Roads between County line Creek & the upper line of this County."

"Court adjourned till Court in Course."

21-41' Court began October 1st, 1754. Held at Eno.

Justices present: James Dickey, Lawrence Thompson, John Gordon, John Pryor, Esquires.

Marks recorded by Mark Morgan, Bazel Brashear, James Latta, and John Boyd, Sr.

"Grand Jury Impannelled & sworn to wit -
John Anderson, James McAllister, John White, Robert Patterson, Henry Shaddock, John Tinnen, Cairnes Tinne, Lawrence Rambo, James Ray, Thos. Whitehead, William Boggan, George Laws."

21-42 William Barnett appointed Commissioner of Roads in the room of James Hendricks.

Inventory of Samuel Harlan dec'd exhibited by Elizabeth & Aaron Harlan Exec'xs. Their securities: John Anderson, Alexander Mebane, Bond: ₤ 1,000 proclamation money.

"Zachariah Headle, Sr appointed Constable in the room of John Duncan."

John West granted license to "keep Ordinary at his dwelling."

Administration on the Estate of William Young dec'd granted to William Nelson, he being the greatest creditor. Bond: ₤ 100.

21-42' Eight deeds proved.

21-43 Six deeds proved.

22-43 Marks recorded by John Boyd, Jr. & Richard Webb.

Patrick Boggan's Ordinary license renewed.

23-44 Three Bills of Sale.

22-44' Bill of Sale

23-45 1 Deed

Court of October 1754 continued -

23-45' .. "following appointed to attend next Circuit Court as Jurors - to wit John White, Thomas Williams, Samuel Bowie, John Patterson, John Pryor, Hugh Dobbin, as Grand Jurors.

John Hurley, Solomon Debow, Hugh Dobbin (C. line), William Copeland, John Dunnagan, William Miers, as Petit Jurors."

23-45' ...."Bastard infant male child named Andrew Sheppeard be bound unto David Pinkerton"..... to learn to read & trade of cordwainer ... if Pinkerton dies before Andrew is 21 years old, he is to be given up to Agnes Leach.

23-46 Four deeds proved, two by affirmation of James Taylor, Quaker.

"John Gray Esq, appointed Commissioner of Roads in the room of Francis Day."

"Ordered that the orphan William Roath (?) brought from Pennsylvania by Samuel Harlan, dec'd, be under the care of John Patterson, Esquire."

23-46' Bogan against Baker Case.

One deed of Sale proved.

24-47 Parish of Saint Mathews (Orange County) to be divided into Districts.

"Alexander Mebane, Esq. late Sheriff of this County came into Court and exhibited a list of Eleven hundred and thirteen Tythables on oath, which he had received and collected while he was Sheriff in the year 1752 and 1753."

Note by Ruth H. Shields. This entire list of "Tythables" was published in the December 1955 issue of the genealogical magazine THE NORTH CAROLINIAN. The name has now been changed to THE JOURNAL OF NORTH CAROLINA GENEALOGY (A Quarterly - $10 per yr.), P. O. Box 531, Raleigh, N. C. Copies of the December 1955 issue can be ordered separately. (The original list is in the N. C. State Archives at Raleigh, N. C.)

James Watson, Josias Dixon & Lawrence Thompson, Esq's, appointed Commissioners and Trustees for the Town laid out on the River Enoe. John Patterson, Esq. appointed treasurer, for the town.

"William Reed granted license to keep an Ordinary near the Courthouse."

24-47'	Bazel Brashear	vs	Edward Southwel	In Case
	John Brown	"	Lewis Howel	" "
24-48	John Martin	"	John Wood	" "
24-48'	Robert Jones	"	Francis Day	" "
	Daniel Weldon	"	John McAdow	" "

"Court adjourned till Court in Course."

25-49 Court of January 1755 begins.

Bill of Sale from Bur (x) Burton "of Enoe in the County of Granville, N.C." to Edward Stone, for £ 14, cattle, etc. Dated 8 June 1752.

25-49' Power of Attorney from Zachariah Martin, Sr. to Zach. Martin, Jr.
25-50 dated 23 Dec. 1754. Witnesses: William and Eliza Reed.

26-51 CASE Joseph Montfort against James Dickey, Esq.

"Court adjourned till Court in Course."

26-51 Court for March 1755 began Tuesday the 11th. Held at the house of James Watson, Esq. Ten Justices present.

26-51' List of Justices appointed for the coming year. No changes. (See 4-7' and 19-37.)

Hugh Smith appointed Constable in the room of John Creig.
Henry Hastings appointed Constable in the room of Thomas Cate.
26-52 John Long appointed Constable in the room of John Morrowmore.
John Fuller appointed Constable on both sides the Western path on the South side Haw River.
Thomas Wilkinson app. Constable in the room of Zachariah Riddle, Sr.
Giles Tillett appointed Constable in the room of Hugh West.

Jane Akin, 13 yrs old next May, to be bound an apprentice to Joseph Davis ... until she is 18.

William Nunn petitions to build a grist mill on the Enoe River "on the land of Col. Corbin and the Town land."

26-52' John Dennis granted license to keep Ordinary.
Alex. Mebane, Esq 's license to keep Ordinary renewed.
Thomas Barkley denied license to keep an Ordinary.

"Grand Jurors appointed to attend the Supreme Court on the 4th Tuesday in May next - to wit -
John Laspie (?), John Rhodes, John King, William Blackwood, Joseph Barbee, Joseph Pinson, Grand Jurors.
Timothy Terrel. Lodowick Clap, Samuel Donaldson, Robert Kilgore, Benjamin Cade, Zachariah Cade, Jr, Petit Jurors."

27-53 "Court adjourned till Court in Course."

27-53 Court of June 1755 begins 2nd Tuesday, 10th day, at the house of James Watson

James Watson, gentleman, qualified as Clerk of Court for Orange.

William Churton, gentleman, qualified as Public Register.

Court of June 1755 continued -

27-53 Mark recorded by Samuel Watt.

James Forrester, Sr. & Wm. Reves app. to appraise "a brown cow & yearling in the posession of Nicholas Culbertson & make return."

27-53' Two items about the Estate of Samuel Harlan, dec'd. Elizabeth Harlan & Aaron Harland, Exec's.

"... appraisment of a small black horse by John Jones & John Wright be recorded." Horse is in the possesion of Daniel Norris.

John McGee's Ordinary license renewed.

"A deed of sale from Hannah McCleland to John Rhodes, for the sixth part of the Estate of William Rhodes, dec'd, was proved in open court by the oath of Duncan Bohannon, Jun. and on his motion was ordered to be recorded." (Hannah was the widow of Wm. Rhodes of Middlesex Co., Va.) See also 31-61.

27-54 "Shadrack Jacobs appointed Constable on Rocky River, Deep River & the Country line" (Creek?).

"Daniel Hollifield appointed Constable on the Waters of Dan River & up the Country line" (Creek).

"William Travis appointed Constable in the room of James Nichols."

James Moss excused from service on Petit Jury.

James May, Constable, cited to appear and shew cause why he did not serve a warrant on John Brown & Josias Wallace.

John Patterson, Esq & William Blackwood were paid for their attendance at the Supreme Court in Edgecombe.

27-54'	Marget Flatt	vs	Michael Synnot	In Case
	Blake Baker	"	Wade & Laxton	" "
28-55	Baker	"	.... Levington	" "

28-55' ...."A child named Jesse Milburn - 2 years March 8th past be bound unto John Roberson" ... until 21.

7 deeds proved.
28-56 8 deeds proved.
28-56' 8 deeds proved.
29-57 6 deeds proved.
29-57' 5 deeds proved.

29-57 Marks recorded by Thomas Dunnagan, James Bowie, Michael Synoot.

29-57' Thomas Lapslie was paid for attending Supreme Court.

Court of June 1755 continued -

29-58 Bill of Sale from Robert Brashear to Hugh Porter, for horse & mare, proved in open court by William Porter, a witness. The other witness was Stephen Merrett.

29-58' "On motion of Mr. Baker, Att'y at law in behalf of John Patterson, Esq, to perpetuate the testimony of William Moore after being duly sworn saith he knew Robert Patterson of Bertie County, living on Meherring Creek, who was the reputed father of the said John Patterson, Esq, and that the said John Patterson was the only male child that the said Robert Petterson had, and that the said John Patterson inherited all said Robert Patterson's land, etc."
(John Patterson was one of the presiding Justices at the opening day of June Court. Robert Patterson's will in Bertie records.)

29-58	Moore	vs	Wilkinson	In Case
29-58'	Churcwell	"	Brashear	" "
30-59	James McGoan	"	David Brunt	Case

One deed proved, Michael Synnot to Thomas Holden, 500 acres.

"Ordered that William Thompson Alias Taylor be recommitted till next court."

30-59'	Othar Brashear	vs	William Porter	In Case
	Othar Brashear	"	George Finley	" "

William Phillips appointed Constable in the room of John Clapp.
30-60 Aaron Van Hook " " " " " " Samuel Sarrat.
John Anderson " " " " " " Thomas Wilkinson.

James McAllister app. Commissioner of Roads in room of James Dixon.

..."Hugh Dobbin be qualified to Execute an Execution against Joseph Dolittle in behalf of James Taylor"

30-60' Mr. ? Thompson granted license to keep Ordinary.

"Court adjourned till Court in Course."

30-60' Court for September 1755 began Tuesday the 10th at James Watson's.

John Jones & John Wright report, the horse taken up by Daniel Norris valued at 1 pound 5 shillings.

Bill of Sale from James Dickey to John Patterson, Esq for cattle. Witness: George Finley.

31-61 Full text of Bill of Sale from Hannah McClayland wife of Daniel McClayland to John Rhodes of Rowan County, N. C., Planter. Witnesses: Duncan Bohannan, Joseph Barbee. Dated 24 April 1755.

Court of September 1755 continued -

31-61' Bill of Sale dated 3 Oct 1755 from Thomas Prestwood of Orange County, N.C. to John Gray, for one negro boy. Witnesses: William Churton, John Pryor.

31-62	Joseph Tate	vs	John Wade	Case
	John Douglas	"	John Grimes	"
31-62	William Baldwin	"	William Johnson	"
31-62'	William Reves	"	Richard Burton	"
32-63	James Cook	"	Thomas Lovelatta	"
	Henry King Jr	"	David Miers	"
32-63'	John McGee	"	James Dickey	"
	Blake Baker	"	Lawrence Banckston	"
32-64	William Eaton	"	William Bobbit	"
32-64'	Thomas Barkley	"	Nathaniel Owens	Petition
33-64'	Thomas Barkley	"	Joseph Barker	"
33-65	Alexander Mebane	"	William Miers	"
	Henry Chambers	"	Henry Reynolds	"
	William Johnson	"	John Lambert	"
	John Dock	"	Robert Allison	"
33-66	Thomas Parker	"	James Dickey	"
	John Anderson	"	" "	"
33-66'	James Alliot	"	" " , Esq.	"
	Thomas Parker	"	Grayham & Reynolds	"
34-67	Osborne Jeffries	"	John Dover	"
	John Hamer	"	Flatt & Henderson	"
34-67'	William Horton	"	George Freeman	"
	William Blackwood	"	Robert Brashear	"
34-68	Charles Johnson	"	" "	"
	William Grant	"	William Goss (Goff?)	"
34-68'	Judeth Shearman	"	John Slater	"
	John Bumpass	"	Andrew Baker	"
35-69	John Boyd	"	Nathaniel Reed	"
	Samuel Williams	"	" "	"
	Thomas Osteen	"	John Phillips	"
35-69'	William Johnson	"	Joseph Dolittle	"
	Richard Knight	"	Thomas Cate, Sr	"
	John Patterson, Esq.	"	Thomas Addison	Debt

35-70 "Court adjourned till Court in Course."

Note: Here begin the meetings of the COMMISSIONERS OF THE ROADS. Some of these entries are duplicated in the Court Minutes.

35-70 Court of - (month blank) - 175_. No date, no place.

35-70 "Commissioners of the Roads for the said county ___

James Dickey, Jno Pitman, & John Allison from the Country line to Haw River ___

Mark Morgan, William Rhodes, & John Patterson, from the lower line of the county up between Nuse & Haw River to the Trading path ___

Timothy Tyrrell, David Miers, & William Miers, from the lower line up the South side of Haw River to the Western path ___

Marmaduke Kimbrough, Henry Bedingfield, & Joseph Boggs, above the western path on the South side of Haw River ___

Lawrence Banckston, Josias Dixon, & James Hendricks, from Hico upwards" ___

"The Commissioners for the District from the County line to Haw River have ordered that a Public Road be laid out & Opened from the County line where it crosseth the Trading path, the best & most convenient way to Orange Court house at Marmaduke Kimbrough(s), thence to the Pine Foard on haw River, to the Oald path of James McGowen under the Inspection of James Dickey. Andrew Bargdel (?)(Bridget?), James Allison, John West, Sr, & John Pittman be Overseer of the said Road."

35-70' March Court 1753. Meeting of COMMISSIONERS OF THE ROADS.

"Present his Majesties Justices, Etc" (No names given.)

"It is ordered that Marmaduke Kimbrough, Henry Bedingfield & Joseph Boggs be appointed Comm's of the Road from the lower line up the S. side of Haw river to the western path in the room of Timothy Tyrrell, David Miers & Wm. Miers who were app. at a former Court."

"On motion of Joseph Teat (Tate?) - "To the Commissioners, etc - It is ordered that a Public Road be opened twelve feet wide from the Court house to Giles Tillet's, thence to the said Joseph Teate's on the East side of little Troublesome and that the said Joseph Tate, John King, Giles Tillet & Joseph Pinson be appointed Overseers of the said road, Etc "-

35-70' "On motion of Mr. Weldon it is ordered that a Public Road be laid out & opened ... from the County line near to where M'Corgan (?) or Morgan (?) Brians Path crosses said line, thence to the upper Sorry Town, thence unto (Y)Adkin River & that William Haltham (?) & James Hampton be appointed Overseers of said Road."

35-70' "Monday, August 6th, 1753, the following Commissioners present -

James Allison, James Dickey, Marmaduke Kimbrough, Joseph Boggs, Henry Bedingfield, Commissioners."

William Reed appointed Clerk to the Commissioners. To be allowed 50 shillings for his services "this present year."

Marmaduke Kimbrough to inspect the road in his District from the Pine ford to the Great Alamance.
Joseph Boggs from thence to Jacob Brooks &
Henry Bedingfield from thence to the County line.

David Phillips Sr. appointed Overseer under Marmaduke Kimbrough.
Jacob Brooks " " " Joseph Boggs.
William Ellis " " " Henry Bedingfield.

36-71 September 1753.

Jacob Brooks app. Commissioner of Roads in room of Henry Bedingfield.
Peter Hilton, Sr. app. " " " " " " Marmaduke Kimbrough.

"Ordered that a Public road be laid out & opened, beginning at the most suitable place on the Western path, thence ... to the County line, leading to Cape Fare (Fear) & that William Barbee be Overseer of said Road from the beginning unto New Hope (Creek) & that Joseph Barbee be Overseer from New Hope to the Country (?) line."

36-71 "At a meeting - held at Marmaduke Kimbrough - 18th day of October 1753.

"Ordered that the Road leading from William Serjants towards Granville Courthouse, be straightened & cleared of all incumbrances for Travellers from between Marlow's Creek & William Barnets & thence to the County line-& that Wm. Serjant, from Hico to Marlow's Creek, be Overseer, & that Hugh Barnet be Overseer from thence to the County line."

Robert Brashear appointed Overseer of Road in the room of John West, Sr under the inspection of John Pittman.

36-71' "Ordered that Francis Day, Alex. Mebane & Robert Erwin be appointed Comm's of Roads for the Old Trading Path from the Country line to Haw River & from thence to the Great Alamanze."

"John Dunnagan Overseer of Road from Granville County line to Michael Synnot's -
Isaac Jackson from thence to the fording place of Enoe River -
James Morrow from thence to Alex. Mebane's Esq.
Hugh Smith " " " Haw River Hill on the S. side of said River

* December 1753

MEETINGS OF COMMISSIONERS OF THE ROADS continued -

36-72 "Ordered that the Old Road leading from this Court House through the Hawfields to Cape Fare (Fear) here (?) be repaired & kept in Order & that the inhabitants on the N.E. side adjoining work on the said road - & that Zachariah Martin Sr. Wm. Copeland & James Collins be appointed Commissioners."

"Robert Cate be app. Comm. of Road in the room of John Patterson, Esq.
Thomas Lloyd " " " " " " " " " Mark Morgan."

36-72 Meeting - 22 April 1754.

"Present: James Dickey, James Allison, Thomas Loyd, Robert Cate, James Hendricks, Francis Day, Robert Erwin, Wm. Copeland, James Collins, Peter Hilton, Commissioners."

A new road to be opened from "the Western Road near Cap't Synnot's to the new road leading to Cape Fare".... beginning on W. path between Cap't Synnot's & John White's ... thence to the Old Ford on Enoe River between where Wm. Reed formerly lived & where Wm. Gross lives, thence to Edward Stone's, thence to the new road leading to Cape Fare - & that Wm. Gross be Overseer under the inspection of Francis Day, - Edward Stone under the inspection of Mr Thomas Lloyd from thence to John Patterson's Esq & thence to the new road leading to Cape Fare --"

36-72' "On motion of sundry Inhabitants of the Governor's Settlement on Enoe for a road to the place Intended for the Seat of Publick Buildings Etc. -- Ordered that a Road be laid out and cleared ... to the place where James Watson, Esq now lives, beginning near the Great lick, on Hus (?) or Hico (?) path ...
Thence etc , & that Thomas Thompson & James Swafer be appointed Overseers under the inspection of Mr. Dickey --"

"On motion of sundry Inhabitants of Hico for a Road to the place where James Watson, Esq now lives --- road to be laid out ... beginning between Adam's Creek & Wm. Barnett's, thence to Flatt river & that John Harley be Overseer under the Inspection of Mr. James Hendricks - that John Cate be Overseer under the Inspection of Lawrence Banckson --"

"Ordered that a road be laid out ... begin ... on Little Troublesome, thence to Orange new road where Nathaniel Allison lives that James Nichols be Overseer under the Inspection of John Pittman & that the said road be 15 feet wide.

37-73 "Ordered that the following persons, Commissioners of this County, who have not appeared at this General Meeting be fined in 20 shillings agreeable to law, Etc --- William Rhodes, Lawrence Banckson, Josias Dixon, Alexander Mebane, Zachariah Martin, Sr, John Pittman, Joseph Boggs, & Jacob Brooks, Commissioners."

MEETINGS OF COMMISSIONERS OF THE ROADS continued -

37-73 "James Hendricks appeared & made a reasonable excuse at the last Genera Meeting on the 1st Monday in August last "- excused. Same for John Patterson, Esq.

"Zachariah Headle appointed Overseer in the room of James McGowen, under the Inspection of James Dickey, Esq."

37-73 July Court 1754

"Ordered that the Tythables between Orange New Road & the Trading path be equally divided & a list delivered the Clerk -

On Orange New Road		On the Trading Path	
1	James McGowen, Sr.	1	James McGowen, Jr.
3	William Creeg (Craig)	1	Hugh Bradley
1	David Steel	1	John McGee
1	Anthony Stanford	1	Thomas Strehan
2	John Hopkins	1	David Black
2	John Boyd	1	Israel Catcham
1	Benjamin Gatham	4	George Irwin
1	William Hopkins	1	James Hopkins
1	Gilbert Strean	1	William Gatham
1	John McCombs	1	William Miers
14	in all	14	in all" (Actually 13)

37-73' "Ordered that Henry Reynolds, Wm. Armstrong & Benjamin King be app. Commissioners of Roads between the Country line Creek & the upper line of this county "-

---

37-73' Monday, August 5th 1754. Fourteen Commissioners present.

John Hendricks app. Overseer of the Road in the room of Wm. Barnett.

..."Thomas Cate, Sr be appointed Overseer from the Camp branch to the Western path in Robert Cate's District & the following persons work on the said road
James Moss, Henry Hunter, John Hastings, John Gray, Henry Leman, James Railey, James Dickey, Charles Fogerson, James Tinnen, Joseph Cate, Richard Cate, & Robert Wiley."

37-74 ...."a Public road be opened 16 feet wide ... beginning at the fork of the road leading to Justice Pryor's thence by the place where Justice Dixon formerly lived, to the new Road where Mr. Van Hook lives, & that James Stewart be appointed Overseer under the inspection of James Hendricks & "that all the inhabitants on both sides of Hico as High as Edward William's work on the said Road."

MEETINGS COMMISSIONERS OF THE ROADS continued -

37-74 ...."Miles Parker appointed Overseer for the lower part of the road leading to Cape Fare under the inspection of Mr. William Rhodes, & Henry Bazell be Overseer from New hope to the head of White oak under the inspection of Thomas Lloyd."

....."Thomas Prestwood appointed Overseer in the room of Wm. Barbee from the Camp Creek to New hope under the Inspection of Thomas Loyd."

The following Commissioners excused for their non-attendance:
Lawrence Banckson was obliged to attend the General Court.
Josias Dixon " " " " " Commissioners for running the boundary line.
John Pitman was obliged to be in Virginia "last meeting."
Joseph Boggs had a fall from his horse.
Jacob Brooks & Zach. Martin did not know of the meeting.
~~Mark Morgan did not~~ know the time of the meeting.

37-74' ..."Mr. John Jones, John Wright & George Hopson be Commissioners for the Cape fare road on the S. side of Haw River from the Western path to the Country line ...."

37-74' October Court 1754.

..."Wm. Barnett appointed Commissioner of Roads in the room of James Hendricks."

37-74' Meeting of April 7th 1755.

38-75 "Joseph Pinson & Wm. Mills, Sr. appointed Overseers of that part of road under the Inspection of John Pittman."

"John King appointed Overseer under the Inspection of Thomas Loyd."

..."Joshua Stroud, George Smith, Thomas Cate, Jr, Richard Owins & Edward Carter ... to work ... under the Inspection of Cap't Robert Cate - John Gray, James Railey, Henry Leman, Henry Hastings & John Hunter ... under inspection of John Gray."

.."James Fruit app. Overseer under Alex. Mebane in room of Hugh Smith."

..."Road from the lower Sorry (Saury) Town to be laid out the nearer way to Orange Court House, & that Thompson Harris be appointed Overseer under the inspection of Benjamin King, & Thomas Bartin ? under inspection of Henry Reynolds."

John Dennis appointed Overseer of Road in room of Isaac Jackson.
Thomas Wilkenson " " " " " " " Zach. Headle.
38-75' James Hart " " " " " " " Thomas Thompson
& James Swaffer.

MEETINGS COMMISSIONERS OF THE ROADS continued -

38-75' Meeting of June 1755.

James McAllister appointed Commissioner for Roads in the room of Josias Dixon, Esq.

Meeting of 4 August 1755.

"Ordered that David Bradford be appointed Overseer in the room of Thoma Wilkinson, who has left this Government."

John White appointed Overseer in the room of John Dunnagan.
James Clark " " " " " " " " .

"Ordered that Thomas Branson, Jonathan Williams, Thomas Lindley, Wm. Miers, Daniel Norris & John Tomlinson be appointed Overseers of the Road to Cape Fare on the S. Side of Haw River."

"On motion of John Jones in behalf of himself & sundry other persons, inhabitants on the S. Side of Haw river, for a road from the Court House - to Mary Williams' on Haw River & thence to the Cape Fare road-Left under consideration until the next County Court."

"On motion of Joseph Mattock requesting a road ... from the Court House to his mill on Enoe River & thence to the Trading Path" -- granted.

"On motion of Wm. Barnett .. for a road beginning at the Virginia line near Holts (?) Mill, thence ... to Taylor's road on the Enoe & thence to the Court House ..." granted. "James Stewart to be Overseer under inspection of Aaron Van Hook, & Lawrence Banckson under inspection of Wm. Barnett."

"James Dickey cooper & Robert Wiley from hence forward, do work on the Trading path Road, & under the Inspection of Major Mebane."

"Court adjourned till Court in Course"

38-76' Court of PLEAS AND QUARTER SESSIONS for December, met at the house of Mr. James Watson, began 2nd Tuesday in 1755.

(No business except suits.)

	James Paine	vs	Thomas Lovelatta	Case
39-77	John & Wm. Baldwin	"	John Bumpass	In Case
	John McGee	"	David Miers	" "
39-77'	William Eaton	"	Wm. Bobbit	" "
	John Doch	"	Robert Allison	" "
39-78	Gilbert Everand (?)	"	John Dunnagan	Case
39-78'	Phillip Pryor	"	Lawrence Banckson	In Case
	Josias Dixon, Esq.	"	Wm. Gutterie	Case
40-79	Richard Dudgen	"	John Beverley	In Debt
	Blake Baker	"	Thomas Wilkinson	In Case
40-79'	James Collins	"	Zachariah Wood	In Debt
	Edmunds & Company	"	John Lyon	Petition
40-80	John Roberson	"	Andrew Banckson	"
	John Dunnagan	"	Thomas Jones	Debt
	Jacob Mitchel	"	Bazell Brashear	In Case
40-80'	Robert Jones, Jr.	"	John Wade	In Debt
	Richard Dudgen	"	John Beverley	Debt
41-81	Blake Baker	"	Thomas Wilkenson	In Case
	James Collins	"	Zachariah Wood	Debt
41-81'	James McCallester	"	John Dunnagan	In Case

"Court adjourned till Court in Course."

41-81' Court of March 1756 began 2nd Tuesday at James Watson's.

(No business except suits.)

	Joseph Bogs	vs	Henry Morgan	Petition
	Joseph Boggs, Esq.	"	Jacob Headle	"
41-82	" " "	"	Clement Reed	"
41-82'	" " "	"	Christian Morris	"
	Hugh Dobbin	"	James Collins	"
	James Cary	"	Richard Simpson	"
42-83	Thomas Lindley	"	~~Zachariah Martin~~	In Case
	William Mouat (?)	"	Alexander Awtree	Petition
	Thomas Wade	"	Moses Ridley	In Case
	James Dogester	"	John Rogers	Petition
	Samuel Benton	"	David Phillips	"
42-83'	William Leachey	"	James Lindley	In Case
	Hosea Tapley	"	William Aldridge	Case

"Court adjourned till Court in Course."

Court of June 1756 began on 2nd Tuesday.

(No business except suits.)

	Copeland & Company	vs	Mark London	In Case
42-84	Robert Jones, Jr.	"	Hosea Tapley	Petition
	" " "	"	John Dunnagan	"
42-84'	William Mouat	"	George Fagan	"
	" "	"	Alexander Awtree	"
43-85	James Dogester	"	John Rogers	"
	William Armstrong	"	George Adams	"
	William Reed	"	James Dickey, Esq.	Original
43-85'	William Eaton	"	Thomas Lovelatta	In Case
	John Wade	"	Barzeel Brashear	" "
43-86	William Eaton	"	William Cox	Petition
	Blake Baker	"	John Brantley	"
	Samuel Benton	"	Gideon Bunch	"
43-86'	John Farral	"	Henry Johnson	"

"Court adjourned till Court in Course."

44-87 Court of September 1756 began on 2nd Tuesday.

(No business except suits.)

	John Dunnagan	vs	Charles Gibson	In Case
	Gideon Linicom	"	John Cate	Petition
44-87'	Thomas Wade	"	Moses Ridley	Or. Attch
	William Eaton	"	Zach. Martin, Jr.	In Case
	John Boyd	"	Isaiah Watkins	Petition
44-88	Thomas Egleton	"	William Moore	"
	Blake Baker	"	William Johnson	"
44-88'	" "	"	Thomas Wade	"
	" "	"	Bazeel Brashear	"
45-89	Thomas Langley	"	John Caston	"
	James Cary	"	Michael Joyce	"
	William Little	"	Brazell Brashear	"
45-89'	Wm. Mouat	"	Wm. Johnson	"
	Francis Mabry	"	John Burt	In Case
	Thomas Lovelatta	"	Moses Chapman	Or. Attch
45-90	Benjamin Landrum	"	George Smith	In Case

"Court adjourned till Court in Course."

Court of December 1756 began on 2nd Tuesday "at the Court house in Corbintown."

45-90 John White's Ordinary license renewed.

.. Glass Caston appointed Constable in the room of James Lattay.

45-90 Three deeds of sale, one deed of Mortgage proved.

Court of December 1756, Continued -

45-90' Daniel Weldon, Esq produced his commission as Deputy to Robert Jones, Jr, Attorney General of the Province of North Carolina, deputy for Northampton, Edgecombe, Granville & Orange.

45-90'	Thomas Grimes	against	Thomas Priestwood	Case
46-91	John Brown	"	Alexander Banckson	In Case

Two deeds proved.

Solomon Debow paid for his attendance at November Superior Court.

46-91 John Patterson Esq's Ordinary license renewed.
Duncan Bohannan, Esq. granted license to keep Ordinary.

Eight deeds proved.

46-92 Five deeds proved.

Stephen McMillion "an infirm person" to be tax exempt.

Thomas Williams was paid for his att. at May 1756 Superior Court.

46-92'	Alexander Mebane	vs	Michael Synnot	In Case
	Robert Jones, Jr	"	James Alliott	" "
	William Boggan	"	Samuel Collins	" "
47-93	Richard Roberts	"	William Hamlet	Debt
	Moses Lovelatta	"	Moses Campbell	Or. Att.
	John Patterson	"	Jesse Brashear	In Case
	John Mooler (?)	"	John McDaniel	" "
46-93'	Michael Synnot	"	John Collins	Petition

Deed of Sale proved. Thomas Holden's mark recorded.

"Orphans of William Williams -
Mary Williams, Wm. Williams & John Williams, orphan children to Wm. Williams, dec'd, be bound to John Rogers, carpenter, until they arrive severally to age, to wit, Mary one year & 4 months, being 17 years old next 16th day of April, William about the age of 14. & John about the age of 11." (See below, and 58-116')

"Mary Potter & Phebee Potter orphan children of Thomas Potter, dec'd, be bound unto William Canady till they severally arrive at age to wit- Mary about 3 years old, & Pheby about 7 months, & that he learn them to read the Holy Bible, spin, sew & knit."

47-94 "Josiah Watkins considering himself aggrieved by the order binding the Williams children to John Rogers - & the Court refusing to appoint him or Elizabeth Williams, supposed mother of the said orphans, who hath not proved herself to be the wife of the said deceased - Guardian, he prays an appeal from the said order to the Supreme Court --"
(See 48-96')

Court of December 1756 continued -

47-94 Ann Anderson & John Anderson, Administrators of John Anderson, dec'd, filed an Inventory of the estate.

Two deeds from Earl of Granville proved. One other deed proved.

Robert Berry against Richard Gibbs. Gibbs was jailed.
Hosea Tapley & Wm. Jay appear & go bail for Gibbs.

47-94' Five deeds proved.

Mr. William Chambers is to made two windows etc. in the Courthouse.

48-95 "On complaint of Wm. Hodges - Thomas Nobles is to be summoned to appear at March Court ... to answer to some ill-treatment given by him to an Orphan Child now in his care."

Thomas Wiley's Ordinary license renewed.

Five deeds proved.
48-95' 8 deeds.
48-96 8 deeds proved.

48-96 "John Slater & Giles Chapman, special Bail for John Beverley, came into Court & Delivered him up- Ordered that the Sheriff take him into custody (He was sued for debt by Richard Dudgen. See 40-79 & 40-80.)

48-96' Administration of Estate of William Williams, dec'd, granted to Isaiah Watkins. Bond: £ 200. (See 48-96')

Thomas Holden appointed Overseer in the room of James Dickey.

..."Joseph Maddox, Wm. Johnson & Freeman Jones appointed Commissioners of the Roads & that they inspect the road from this Courthouse, to Mary Williams' Ford on Haw river, thence to Rocky River."

"A list of the present Commissioners of Roads Monday April 26, 1756-

Thomas Holden	Thomas Lloyd	
John Pittman, Esq.	Robert Cate	Rob't Cate fined 30 shillings.
James Allison	Thomas Rhodes	
Lawrence Banckson	Joseph Boggs	
James McCallister	Jacob Brooks	
William Barnett	Peter Hilton	
John Gray	William Collins	
Alexander Mebane	James Collins	
Robert Erwin	Zachariah Martin	
William Armstrong	John Jones	
Henry Reynolds	George Hobson (Hopson?)	
Benjamin King	John Wright"	

Court of December 1756 continued -

48-96' William Nunn appointed Overseer of Road in room of John Dennis.
49-97 William Blackwood " " " " " " Henry Lemon.
Lodowick Clap " " " " " " John Fuller.
George Erwin " " " " " " James Fruitt.
Paul Proe (?) " " " " " " Daniel McDaniel.
Thomas Lowe " " " " " " Nathaniel Reed.

"Memorandum, that at the Supreme Court 1755, Thomas Brooks & Gilbert Patterson, was appointed Commissioners of the Roads, leading down Cape Fare S. Side of Haw River, with the other Commissioners."

James Allison, George Hobson & William Rhodes excused for not attending the last meeting of the Commissioners.

..."Josiah Hadley Overseer from the Court House to Mary Williams' Fording over Haw River & that the following Tythables work on the said Road - John Hadley, John Marshal, William Johnson, Charles Johnson, John Johnson, Mathew Woods, Thomas Cate, Jr., Thomas Cate, Sr., Robert Cate, Jr. & Cap't Robert Cate, Joseph Cate, Robert Wil(l)ey, Wm. Roseberry & Edmund or Edw'd Davis."-

49-97' "Ordered that James Stewart be continued Overseer of the Road from the Virginia line near Holls (Holt's?) Mill, to Taylor's Road on Enoe." -

John Powel appointed Overseer of Road in the room of David Phillips.

Hugh Porter appointed Commissioner instead of John Pittman.
John McGee " " " " Jacob Brooks.

"A list of the present Commissioners taken Monday August 2, 1756.

Thomas Holden	.John Gray	.Thomas Brooks
Hugh Porter	.Alex. Mebane, Esq.	.Gilbert Patterson
James Allison, Esq	.Robert Erwin	Thomas Sullivant
Robert Cate	William Copeland	John White
.Thomas Loyd	James Collins	Reuben Freshwater
William Rhodes	Zach. Martin, Sr	Samuel McDuff
Lawrence Banckson	William Armstrong	Lawrence Thompson
.James McAllister	Henry Reynolds	John Crawford
.William Barnett	Benjamin King	Robert Lanier
.Joseph Boggs, Esq	.John Jones	Samuel Jones
John McGee	.George Hopson	Isaac Jones"
.Peter Hilton, Sr	.John Wright	(35 on this list)

49-98 "At a general meeting of the Commissioners for Roads at the Court house on Monday, August 2, 1756," there were fifteen Commissioners present. (the 13 checked on above list, plus Joseph Maddock & Francis Jones.)

Court of December 1756 continued -

49-98 "John Landrum appointed Overseer of that part of the Road leading to Cape Fare, from Rocky river, to Terrell's to Gravel Banck under the Inspection of Francis Jones, Commissioner. Also that John Pyle be appointed Overseer from the Gravel Bank, on said Road unto John Wood's at Mary Williams' at Haw River ...."

"Cape Fare road to be extended from the Western path where (?) Cap't Boggs .... to the Country line, to the reedy fork at the head of Haw river & that Wm. Wiley be Overseer under the inspection of Joseph Boggs, Esq...."

"a road from Crown (?) Ford on Haw river to Hogan's Ford on Deep River & thence to the Cape Fare Road be opened ... at the expense of the petitioners ...& that Charles Fooshe be Overseer of said Road ..."

"Court adjourned till Court in Course."

49-98' Court of March 1757 began on second Tuesday.

Plunkett Ballard, Attorney, qualified to practice at Orange Court.

Estate of Rev. William Williams dec'd to be sold 2nd Tuesday in April.

"James Dorchester appointed Constable on the waters of Hico."

Jane Boggan, wife of William Boggan, examined about a deed.

Hugh Porter proved an Account of £ 10 Pa. money against James Gilchrist of Lancaster County, Pa.

Joseph Barbee app. Commissioner of Roads in the room of William Rhodes

James Railey's mark recorded.
50-99 Marks recorded by Mathew Cary, Joseph Reed, William Comb, Patrick Rutherford, John Ambree, & James Murdock.

"Ordered that the Sheriff pay Joseph Maddock for building the Prison and other matters relating thereto."

Three deeds proved.
50-99' Four deeds proved.
Marks recorded by John King, John Tomlinson, & Thomas Couch.

50-100 The will of Joseph Wade, dec'd. was proved by William Burford and Samuel Burton. James Wade and Joseph Powel qualified as Execs. (This will is recorded in Book A-67, also in GRIMES.)

Three deeds proved.

Court of March 1757 continued -

50-100 Captain Snow, a Catawba friendly Indian - says a horse now in the possession of Michael Synnot was stolen from him a year ago -

"On motion of Plunkett Ballard, Atty at Law, in behalf of Miles Parker & Peter Parker, Jr, being charged by John Copeland of Cumberland County with stealing a cow - that the said Parkers be discharged ... not granted."

50-100' Hugh Smith appointed Constable in the room of John Johnson.

William Copeland	against	Mark London	In Case
Francis Mabry	"	John Bert (?)	Writ of Inquiry

51-101 Two deeds proved.

"The following persons appointed to attend the next Supreme Court at Salisbury for the counties of Orange, Rowan, & Anson.
John Patterson, Esq., Mark Morgan, John McGee, Cairns Tinnen, Hugh Dobbin, William Barbee, Grand Jurors.
Jno West, Sr, Lodowick Clap, Thomas Bradford, Luke Bynum, Robert Patterson, & William Creege, Petty Jurors".

Jonathan Fincher fined 5 shillings for contempt.

Hugh Smith	against	Jacob Mason	Petition

51-101' Five deeds proved.

James Downing appointed Constable in the room of William Murrah.

51-102 "Deed of Sale from Glass Caston & John White & Ann White his wife for William Nunn for a Lott in Corbintown was proved in the following manner - to wit - Glass Caston by the oath of Wm. Reed, John White by the oath of Daniel Cain & Ann his wife acknowledged in open court her right of dower .. etc.."

Peter Noe app. Commissioner in the room of Peter Hilton, Sr.
Wm. Wiley, Sr. app. " " " " " Cap't Boggs "on the Cape Fare Road."

Thomas Cate appointed Constable in the room of James Dickey.

John Patterson, Lawrence Thompson & Alex. Mebane, Esq's recommended to the Governor as candidates for Sheriff.

51-102' John Slater app. Constable in Corbintown in the room of Glass Caston.
Samuel Watt " " " the room of Daniel Hollyfield.

"Samuel Lane, Orphan of Edward Lane 7 yrs old the 6th day of this Instant be bound apprentice to Thomas Wiley until he arrive at age."

Court of March 1757 continued -

51-102'	William Stroud	vs	Thomas Collins, Jr		Petition
52-103	Samuel Collins	"	William Stroud		"

"Read the Petition of William Halcombe who is in Prison at the Suit of Michael Synnot & prays to have the benefit of the Insolvent Act. etc. - not granted."

52-103'	Church Wardens	vs	Prestwood	Or. Attachment
	Halcombe	"	Synott	In Case
52-104	Hosea Tapley	"	William Aldridge	" "

Two deeds proved.

52-104' Two deeds proved.

	Robert Berry	vs	Richard Gibb	In Case
53-105'	Mr. Weldon	"	Henry Shaddock	Debt

Deed of sale proved.

James Lea proved his attendance for Pltf. in the suit Tapley vs Aldrid

Wm. Gold proved his att. for plaintiff in suit Tapley vs Aldridge.

53-106 Lawrence Winfield proved his attendance in suit Berry vs Gibb.

Lawrence Kelly came into Court & acknowledged himself indebted to the King, to keep the Peace until next Court.

John Wood came into Court & acknowledged himself indebted to the King.

John Russell proved his attendance in suit Berry vs Gibbs.

Phebe Ran proved her attendance in suit Berry vs Gibbs.

The King against Robert Huart (?) Issue of Traverse.

53-106' Thomas Laxton, Jr and Samuel Cobb proved their attendance as Evidences in the Suit - Taylor vs Reynolds.

John Cate and Margery his wife proved their attendance as Evidences in the Suit Berry vs Gibbs, for the Plaintiff.

Hugh Taylor against Nathaniel Reynolds In Case

54-107 William Saunders & David Stevens, who were summoned as witnesses in the suit Taylor vs Reynolds, failed to appear.

Michael Dixon's mark recorded. Deed of Sale proved.
John Hunter proved his attendance in the suit Widow Hunter vs Jos. Mon
Henry Gold proved his " " " " Taypley vs Aldredge.

Court of March 1757 continued -

54-107 "Ordered that John Patterson, Esq, James Taylor & Lawrence Thompson, Gentlemen, Commissioners for the Cape Fare Road, do hire some persons to Poilet them and to mark said Road ...."

Provision is made to reimburse persons entertaining the Indians traveling to or from Virginia. (See page 62-123)

54-107' Michael Synnot against Beer Barton Debt.

"Josias Dixon, Esq and Lawrence Thompson, Gentlemen, Guardians to Mary Douglas and John Douglas orphan children of Jeremiah Douglas" to exhibit their account at next court to be held in March.

More Justices of the Peace are to be nominated.

Stocks and Pillory and Whipping Post to be built.

..."Mrs. Kilpatrick late widow of William Kilpatrick" to have "two of her taxables ... abated for the year 1756".

54-108 Joseph Barbee app. Commissioner of Roads in room of William Rhodes. "William Wiley app. Commissioner of Cape Fare Road in room of Cap't Boggs."

General Meeting of the COMMISSIONERS OF ROADS - held at the Court House in Corbintown, Monday the 18th of April 1757. Twelve present.

John Hunter app. Overseer of Road in room of William Blackwood.
William Mians (?) appointed Overseer of Road in room of George Erwin.
"..Joseph Powel " " " " from Michael Synnot's to Little River in the room of John White."
"...Joseph Powel appointed Overseer of Road from Little River to the County line in the room of John White.

John Marshal appointed Overseer of Road in room of Joshua Hadley.
William Craig " " " " " " " David Bradford, Jr.

54-108' "..Gilbert Stream appointed Overseer of Road from the Court house to the road leading to the hawfields."

William Combe appointed Overseer of Road in room of William Nunn.

".. Public road ..be laid out...from George Finley's at the County line ... to Boyd's Road & that Peter King be Overseer."

"Adam Trollinger app. Overseer of Road from Haw River to the Great Alamance."
Joseph Gold appointed Overseer on the S. Side of Hico.
John Warren " " " " N. Side of Hico.
Solomon Derbe (?) Overseer in the room of William Serjant.

Court of March 1757 continued -

54-108' All absent Commissioners are to be fined.

Public road to be laid out ... from William Jay's to the Sorry (Saury) Town ... Peter Banckston, James Henricks & James Satterfield to be Overseers.

Lawrence Redman appointed Overseer in the room of Henry Gold.

List of 28 Commissioners of the Road:

54-109 "Thomas Holden, Hugh Porter, James Allison, Thomas Loyd, Robert Cate, Joseph Barbe, Lawrence Bancson, James McAlister, William Barnet, William Armstrong, Benjamin King, George Hopson, Thomas Brooks, Joseph Maddock, Joseph Boggs, William Wiley, John McGee, Peter Noey, John Gray, Alexander Mebane, Robert Erwin, William Copeland, James Collins, Henry Reynolds, John Jones, John Wright, Gilbert Patterson, Francis Jones"

SUITS -

55-109'	William Eaton	vs	Zachariah Martin	In Case
	John Robinson	"	John West, Sr.	Debt
55-110	Robert Jones, Jr	"	James Elliott	In Case
55-110'	Blake Baker	"	Josias Dixon	Petition
	John Steel	"	Thomas Laxton	"
	John Offill (Ossil?)	"	Hugh Smith	"
56-111	Michael McDaniel	"	Robert Cate, Sr	"
	Hezekiah Collins	"	William Howlett	"
56-111'	Hugh Smith	"	Jacob Mason	"
	Wm. Henderson	"	Lawrence Winfield	"
57-112	Samuel Watt	"	John Smith	Or. Att.
	Ann Hunter	"	Joseph Money	Petition

"Court adjourned till Court in Course."

56-112' Court of June 1757. Six Justices present.

Commissions as Justices of the Peace to:
"James Watson, Alexander Mebane, John Gray, John Pryor, Joseph Boggs, Lawrence Thompson, Josias Dixon, John Patterson, James Allison, Andrew Mitchel, Lawrence Banckson, John McGee, Thomas Loyd, William Reed, William Churton, Robert Abercromby (new), Hugh Porter, and Jacob Brooks, Esquires." (18 named)
"and of whom ware qualified the worshipful John Pryor, William Churton, Joab Brooks, Richard Parker, Thomas Loyd, & William Lea, Esquires".

Letter of Attorney from John Campbell & Alexander McCulloch to Robert Rainey, proved by John Rainey, a witness.

Court of June 1757 continued -

57-113 Joseph Walker's mark recorded, also Joseph S or Lattons (?)

William Reed's Ordinary license renewed.

John Brooks, Jr, appointed Constable in the room of Shadrick Jacobs.

Thomas Bradford to be paid for his attendance at Salisbury Court of May 1757 as Petit Juror.

Thomas Hide, a poor man, aged 64, to be excused for taxes for 1756.

57-113' Power of Att'y from Henry McCulloch of England, & Joseph Willock of Bristol, England, to Robert Rainey (late of Ireland) to sell lands on Peedee and Haw Rivers, 100,000 acres each - two and a half pages about this.

57-114' Deed from Enoch Lewis to Wm Reed for one-half of Lot #6 in Corbintown, proved by oath of John Sims.

Deed from Wm Boggan & Jane his wife to James McCallister, 419 acres.

58-115 Deed from Wm Reed to "Justices of this Court" for ground whereon the prison stands.

Deed from Wm Reed to Wm Churton for Lots 3,4 & 5 (in Corbintown).

Deed from John Slater to John Stubs for one-half of Lot #89, in Corbintown.

Deed from Wm Churton to Wm Combe "for a Lot in Corbintown-K-."

Deed from Wm. Churton to Enoch Lewis for a Lot in Corbintown.

57-114'	Thomas Wade	vs	Moses Ridley	In Case
58-115	Dunnagan	against	Canady	Case

Gilbert Patterson granted license to keep a Ferry on Deep River.

58-116 Deed from Wm Churton to Enoch Lewis for Lot of Land marked G.

William Goss, Constable, fined 5 shillings for Contempt of Court.

William Howlett acknowledged himself indebted to the King, James Collins and Hosea Tapley are his Securities.

Cairnes Tinnen to be paid for his attendance at May Salisbury Court as Grand Juror.

58-116' Samuel Watt is appointed Guardian to Mary Williams and John Williams, orphan children of Rev. Wm. Williams, dec'd.

Two other items about Wm. Williams' estate.

Court of June 1757 continued -

58-116' Wm Stroud, Jr proved his attendance for Plaintiff in the suit Stroud vs Collins. John Carragan proved his attendance for Defendant.

Two deeds proved.

59-117 Six deeds proved.

59-117 "Wm Reed proved an account of Ⱡ 2.. 1d for dyating 56 Catawba Indian and corn for eleven horses on their return from Virginia since last March Court."

59-117' Lodowick Clap recorded his mark. He was paid for his attendance at Salisbury Superior Court 1757.

Samuel Allen's Ordinary license granted.

Thomas Lovelatta Jr app. Constable "in the upper part of the County."

59-118 Zach. Martin. Jr granted license to keep Ordinary at his dwelling house on Rocky River.

Jacob Mason granted license to keep Ordinary in Corbintown.

59-118' James Watson's Ordinary license renewed.

59-118	Collins	vs	Martin, Sr	In Case
	Watt	"	Smith	Or. Attach.
59-118'	Wm. Boggan	"	Samuel Collins	In Case
	Rich'd Simpson	"	Edward Southwell	" "
60-119	Thomas Lovelatty	"	Moses Campbell	Or. Attach.

"Wm Wiley ..hath in his hands - 8 shillings - a fine recovered from Jacob Summers, a defaulter on the roads."

"Hugh Smith, an Overseer of the Road, under the Inspection of Robert Erwin, Commissioner of the Western path", says warrants were issued against John Madow & against Wm Gattren (?), he thinks directed to John Craig, Constable.

60-119' "David Roper appointed Overseer of the Road from Hogan's Creek to the Country line Creek & James Crawford from thence to Solomon Dobbs.

"Court adjourned till Court in Course."

60-119' Joseph Boggs was the only Justice who appeared on the 2nd Tuesday, September 1757. "Adjourned till tomorrow."

Next day - present: Joseph Boggs, Thomas Lloyd, William Lea, Esqs.

60-120 Marks recorded by James McCarver, Wm. Boyd, Wm Wiley, James Asspey.

Court of September 1757 continued -

60-120 Lawrence Thompson, Esq qualified as Sheriff of Orange County. James Bowie & Samuel Sarat qualified as under Sheriffs.

Daniel Weldon presented a motion "on behalf of James Dickey who intermarried with a certain Mary Kilpatrick late widow & relict of Joseph Kilpatrick, dec'd, that letters of Administration be granted to him ..." Bond: Ŀ 50.

Wm Craig paid for attending Salisbury Court as Juror, May 1757.

60-120' Marks recorded by James Couch, Henry Morris.

Deed from Jacob Mason to John Woods for a Lot in Corbintown.
" " Wm Churton " James Watson " " " " " .
" " " " " Andrew Corbin Reed - Lot in Corbintown.
" " " " " The Vestry for a " " " .

Deed of Gift. Deed of Sale.
61-121 Four deeds of Sale.

Petit Jurors who failed to appear:
Daniel Cane, John Allison, Thomas Easkin (?), Wm. Armstrong, John Davis, James Barnhill, James Fruit, Patrick Rutherford, & Wm Copeland.

61-121' William Howlett vs John Rogers CASE

Henry Webb's Ordinary license renewed.

James McAllister, John Tinnen & James Taylor to appraise five stray steers, at the plantation of Daniel Cain ...

Ezekiel Dollahide appears - no person appearing to prosecute him, he is discharged.

61-122 Richard Simpson to be summoned for Contempt of Court.

Marks recorded by Samuel Temples (?) & Joseph Allison.

Hannah Hilton, widow and relict of Peter Hilton, dec'd, appointed Administratrix of his Estate.

James Dickey exhibited an Inventory of the Estate of William Kilpatrick. Sale ordered.

61-122' Mrs. Ann Anderson's license to run an Ordinary in Corbintown, renewed. Her securities: Thomas Lapsey and James Taylor.

Ordinary rates listed.

Deed from Adam Trollinger to Jacob Mason, 1 acre in Corbintown.

Court of September 1757 continued -

61-122' .."Following persons to attend next Superior Court at Salisbury - Cap't David Holt, Joseph Powel, Gilbert Strean, Henry Webb, David Steel Richard Simpson, David Holt, for Grand Jurors.

For Petit Jurors:
Mark Morgan, John Pryor, George Laws, Michael Dixon, Hugh Smith, & Hugh Woods."

62-123 "Ordered that James Watson, John Gray & James Taylor (Gent) be appointed a committee to examine the accounts brought in by sundry persons of this county for the Damages & Expenses of the Indians Traveling through this county to Virginia, & that Thomas Loyd give his attendance, and that they report to the next Court."

	Phillip Howard	vs	Bazell Brashear	In Case
62-123'	Thomas Williams	"	William Bobbitt	Case
	William Richmond	"	Thomas Barkley	In Case
63-124	Anthony Strother	"	Robert Patterson	" "
63-124'	Margaret Flatt	"	John Boyd, Sr	Slander
	William Gibson	"	Hosea Tapley	Petition
63-125	John Robinson	"	William Grimes	"
	James Woods	"	William Bobbitt	Debt
63-125'	David Steel	"	Joseph Money	In Case
	John Dunnagan	"	Thomas Wade	Case
63-126	Robert Rowan	"	John Robinson	"
	William Howlet	"	John Rogers	"
63-126'	William Persons	"	Thomas Lovelatty	Debt
64-127	Exec's of John Boyd	"	William Logan	Petition
	Jonathan Fincher	"	William Gordon	"
64-127'	John Steel	"	Law. Banckson, Esq	"
	William Reed	"	Henry Johnson	"
64-128	James Cary	"	George Haygood	"

"Court adjourned till Court in Course."

64-128' Court of December 1757 began 2nd Tuesday.

One deed proved.

Elizabeth Neblet an orphan child aged 6 yrs & 6 months to be bound to William White until she is 18 years old.

Alexander Mebane's Ordinary license renewed.

65-129 Mathew Woods granted license to "keep Ordinary at his house in Corintown."
Benjamin Jackson granted license to "keep Ordinary at his house in Corbintown".

Court of December 1757 continued -

65-129 John Green granted license to "keep Ordinary at his house in the Hawfields".

Mark recorded by Robert Harris.

Deed proved, Robert Jones, Jr to John Warren, 200 acres.

Thomas Goss is granted Administration on the Estate of his brother William Goss, dec'd. Bond: £ 200. Securities: Thomas Robinson, James Couch and Edward Stone.

65-129' Deed from James Taylor to Isaac Gaddis 250 acres
" " " " " John Tinnen 100 acres
" " " " " Ann Anderson 409 acres

Deed from John Rutherford, Esq to James Taylor for 770 acres, proved "by the affirmation of Robert Taylor (Quaker)..."

65-130 A few lines below we read - "Deed of Sale from John Rutherford, Esq. to James Anderson for 313½ acres - "proved in open court by the oath of Robert Taylor." (Is this a slip of the Clerk, or were two men named Robert Taylor proving deeds on the same day?)

65-129' John McDaniel Jr's mark recorded.

65-130 Three deeds proved.

Lodowick Clap granted Administration of "estate of Ball Seboon(?) late of Orange County, dec'd." Bond: £ 100. Securities: Joseph Boggs, Jacob Boon.

65-130 "Patty Bohannon, widow of Joseph Bohannon, late of the said County, dec'd" granted Letters of Administration. Bond £ 500. Bondsmen: John Patterson and Thomas Tinden (?).

Will of Jonathan Fincher submitted, "but no evidence appearing to prove the same" - put off until evidences appear. (Recorded in Book A, page 3). See Court of March 1758.

65-130' "Ordered that Justice Stroud, natural child of Elizabeth Stroud, aged 2 years the 6th of January next - be bound to William Stroud ... to have 2 years schooling after he is ten years old."

Watts vs Brown T.A.B.

66-131 John Slater's Ordinary license renewed.

Marks recorded by Robert Brashear & Wm Reed, Sr.

Court of December 1757 continued -

66-131 The King vs William Halcomb, Issue of Traverse. Not guilty.

66-131'	Charles Gibbons	vs	Joseph Collins	T.A.B.
66-132	Thomas Williams	"	William Bobbitt	In Case
	Boggsn's Admin's.	"	William Halcomb	Case
66-132'	Wm Richmond	"	Thomas Barkley	In Case
67-133	Wm Williams	"	John Dover	Case
	Wm Gibson	"	Hosea Tapley	Petition
67-133'	John Murry	"	Christian Tyrie	Case
	James Moss	"	James Couch	Debt
67-134	Hugh Smith	"	John Lambert	Case
67-134'	Michael Synnot	"	Joseph Collins	"
68-135	Cairnes Tinnen	"	Bazel Brashear	Petition
68-135'	Blake Baker	"	Francis Day	"
	" "	"	John Brantley	"
	John Martin	"	John Byars	"
68-136	James Cary, Jr	"	Charles Conally	"
	James Cary, Jr	"	William Howlet	Debt
	Cary & Weldon	"	John Collins	"
68-136'	John McCullom	"	Wm. Miller	Petition
	William Wiley	"	Hugh Foster	Or. Attach.

"Court adjourned till Court in Course."

69-137 Court of March 1758 begins.

Deed of Sale proved.

Francis Fruit appointed Constable in the room of Hugh Smith. "Ordered that George Smith be continued Constable."

"Ordered that Paul Fountain, orphan child of Paul Fountain, aged 14 the 16th day of May next, be bound to James Stewart"... till 21 years of age ... to read and write, etc.

James Downing's mark recorded.

"Ordered that the Charter for the County of Orange be registered."

69-137' "Alex. McCracken have license to keep Ordinary at the house of Moses and John Ambee in Corbintown." Securities: James McCallister and Cairnes Tinnen.

..."James Copeland app. Constable down the Haw River towards the lower part of the county."

Marks recorded by David Pinkerton and Robert Tate.

Patrick Mahen (?) granted license to keep Tavern at his dwelling house in the Haw Fields.

Court of March 1758 continued -

69-137' Samuel Stewart granted license "to keep Tavern at his dwelling house in Corbintown." Securities: Hugh Smith, Cairns Tinnen.

..."following were qualified as Grand Jurors - Thomas Thompson, Robert Lyttle, James Hart, Daniel Cain, David Mitchell, George Allen, Michael Dixon, Joseph Dunkin, Alex. Lackey, William Creig, John Grist, James McCallister, James Rea, Thomas Holden, Henry Watson, & William Blackwood."

69-138 "The Orphan Court opened - Present: Alexander Mebane, William Lea, Richard Parker, Esquires."

"Thomas Goss, Adm, filed an account of sales."

John Pryor, Esq appointed Commissioner of Roads in the room of William Barnett.

Robert Stubblefield to build a Public Grist Mill on his own land on Hogan's Creek.

Bill of Sale from John Rogers to Thomas Erksine for a negro man, proved by Samuel Sarratt.

69-138' Lodowick Clap, Adm of Bale Seboon, filed an Inventory of Estate.

"Patty Bohannon, dec'd. Exhibited an Inventory of Estate." Perishable part of the property to be sold 2nd day of April next at the house of John Patterson.

Administration on the Estate of William Barbee granted to Raichel Barbee, his widow. Bond: £ 500. Bondsmen: John Patterson, Joseph Barbee and Micajah Pickett.

Administration on the Estate of Jonathan Fincher granted to "Jane Fincher and Jonathan Fincher her son". Bond: £ 1,000. Bondsmen: Thomas Holden, James Bowie, and Robert Taylor.

(The above is the last entry in the first volume.)

VOLUME TWO

1-139 Six deeds proved.
1-139' Six deeds proved.

1-140 Deed from James Taylor to William Few for 640 acres proved by the "affirmation of Robert Taylor".

Court of March 1758 continued -

1-140 "Isaiah Phipps - aged 11 years, 3 months & 6 days ...."

James Satterfield, Jr appointed Constable in room of Samuel Bumpass.

"Wm. Reed proved his account of 1 hog delivered to Cap't Bull and his Company of Cherokee Indians on their Journey to Virginia..."

James McGowen, Jr. app. Commissioner of Roads in room of Thomas Holden
Cairnes Tinnen " " " " " " " Thomas Holden

1-140' Alexander Lackey appointed Constable in room of John Tinnen.
Joseph Brown " " " " " Thos Lovelatty, Jr.

Marks recorded by Mathew Durham, Thomas Durham & John Edwards.

Two deeds proved.
2-141 Five deeds proved.

"following to attend next Superior Court at Salisbury - Alexander Mebane, John Lea, Lawrence Vanhook, John Tinnen, Thomas Hart, & Gilbert Strean, Grand Jurors.

2-141' Richard Simpson, Joseph Powel, William Riley, Daniel McCullom, James McGowen, and Thomas Reaney, Petit Jurors."

John Dennis, a Quaker, claims that a horse delivered by John Frohawk to Thomas Capper - was the property of said Thomas Capper & supposed to be taken away by the Indians some time ago.

Two deeds proved.

2-142 James Espey appointed Constable in the room of John Stabler.
Joseph Allison " " " " " " John Tinnen.

George Harren (Herndon) appointed "Constable in the North Settlement of New Hope and parts adjacent." (See August 1761, page 36.)

William Boggan appointed "Constable on the N. Side of Enoe to the Country line Eastward,"
"Samuel Burton appointed Constable on the S. Side of Enoe & down Nuse to the Country line."
"Robert Willey appointed Constable in the District between James Fruit's District & James Espey's."

	Hugh Barnett	vs	Robert Barnett	Case
2-142'	Fielding Lewis, Esq	"	Francis Cox	"
	John Stubblefield	"	Isaiah Watkins, Adm.	"
3-143	Michael Dixon	"	William Wilson	Petition
3-143'	John Jones	"	William Bobbitt	"
	John Money	"	Zach Martin. Jr	"
	Gabriel Everand	"	John Slater	Debt

Court of March 1758 continued -

3-144	Timothy Terrel	vs	John Slater	Case
3-144'	James Carey, Jr	"	John Mayner	Petition
	Hugh Smith	"	Joseph Sharp	"
4-145	William Blackwood	"	Robert Brashear	"
	Thomas Williams	"	William Bobbitt	"
4-145'	Gabriel Everand	"	John Boyd	Case
	Rice Curtis	"	John Graves	Debt

"Court adjourned till Court in Course."

4-146 Court for June 1758 began 2nd Tuesday, at the Courthouse in Corbintown.

Philemon Edwards judged father of Tabitha Rigsby's "bastard female child". Edwards' bondsmen were: John Edwards & Henry Brewer.

Josiah Dixon, Esq qualified as Sheriff of Orange County.

4-146 "Richard Braswell admitted to keep a Public Ferry at his Plantation on the N. West of Cape Fare River." Fares listed.

4-146' The following persons were in the coustody of Lawrence Thompson, late Sheriff: "Catherine Gordon, committed on the Vagrant Act". "Elizabeth Samp (alias Gordon) on suspicion of aiding her husband - to wit- James Samp (alias Gordon) & a certain John Samp (alias Gordon) to break the prison... from whence the said prisoners escaped." Jacob Mason, a debtor. "Patrick Mehone at the suit of Oliver Stroud," Debt.

Mr. William Cummings, Attorney, qualified to practice in Orange.

5-147 Peter Noe granted license to keep Tavern at his dwelling house. Giles Chapman's Ordinary license renewed.

"On reading the petition of Daniel Henlen, it is ordered that Patrick Rutherford be summoned to appear with Mary Butts, the apprentice, & William Grace be and appear at the next Court, etc."

The Sheriff to be fined 5 sh. for not attending this Court. George Miller fined 5 shillings for Contempt of this Court.

Marks recorded by Valentine Hollingsworth & John Pyle.

5-147' Ann Bohannon granted Administration on Estate of her late husband Duncan Bohannon. Bondsmen: John Gray, James Bowie.

Susannah Fooshe, widow of Charles Fooshe - the will "not being signed or sealed" .... Joseph Fooshe testified as a witness. He was granted Administration. (This will was recorded twice in Book A, on page 2 and 62.)

Court of June 1758 continued -

5-148 John Barbee appointed Guardian of Francis Barbee, son of Wm. Barbee, dec'd.

Raichel Barbee, Adm'x of Wm. Barbee, filed an Inventory.

William Lea, Esq appointed Commissioner of Roads in the room of Lawrenc Banckson, Esq.

Joseph Money to give security for his good behavior.

5-148' William Burney and Thomas Stubbs fined for Contempt of Court.

James Aspey and John Slater and James Bowie accused of aiding James & John Seamp to escape from prison.

6-149 James McCallister called to give evidence against Richard Burton who is charged with cursing King George the Third.
6-149' Robert Harris & Samuel Burton are bail for Richard Burton.

Six deeds proved.

6-150 Joseph Pevey (or Percy?) appointed Constable in room of David Phillips.
William Boggan who was appointed Constable has failed to qualify.
David Knight appointed Constable.

Catherine Gordon was discharged - she is to "Immediately depart this County."
6-150' Elizabeth Samp acquitted.

2 deeds proved.

Thomas Stag granted license to keep tavern at his dwelling on Flatt River.

7-151 Robert Alsup accused of stealing a saddle and bell from Samuel Sarratt. He is committed for trial at next court.

7-151' CASE Joseph Powel against Micajah Pickett.

7-152 Five deeds of sale, one deed of gift proved.

William Lea's mark recorded.

7-152' Thomas Wiley's Ordinary license renewed.

Deed from Wm Churton to Alex Mebane for Lot #120 in Corbintown.

8-153 William Horton appointed Constable in room of James Wilkerson.

Joseph Maddock did not finish the prison according to his agreement.

Court of June 1758 continued -

8-153	Charles Turnbull	vs	James Docherty	Petition
8-153'	Robert Boran	"	John Roberson	Case
	Ann Seals	"	Isaiah Watkins' Adm's	Case
8-154	John Gray	"	William Copeland	Case
8-154'	Thomas Wade	"	Joseph Dolittle	Petition
	William Churton	"	John Slater	Case
9-155	Francis Day	"	Benjamin Sexton	"
9-155'	George Flynn	"	John Byas	Petition
	John King	"	Samuel Stewart	Or. Attch.
	Giles Chapman	"	James Lindley	Case
9-156	Jacob Mason	"	Shadrick Jacobs	Petition
	John Gray	"	Thomas Hooper	"
9-156'	Robert Jones, Jr	"	Hosea Tapley	"
	James Cary, Jr	"	James Woods	"
	Mark Morgan	"	John Bohannon	"
10-157	Daniel Weldon	"	Nelson & Knight	"
	James Cary, Jr	"	John Tabor, Sr	"
	Edward Stone	"	Jacob Mason	"
10-157'	Jacob Mason	"	John Dennis	"
	Daniel Weldon	"	Samuel Collins	"
	James Taylor	"	William Willson	"
10-158	John White	"	Robert Hamlet	"
	Sherrod Halley	"	John Falconer	"
	George Allen	"	Dover & Martin	"
10-158'	Thomas Lapsey	"	John Armstrong	"
	George Dowthet	"	Adam Hannan, Sr	Debt
	Jacob Mason	"	Bazel Brashear	Petition
11-159	" "	"	Robert Brashear	"

"Court adjourned till Court in Course."

11-159' Court for September 1758 began 2nd Tuesday, at the Courthouse in Corbintown.

Jacob Mason's Ordinary license renewed. Deed of sale proved.

Susannah Fooshe, Exec'x of Charles Fooshe returned an Inventory.

11-160 Eight deeds proved.
11-160' Eight deeds proved.
12-161 Three deeds proved.

Marks recorded by Christopher Rhodes & William Couch.

James Vessey appointed Constable in room of William Horton.

"Court adjourned till tomorrow Morning at 8 o'clock."

Court of September 1758 continued -

12-161 Court Met: Present: Joseph Boggs, John McGee, Joab Brooks, William Churton, Esquires.

12-161' Daniel McDaniel vs Absolom McDaniel Warrant

"Joseph Pevey (?) appointed Constable on the S. side of Haw River on both sides the trading path."

William McMath, a poor & sickly man" excused from tax.

12-162 Eight deeds proved, 7 of them from Earl of Granville, the other John Patterson to Charles Johnson for 530 acres.
12-162' Four deeds proved.

Conrod Lowe, David Lowe and George Angle appointed "Commissioners of the Buffalo Road leading from Lowe's Mill to King's Mill."

Raichel Barbee, Adm'x of William Barbee, filed an Inventory. Negroes belonging to the Estate to be sold.

13-163 Isaiah Watkins, Adm of Estate of Rev. Wm. Williams files a further inventory. Two other items about this Estate.

"James Dickey who intermarried with Mary the widow and Adm'x of Joseph Kilpatrick, dec'd, exhibits an account of the sales of the said Estate."

13-163' "Ordered that Lurania Carter an orphan child be bound an apprentice to David Nelson" ..she was formerly bound to James Wright.

Ann Bohannon, Adm'x of Duncan Bohannon, dec'd, filed an Inventory.

13-164 A set of weights and measures is to be bought for Orange County.

13-164' William Nunn's Ordinary license renewed.

Phillip Gee granted leave to build a water grist mill on Boling's Creek

14-165	Michael Synnot	vs	Andrew Baker	Case
	Arthur Gibbons	"	Edward Moore	"
14-165'	Robert Carver	"	James Lindley	"
	Jacob Mason	"	Thomas Dunnagan	Petition
14-166	John White	"	Joshua Brent (?)	"
	James Boyd	"	" "	Or. Attch't.
14-166'	" "	"	Dennis Sullivant	Case
	Plunkett Ballard	"	Francis Day	Petition
	" "	"	Edward Moore	"
15-167	Lewis Robinson	"	Hosea Tapley	"
	George Carrington	"	Phillip Huings (?)	"
	James Cary, Jr	"	" Hugings	"

Court of September 1758 continued -

15-167'	John Richardson	vs	Frederick Nall	Petition
	James Cary, Jr.	"	Michael Murry	Case

"Court adjourned till Court in Course."

15-168 Court of December 1758 began 2nd Tuesday, the 12th day, at the Courthouse in Corbintown.
Negroes belonging to the Estate of William Barbee to be sold Friday the 22nd.

Daniel Cain granted license "to keep Tavern in the house where William Reed formerly lived".

15-168' Three deeds proved, then -
Deed from John Watson to James Cary, Jr for 2 lots and improvements in Corbintown (#4), proved by Alex. Emsley.

Hugh Smith and Henry Watson paid for their attendance as Jurors at Salisbury November Court 1758.

John Barbee app. Guardian to Christopher Barbee, son of William Barbee, dec'd.

Samuel Allen, Jr's Ordinary license renewed.

16-169 Deed of Sale from Josias Dixon, Esq & Elizabeth his wife,to Joseph Armstrong, proved.

CASE Robert Jones, Jr against Margaret Boggan, Adm'x.

William Brazier appointed Constable on S. Side Haw River.

16-169' Ann Anderson's Ordinary license renewed. Securities: Alex. Mebane & Wm. Reed, Esq's.

Sheriff ordered to pay James Bowie £ 6-2-4 "for carrying Gordon and Erwin prisoners to Salisbury Court."

Sheriff ordered to pay Samuel Stewart, Jailor, 29 shillings, 4 pence "for his Prison fees and Dyating Gordon and Erwin".

CASE James Watson against Jacob Mason.

Bill of Sale from James Ross to Richard Wood, for a bay horse, proved by oath of Hugh McConnel.

16-170 William Chambers, Sr. to build a Water Grist Mill on Marlow's Creek - Michael Dixon summoned.

Court of December 1758 continued -

16-170' "...William Lea appointed Commissioner of Roads in room of Wm. Armstr
John Graves " " " " " " " Benjamin Kir

Barnaby Cabe's mark recorded.

Joshua Fincher fined 20 shillings for Contempt of Court.

16-170' "Nathaniel Cary, Security for Bendal Strayham (?) delivers him up..."

Sheriff to pay James Spratt his account, when it is proved.

	John Williams	vs	Howell Brewer	Traver
17-171	Robert Lyttle	"	William Moore	Case
	Giles Chapman	"	James Lindley	"
17-171'	Hector McNeel, Esq	"	John Brantley	"
17-172	Blake Baker	"	Richard Copeland	"
	" "	"	William Lacey	Petition
17-172'	Michael McDowel	"	John Davison	"
	William Richmond	"	Jacob Mason	Case
18-173	Jacob Mason	"	Andrew Crawford	Petition
	Joshua Fincher	"	James Espey	"
18-173'	Mark Morgan	"	" "	"
	James Carey, Jr	"	William Berry	"
	James Carey, Jr	"	Aaron Vanhook	"
18-174	Eliz Underhill, Adm'x	"	John McDaniel	"
	Timothy Terrell	"	John Armstrong	"
	James Dickey	"	John Dover	"
18-174'	James Cary, Jr	"	Samuel Sarratt	Debt
	" " "	"	John Cantril	"
	" " "	"	John Boid	"
19-175	" " "	"	Jacob Haggins	"
	" " "	"	John Raney & Mordecai Gwinn	Debt
	" " "	"	Hugh Dobbin	"
19-175'	" " "	"	Jacob West	"
	" " "	"	Richard Cheek	"

"Court adjourned till Court in Course."

19-176 Court of March 1759 began 2nd Tuesday, Corbintown.

Deed of Sale from Hector McNeel to John Brantley, for 148 acres.

"The following persons were sworn as Grand Jurors:
Aaron Van Hook, Thomas Clark. Thomas Thompson, Thomas Dobbin, Robert Patterson, Thomas Whitehead, Lawrence Rambo, James McGowen, William Basket, Henry Leman, John Satterfield, Hugh Wood, Gabriel Davey, Andrew McBroom, Robert Berry, Robert Donalson, James Dinkins, & Hugh Smith."

Court of March 1759 continued -

19-176 William Williams and Benjamin Williams. orphan children of Edward Williams. dec'd. to be apprenticed to Thomas Williams - to learn to read and write and "the first five rules in arithemtic."

19-176' Six deeds proved.

"Letter of Attorney from Jesse Hollingsworth to Herman Husbands, proved by the affirmation of Joshua Gregg..."

20-177 "Stephen Howard, a Baptist,"has refused to "qualify as Evidence on pretense of Tenderness of Conscience ..."

George Gouge, dec'd - "his orphan children" - Micajah Pickett is to be restrained from removing any of Gouge's estate.

Winnifred Pickett sues Micajah Pickett. William Reaves and Thomas Velvin are summoned on behalf of Winnifred. (See 23-183)

The will of Henry Webb, dec'd proved by oath of George Laws. Elizabeth Webb, sole Executrix. (See GRIMES 395)

"Elizabeth Webb, alias Harris came into court and relinquishes all advantages that she might receive by the will of her deceased husband, Henry, and desires to have the provision made to her by law, Etc.."

James Thompson app. Constable in the room of Joseph Brown.
20-177' Edward Wilburn " " " " " " Edward Chambers.
Samuel Stewart " " " " " " Samuel Espey.
Samuel Allen, Sr. " " " " " James Frewit (Fruit).

"Ordered that Thomas Harris be appointed Guardian to Ann Webb orphan child of Henry Webb, dec'd." Bond: Ŀ 500 Sterling. Bondsmen: Robert Harris, Tyrie Harris.

James Wade appointed Guardian to Thomas Webb orphan of Henry Webb. Bond: Ŀ 500 Sterling. Bondsmen: Thomas Harris, Warham Glenn.

Robert Patterson fined 5 shillings for being drunk while serving on the Grand Jury.

John Graves granted license to keep Tavern at his house.

20-178 Sheriff to pay John Cook 4 shillings for plank to make a coffin for John Morgan, deceased.

Further reports on Estates of William Barbee, Duncan Bohannon and Jonathan Fincher.

20-178' "Ordered that Jane Sawyer, a child of five years, be bound to John Raney" until she is eighteen years old.

Court of March 1759 continued-

20-178' "Ann Morrow, widow of Benjamin Morrow" granted letters of Administrati on his Estate. Bond: £ 200 Proclamation Money. Bondsmen: William Lea, William Jay.

Five deeds proved.
21-179 Deed from Wm. Reed, Esq to Jacob Mason for 2 lots in Corbintown.
" " Jacob Mason to Wm Reed for 2 lots (in Corbintown?).
Two other deeds proved.

James Spratt to be paid 5 shillings for "Smith's work done to the Prison."

John Pryor, John McGee and William Reed Esq's recommended as candidates for Sheriff of Orange County.

Grand Jurors for next Superior Court to be held at Salisbury: William Reed, John Dowell, James Murry, John McFarlin, John Woods, William Anderson, John Powell, Michael Holt, Daniel McCullom, Joseph Walker, George Allen, & Peter Hilton.

Deed from James Downing to George Allen for 100 acres of land, proved by the affirmation of James Lindley (Quaker).

21-179' Two deeds proved. Nathaniel Jones' mark recorded.

No liquors to be sold in Corbintown except by licensed public taverns.

Jonathan Greenal's Securities deliver him to the Sheriff.

21-180	David Gordon	vs	William Barbee	Petition
	Peter Legrand	"	Lawrence Vanhook	Traver
21-180'	James Espey	"	Thomas Winchester	Petition
	Jacob Mason	"	Conrod Lowe	"
22-181	Nathaniel Cary	"	John Collins	"
	John Wright	"	Joseph Boggs	"
22-181'	Charles Jones	"	Francis Day	"
	Peter Noe	"	Jacob Mason	"
	Thomas Alexander	"	Moses Hunter (?) or Winter (?)	"

"Court adjourned till Court in Course".

22-182 Court began 2nd Tuesday in June 1759, at "Corbin Town."

Bill of Sale from Andrew Crawford to John Green, for a mare, proved by oath of Hugh McConnel.

Samuel Walker to build a Public Grist Mill on Sandy Creek, "he having land on both sides thereof."

Court of June 1759 continued -

22-182 Thomas Laxton to build a Public Grist Mill on Country line Creek, "he having land on both sides thereof."

Ann Morrow, Adm'x of Benjamin Morrow, dec'd, filed an Inventory.

22-182' "Ordered that Jonathan Anderson, orphan child of (blank) Anderson, aged about 16 years and 4 months be bound apprentice to Samuel Barnett (Blacksmith) to learn his trade and that his master learn him to read write and cypher."

Bill of Sale from William Cox to James Watson for a negro boy was proved by the oath of Enoch Lewis.

23-183 Patty Bohannon, Adm'x of Joseph Bohannon filed a "further Account of Estate."
Ann Bohannon, Adm'x of Duncan Bohannon, filed a "further Inventory."

Will of Robert Melton. dec'd exhibited by Nathan Melton, was duly proved by oath of Richard Parker, one of the witnesses.
Other witnesses were James Sellers and Mary Stratton, to be summoned to appear at next Superior Court. (See GRIMES page 246.)

Suit of Winnifred Pickett against her husband Micajah Pickett. Bond of £ 100, for his good behavior for 1 year.

23-183' Thomas Harris and Elizabeth his wife, Administrators, filed an Inventory of the Estate of Henry Webb.

Thomas Stagg, Samuel Burton and Thomas Loyd are appointed to divide the Estate of Henry Webb.

Wentworth and John Webb acknowledged a certain agreement with Elizabeth Webb.

23-183' to 24-185' Eleven deeds from Henry McCulloch and sixteen deeds from Earl of Granville proved.

24-185' Hercules Ogle to build a Public Grist Mill on Deep River in the Earl of Granville's District. Surveyor to lay off 2 acres - land to be appraised by Jacob Brooks, Esq, Zachariah Martin, Thomas Dark & Timothy Terrell. Earl of Granville agents to have notice.

24-186 Joseph Maddock and John Jones, Executors of the last will of John Stanfield, dec'd, exhibited an account of Estate.

Four deeds from Earl of Granville.
24-186' Two deeds proved.
Six deeds from Earl of Granville.
25-187 Three deeds proved.

Court of June 1759 continued -

25-187 Joseph Maddock to be paid 14 shillings for mending the prison, etc.

Micajah Pickett gives bond for his good behavior. Richard Burton, Benjamin Phillips, John Holt and James Burton, "acknowledge themselves severally indebted to the King" as Pickett's bondsmen.

John Collins proved his attendance in suit of Thomas Jennings aganist Isareel Eastwood.

25-187' Seven deeds proved.
25-188 Five deeds proved.

25-188' "Ordered that Edward Stone, William Rhodes, William Cox, Joseph Barbee, George Herendon, John Barbee, Christopher Barbee, John Patterson, William Pickett, John West, James Acock and Arthur Cook be appointed as a Jury to lay out a Road leading from Orange County Court House to the County line and from thence to Tower Hill where the seat of Government is directed to be fixed and that the Sheriff summon the said Jury to meet at the Court House in Corbintown on the 25th Day of July next in order to be qualified and that they make return of their proceedings to next Court, and that Edward Stone be Overseer from the Court House to William Rhodes, and John Patterson from thence to Joseph Barbee's, and the said Barbee from thence to the County line." (See ASHE'S "History of North Carolina" pages 293 & 296, Vol I, concerning Tower Hill.)

"Ordered that James Wade, John Mitchel, Nathaniel Kimbrough, John Alston, Samuel Burton, William Reaves, James Ray, Micajah Pickett, Watson Bromfield, Warham Glenn, John Woods & Richard Burton be appointed a Jury to lay out a road ... leading from the Plantation Thomas Hart's to the road that leads to Tower Hill from Orange Court House..... James Wade be Overseer from the beginning to William Moore's, John Alston from thence to Nathaniel Kimbrough's, and the said Kimbrough from thence to the County line."

25-189 A Public Road to be laid out from Plantation of Alexander Mebane to the County trading path leading to the new Warehouse on Peedee River - and that William Murry, George Allen, Hugh Smith, George Johnson, Ralph Croft, Mathew Woods, James Fruit, Jacob Smith. Daniel McDaniel, William Mebane, Lanclott (?) Armstrong, John Wright and James Campbell be appointed a Jury to lay off the said road from the beginning to the Quaker Meeting at Cain Creek, - and that Thomas Brooks, Joel Brooks, Zachariah Martin, Ambrose Smith, John Gardenor, Daniel Norris, Peter Youngblood, James Williams, Hugh Laughlin, Shedrick Jacobs, John Rhodes and Aaron Pinson be appointed a Jury to lay off the said road from the Meeting House to the County line and that George Allen and John Wright be app. Overseers of the first part of the road to the Meeting House, and that Zachariah Martin and Aaron Pinson be app. Overseers from the Meeting House to the County line. The Sheriff to summons the first Jury to meet at Alexander Mebane's, Esq - the last-mentioned Jury to meet at the Court House in Corbintown.

Court of June 1759 continued -

25-189 "George Horner appointed Overseer of trading path road from the house of Alexander Mebane to the river Enoe."
George Allen from Alex. Mebane's to Haw River.
Benjamin Jackson from Eno River to Cap't Synnot's.
Thomas King from Synnot's to the County line.

26-189' "Ordered that in the suit Messers Cary against Robert Boyd that a Dedimus Issue to Thomas Hall and Alexander McCulloch or William Richmond, Esq to Examine John Gibson, Gabriel Everand & John Alston the Younger returnable to next Court."

Hugh Dobbin proved his attendance in the suit Thomas Dobbin against Watt and Boyd.

Two deeds from Earl of Granville proved.

Lodowick Clap and Thomas Lowe appointed Overseers of the "the Western path or Great Road from Haw River to the County line."

26-190 James Watson & William Reed, Esq's are appointed to see to repair of county prison.

Eli McDaniel app. Constable on the S. Side of Haw River.

	Francis Day	vs	Thomas Dunnagan	Case
26-190'	Thomas Jennings	"	Israel Eastwood	F.V.A.
	Oliver Stroud	"	Alex. McCracken	Debt
27-191	Wm. Lowther & Co.	"	Jacob Mason	Case
27-191'	Peter Legrand	"	Lawrence Vanhook	Traver
	Jacob Mason	"	George Mills	Or. Attch.
27-192	James Ball	"	George Rose	" "
	Henry Tollinger	"	Charles Mills	" "
27-192'	Joseph Moobry (?)	"	Paul Collins	Debt
	Henry Evans	"	Richard Burton	F.V.A.
28-193	Thomas Dunnagan	"	Francis Day	Case
	George Smith	"	Moses Winter	Petition
28-193'	William Spruce	"	Howell Brewer	Debt
28-194	James Graves	"	James Cheney	"
	Robert Hammett	"	John White	"
28-194'	John King	"	James Allison, Esq	Petition
	James Espey	"	Jonathan Greenels	"
	Henry Brewitt (?)	"	William Howlett	"
29-195	Thomas Dobbin	"	Samuel Watt & Boyd	Case
29-195'	Alex. Mebane, Esq	"	William Howlett	"
	Nathaniel Cary	"	David Lile	"
29-196	James Watson	"	William Hunphrys	Petition
	John Patterson	"	William Moore	"
29-196'	Alexander Emsley	"	William Bobbitt	"

Court of June 1759 continued -

29-196'	Lazarus Benton	vs	Titus Benton	Petition
	Robert Patterson	"	Francis Cyprus	Case
30-197	Henry Whitfills	"	Wolrie (?) Keasey	Petition
	Thomas Anderson	"	Edward Williams	Or. Attch.

"Court adjourned till Court in Course."

30-197' Court began on 2nd Tuesday, 11th day, September 1759. "Corbin Town."

James Collins, Jr to build a Water Grist Mill on his own land on East side of Haw River.

Last will of James Hopkins, dec'd proved by oath of Alexander Fogerson, John Dobbin & David Smith. William Hopkins, William Phillips & John Hopkins qualified as Executors and returned an Inventory of Estate.

Solomon Deboe's mark recorded.

Letter of Attorney from Benjamin Davis to Elnathan Davis recorded.

30-198 John Dowell granted license to "keep an Ordinary at his Dwelling in Corbintown."
Mathew Wood granted license to keep Tavern at his dwelling in Corbintown.
Thomas Hadley granted license to keep Tavern at his dwelling.

Isaiah Watkins, Adm. of Estate of William Williams, exhibits a further Inventory. John Pryor & David Hart, Esq's are appointed to settle his accounts.

"Ordered that a road be opened ... from Hogan's Creek to Orange Courthouse & that Daniel McCulloch, Benjamin King, Thomas Hughs, Edward Denney, William Grimes, Nathaniel Hart, John Cantril, William Savage, Joseph Cantril, Thomas Thompson, Christopher Logue, Cairns Tinnen, Benjamin Keadle, Zachariah Keadle, Jr be a Jury to lay out the same & that John Cantril & Wm. Savage be Overseers of the same."

30-198' "Benjamin Cantril proved an account of £ 1-15-0 against the Estate of Andrew Culbertson dec'd for funeral charges and attendance upon the said deceased."

"Ordered that John Cate and Patrick Rutherford make an equal Division of the hands that work on the Road in their District."

Court of September 1759 continued -

30-198' "Ordered that a road be laid out leading from the Great Road that leads to Cape Fare where James Trice lives to the County line leading to Halifax - & that Joseph Barbee, John Barbee, Sr, Henry Beasley, Christian Rhodes, James Trice, Edward Trice, John Trice, Mark Morgan, Hezakiah Rhodes, Nathaniel Kimbro, Jacob Bledsoe & Benjamin Saxon, be a Jury to lay out some - & that Nathaniel Kimbrough & Benjamin Saxon be Overseers - etc."

"Ordered that John Gaddis remain under thecare of Edmund Denney until the next County Court --"

John Landrum petition to build a Public Water Grist Mill on land belonging to the Earl of Granville.

Thomas Cate and Thomas Rainey appointed Overseers of road leading from Court House to John Woody's Ferry.

31-199 "Ordered that David Hopkins orphan child of James Hopkins be bound to John Hopkins until he come of age..."
"And that Mary and George Hopkins be bound unto Andrew Bridges (?) until they come of age..."
"And that Aron Hopkins orphan of James Hopkins, dec'd be bound unto William Hopkins to learn to read and write and the trade of a shoemaker."

Deed from Earl of Granville to Gilbert Strean (Strayhorn).

"Ordered that a Road be laid out... from that part of the Western Path where Alex Mebane Esq lives to John Woody's Ferry on Haw River & that David Nelson, Robert Holloway, Robert Allison, William Blackwood, James Ross, Martin Doyle, James Ayliot (Elliott), George Johnson, Richard Woods, William Mebane, Thomas Rainey and Samuel Moore be appointed a Jury to lay out the same, and that Thomas Hadley and Robert Rainey be Overseers thereof."

31-199' Six deeds proved.
31-200 Two deeds proved.

.."Piece of writing said to be the last will"...of Charles Foshe.... Joseph Foshe named as Executor came into Court and renounced the aforesaid Executorship.

31-200' Widow of Charles Fooshee ordered to appear at next court and give security of children's part. Estate is in danger of being wasted. (The widow, Susannah Fooshee, died not long after this date. See Court of June 1764, page 105 in next volume, and below).

Court of September 1759 continued -

31-200' "William Craig appointed Overseer "of that end of the Cape Fare road next the Court House so far as New Hope including the Ford - Thomas Capper from thence ten miles towards the County line - William Barbee from thence to the County line."

32-201 William Nunn's Ordinary license renewed.

William Comb's mark recorded.

Thomas Lloyd, Esq, Thomas Stagg & Samuel Burton appointed to divide the Estate of Henry Webb"amongst the widow & heirs & make report..."

Harman Husbands has leave to build a Public Grist Mill on his own land on waters of Deep River.

Following to attend as Jurors at November Salisbury Court - Mark Morgan, James Ray, Tyrie Harris, James McAllister, David Hart & Lawrence Rambo.

Petit Jurors:
David Steel, James Wilkinson, George Finley, Nathaniel Jones, James Stewart & George Brantley.

32-201' William Brown, a bastard child, to be bound to William Comb for the term of 5 years & 9 months...

John Tinnen fined 5 shillings for his Contempt of Authority.

Jacob Mason's Ordinary license renewed.

32-202 "..Joseph Brown & Dunkin Lewis, two Evidences summoned in the Suit Hugh Porter, Esq Plt'f against John Bickerstaff be fined 20 pounds each" for not appearing.

	John Dunnagan	vs	Grace Mier	F.V.A.
32-202'	James Watson	"	Jacob Mason	Case
33-203	Israel Eastwood	"	Thomas Jennings	Debt
	Robert Brashear	"	John Hallum	Debt quietem
33-203'	Robert Jones, Jr	"	John Wood	Case
33-204	David Mimms	"	Sampson Williams	"
	Hugh Smith	"	David Sharp	Petition
	Thomas Copestick	"	Benjamin Povey	"
33-204'	John Wright	"	John Slater	"
	James Watson	"	John Hinchey	"
34-205	" "	"	Michael Waldrop	"
	" "	"	Shadrick Jacobs	"
	Willie Jones	"	John Hatley	"
34-205'	William Taylor	"	Bendal Strahan	"
	Shadrick Jacob	"	Jamey Welsh	"
	Joseph Boggs, Esq	"	Mary Fuller	"

Court of September 1759 continued -

34-206 William Reed, Esq	vs	Zachariah Martin	Petition
James Cary, Jr	"	James Graves	Debt
" " "	"	John Slater	"

"Court adjourned till Court in Course."

34-206' Court began 2nd Tuesday in December 1759, Corbin Town.

Deed proved from Richard Braswell to David Mims.

Perishable Estate of Robert Melton, dec'd to be sold.

William Churton, Esq recommended to be Public Surveyor.

James Watson, Esq produced his Commission as Entry Taker for Orange County.

35-207 John Douglass & James Barnhill appointed Overseers of Road from the Courthouse to the Pine ford on Haw River.
George Finley app. Overseer from John Roberson's to the County line.
George Adams app. Overseer from Henderson's Creek towards Peter King's.

Peter Noey's Ordinary license renewed. Two deeds proved.

Deed from William Reed, Esq to Walter Ashmore, lot in Corbintown.

35-207' Deed proved.

"On motion of Plunkett Ballard, gentlemen, in behalf of Sarah, a poor Orphan living with Thomas King"... she complains... and "said John? King be summoned to appear ..."(Her last name not stated).

Marks recorded by Samuel Money & William Churton.

Two deeds proved.
35-208 Three deeds proved.

Complaint against Susannah Fooshee, Exec'x of Charles Fooshee, dismissed.

35-208' John Dowell to give evidence against James Espey and John Wood (for passing false money). John Woods discharged.

36-209 "Ordered that Isaiah Watkins, John Smith, Thomas Lovelatty, John London, Francis Cox, Joshua Brown, Marshal Lovelatty, Mark London, Joseph Thrasher, John Delishment (?) & John Smith be appointed to lay out a road from the County line near Pinson's Ferry on Dan River to John Cunningham's Road on Haw River that leads to Salisbury in Rowan County ...Daniel Allen appointed Overseer thereof."

Court of December 1759 continued -

36-209	Nicholas Perkins	vs	Joseph Dolittle	Debt
	Nathaniel Cary	"	James Espey	Petition
36-209'	James & Nath. Cary	"	John Slater	"
	James Cary, Jr	"	William Howlett	Debt
36-210	" " "	"	William Stroud	"
	" " "	"	Thomas Hughs	"
36-210'	" " "	"	William Cox	"
	Nathaniel Cary	"	William Birk	"

"Court adjourned till Court in Course."

37-211 Court began on 2nd Tuesday in March 1760, in Corbin Town.

Letters Testamentory "to Anthony Chamness & John Marshall, Exec's of the last will of Henry Mayner, dec'd, proved in open court by the affirmation of Charles Davis and John Pyke..." (Recorded in Book A, page 12)

Joseph Maddock "one of the Executors of John Stanfield, dec'd, exhibited a receipt from Hannah Stanfield, widow."

Marks recorded by Hackley Warren & Edward Moore.

Gilbert Patterson - "poor, aged, infirm", to be tax exempt.

37-211' Dyall Pevey's mark recorded.

Robert Davis app. Overseer of Road in room of James Murdoch.
Andrew McBroom " " " " " " " Patrick Rutherford.

Last will of Maryann Currie proved in open Court by the oath of Edward Nash. Letters Testamentary to James Currie, Exec. Bond £ 50. (Recorded in Book A, page 11)

"Ordered that William Serjant, Stephen Serjant, Samuel Bell, John Campbell, George Bagley, John Fogerson, Thomas Dobbins, John Lea, James Dochester, Thomas Willson, John Walker & Charles Mulholland be a Jury to lay out a Road beginning at John Roberson's, Thence by John Campbell's & thence by Stephen Serjant's unto the Great Road that leads near to Solomon Debow's & McCoy's Mill and that William Lea be appointed Overseer thereof."

37-212 William Grace granted license to keep Ordinary at his Dwelling.
Overseers of Roads appointed -
Benjamin Pickett from Stinking Quarter to Cain Creek.
Charles Davis from Cain Creek to Rocky River District.
Samuel Dark for Rocky River District.
James Williams for Lick Creek District.
Samuel Norris from Bear Creek to Deep River.
John Tomlinson from Deep River to the County line.

Court of March 1760 continued -

37-212 "Ordered that William Morrow be appointed Overseer of Cape Fare Road from Woody's Ferry to Terrell's Creek, and Joshua Hadley from thence to the fork of the Road."

Cairns Tinnen appointed Overseer in room of Alexander Lackey.

Letters of Administration on Estate of James Forrest, dec'd, granted to William Forrest. Bond: £ 300. Bondsmen: Benjamin Forrest, Thomas Forrest, James Forrest, Abraham Nelson.

37-212' Thomas Pugh appointed Overseer of Road in room of Samuel Allen. Andrew McBroom appointed Constable in the room of Joseph Allison.

"Ann Morrow, Adm'x of Benjamin Morrow dec'd exhibited a full discharge from two of the children for their share of the Estate ..." their names are not stated.

Michael Trollinger to keep a Public Ferry near the Pine ford on Haw River.

Nathan Melton, Exec of Robert Melton, dec'd filed an account of sales.

Sackfield Brown appointed Constable in the room of George Smith.

38- 213 Daniel Cain appointed Constable "in the District where Samuel Stewart lives near the Courthouse."
Mordecai Gwin appointed Constable "in the room of (blank) Thompson in Pinson's Settlement."

Gilbert Strean app. Overseer of Cape Fare Road in room of William Craig.

John Grace's Ordinary license renewed.
Zachariah Martin's Ordinary license renewed.

William Reed exhibits his Commission as Sheriff of Ornage County.

"Ordered that an Orphan boy named John Gaddis of the age of 17 years be bound unto Edmund Dennice" until 21 years old.

38-213' Samuel Allen, Jr. App. Constable in room of Samuel Allen, Sr.

Item about James Hopkin's Estate.

Marks recorded by Giles Chapman and Samuel Chapman.

James Bowie, Thomas Whitehead and John Dowell qualified as Deputy Sheriffs.

38-214 Fifteen deeds proved.

38-214' "Court adjourned till Court in Course."

39-215 Court began 3rd Tuesday in August 1760, in Corbin Town.

Anthony Chamness and John Marshal (Quakers) Exec's of Henry Maynor, dec'd, exhibited an Inventory.

"On motion of William Cummings, Esq att'y in behalf of Jane Mayner widow of Henry Mayner, dec'd, that the said Jane may be appointed Guardian to the two youngest children of the said Henry to wit Betty and Ann and that she appear at the Court to enter into Bond..."

William Reed, Esq appointed Standard Keeper of Orange County.

William Fletcher appointed Constable in the room of John Burks.

39-215' Letters of Administration to William Reed, Esq on the Estate of Mary Douglass, dec'd. Bond £ 40. Bondsman: James Bowie.

William Hart appointed Constable in the room of John Brooks.
Thomas Stagg " Overseer of Road in the room of Thomas King.
Semore York " " " " " " " Thomas Lowe.

Sherrod Reynolds to build a "Public Grist Mill at the place where he now lives on Little Barton's Creek." Agents of Earl of Granville to be notified.

Letters Testamentory to Catherine Vanhook, widow & Exec'x of Aaron Vanhook, dec'd. The will proved by oath of Lucy Vanhook. (Recorded Book A page 9)

"Ordered that James Daniel be appointed Guardian to John Gouge Orphan child of John Gouge, deceased." Bond £ 200. Bondsmen: Thomas Harris, William Reaves.

39-216 Marks recroded by James Aycock, William Reaves, Jr. & Wm. Wireman.

William Forrest, Adm of James Forrest, dec'd, filed an Inventory.

Letters of Administration to Jane Wade on the Estate of James Wade, dec'd. Bond: £ 500. Bondsmen: Robert Abercromby, Hugh Wood..

Letters of Adm. to John Spann on the Estate of Joshua Ambrose Smith. Bond: £ 300. Bondsmen: Benjamin Blake, Benjamin Saxon.

39-216' Nathaniel Walton records his mark.

James Dinkins appointed Overseer of Road in room of Lawrence Redman.
Joseph Money " " " " " " " George Horner.

John Pryor, Esq, William Churton, Esq, George Lowe, Thomas Stagg, Luke Bynum, Thomas King, to attend next Superior Court for District of Halifax on 1st September as Jurymen.

Court of August 1760 continued -

39-216' "Grand Jury Impanelled and Sworn to wit-

Joseph Barbee	Thomas Holden	William Barnes
James Ray	Benjamin Blake	Tignal Jones
Nathaniel Jones	John Bohannon	Joseph Walker
John Stewart	Arthur Cook	Daniel McCullom
Samuel Watt	Thomas Stagg	Hugh Wood"
Edward Stone	Hugh Smith	

40-217 Jacob Mason's Ordinary license renewed.
Daniel Cain's " " " .

"Ordered that Nathaniel Hart, David Hart, Thomas Hughs, Edmund Denney, Daniel McCullom, Samuel Cobb, John Cantril, Joseph Cantril, John Thrasher, Robert Wells, & Samuel Watt be appointed a Jury to lay out and open a road ... from Daniel McCullom's Plantation to Taylors Road leading to the Courthouse,..and that Benjamin King be appointed Overseer of the upper part & John Cantril of the lower part of the said road."

"Ordered that the following persons be appointed a Jury to lay out a Road beginning near Robert Patterson's Plantation, thence to Colling's Ford on Haw River, thence... to Hoge's Ford on Deep River, thence down Cape Fare to the County line, to wit - John Brantley, Richard Braswell, Moses Ginn, Joseph Kirk, Charles Clanton, William Petty, Sr, James Crawford, Thomas Tucker, Joseph Brantley, Nicholas Copeland, Hercules Henderson, John Stewart, & that John Brantley be appointed Overseer of the Lower part, and James Copeland for the Upper part."

40-217' Hugh Bradley, a poor man in Saint Mathew's Parish to be tax free.

John Fuller appointed Constable on the S. Side of Haw River.

Peter Noey app. Overseer of Road from Haw River to the Great Alamance.

"Ordered that the Sheriff get an Iron Collar made & that he cause it to be put on the Negro man said to belong to Benjamin Cook (called Jack) now in the Goal of this County, & that the said Sheriff hire out the said Negro agreeable to law."

"Ordered that Samuel Watt bring Winnifred and Judith Mitchell to next Court to have them bound to the said Samuel Watt."

Daniel Cain appointed Constable in the room of John Thomas.

	Henry Temple	vs	Sampson Williams	Debt
40-218'	James Cary, Jr	"	Timothy Lea	Petition
	Edward Herren	"	Sherrerd Reynolds	"
	Alex. Torrington	"	Wm & Alex. Spencer	Or. Attch.
	Thomas Harriss	"	James Bowie	Debt

Court of August 1760 continued -

40-219'	Thomas Harriss	"	Thomas Loyd	Debt
	" "	"	James Boyd	"
40-220	" "	"	Samuel Burton & Thomas Stagg	"
	Luke Bynum	"	Jacob Mason	Petition

"Court adjourned till Court in Course."

41-220' Court began on 3rd Tuesday in November 1760.

Estate of James Wade to be sold 11 December 1760. Jane Wade, Adm'x filed an Inventory of Estate.

"Grand Jury Impannelled and Sworn to wit -

Thomas Stagg	Hugh Wood	John Mitchell
William Reaves	Samuel Burton	James Trice
Benjamin Saxon	William Grimes	David Hart
William Wiley	John Wood	John Slater
Richard Holman	Samuel Temple	James Horton."

41-221 Will of Joshua Hadley, proved by oaths of Patience Hadley and Joshua Hadley, Exec's.

"Alexander Young, a boy twelve years old to be bound to James Henderson (cooper) till he arrive to the age of 21". (Reconsidered later, and held over until next Court.)

Thomas Stagg's Ordinary license renewed.

Letters of Adminstration to Josias Dixon on the Estate of James McCall, dec'd. Bond £ 120. Bondsmen: Thomas King, Thomas Harris.

41-221' Catherine Vanhook, Exec'x of Aaron Vanhook, dec'd, filed Inventory.

Henry Leman & Thomas Watkins appointed Overseers of Road leading from the Courthouse to Woody's Ferry.

Thomas Stagg, Luke Bynum & Thomas King to be paid for their attendance at Superior Court of Halifax, 1760.

John Dowell's Ordinary license renewed.

William Grimes appointed Overseer in the room of Nathaniel Hart - "beginning at Isaac Durham's to the head of Hogan's Creek, thence to the head of Country line Creek thence to fork of said Creek."

42-222 John Almond appointed Constable in room of James Satterfield. Thomas Hendricks app. Overseer of Road in room of David Vanhook.

Court of November 1760 continued -

42-222 Estate of Joshua Ambrose Smith to be sold Monday, 15th December.

"Ordered that James Daniel be appointed Guardian to John Gouge an orphan child of John Gouge, Dec'd". Bond: £ 200. Bondsmen: Thomas King, Thomas Harris.

Thomas Capper's mark recorded.

Thomas King granted license to keep Ordinary at his house in Corbintown.

Deed of Sale proved.

Edward Tyrie app. Overseer of Road in room of Joshua Hadley, dec'd.

Mr. James Cary to be paid " £ 55.16.8 Proclamation Money for a Standard of Weights and Measures, .. and £ 5 for his services therein" and "the Land Carriages thereof from Hallifax."

42-223 Jury to lay out a road from Childsburg to Johnston County Line - Mark Morgan, Joseph Barbee, Henry Beasley, John Patterson, *George Herndon, John Barbee, James Trice, Christopher Barbee, Christopher Rhodes, William Rhodes, Thomas Capper, James Aycock, Edward Stone, William Cox, Benjamin Saxon, William Pickett, Arthur Cook and William Williams. They to appear at the Court House in Childsburg on 2nd Tuesday in February, (formerly Corbintown.)

Three deeds from Earl of Granville.
43-223' 8 deeds Earl of Granville. 42-224 Eight deeds Earl of Granville.
43-224' 8 deeds " " " .

43-225	Charles Jones	vs	John White	Or. Attch.
	Thomas Bowman	"	Joseph Sutton	Case
43-225'	John Kelly	"	Joshua Fincher	Debt
	Joshua Fincher, Ass.	"	Hugh Smith	Case
43-226	Leonard Clayborne	"	William Petty	Petition
43-226'	A. Dixon	"	John Meherg	Ass'. & Batt'.
45-227	Michael Boyl Etc?	"	Daniel Caine	Debt
	John Cox	"	Thomas Capper	Case
45-227'	Thomas Anderson	"	Daniel Dean	Or. Attch.
	Reason Ricketts	"	Joseph Voss	Debt
45-228	William Cummings	"	Conrod Lowe	Case
	John Kelley	"	Joseph Benton	Or. Attch.
	David Bradford	"	Michael Boyl	Case
	Benjamin Posey	"	Thomas Landrop	Or. Attch.
45-228'	Wm. Cummings, Esq	"	Notley Hollis	Petition

"Court adjourned till Court in Course."

---

*Note by Ruth H. Shields. I am a descendant of George Herndon and William Rhodes. I also have information on the Barbee, Morgan, Patterson, Pickett, and Trice families. I have no information on the other names.

46-229 Court of February began 17th, 1761

Hugh Laughlin appointed Overseer of Road in room of William Morrow.
Laughlin Campbell app. Overseer of Road in room of Benjamin Jackson.

Ralph Croft appointed Constable in room of Samuel Allen, Jr.

John Graves cattle mark recorded.

"Ordered that the following persons do attend the Superior Court at Halifax, the 1st day of March --
James Allen, James McAlister, & Robert Abercromby, as Grand Jury.
William Horton, James Clarke, & Hugh Woods as Petit Jury."

46-229' James Linley granted license to keep Ordinary at his dwelling.

"Grand Jury impanelled and Sworn - to wit

Thomas Stagg	Benjamin Carter	Moses Hollis
Richard Simpson	Joseph Atkins	Hugh Porter
Jesse Brashear	John Hunter	Ephraim Gold
Henry Reynolds	William Willson	Phillip Preather (?)
Nathaniel Reynolds	Alexander Going	Thomas Willson."

"Ordered that Barnett Troehsdale (Trousdale ?) & Henry Slater have liberty to build a Water Grist Mill on their own land"....

"Peter Perkins proved his attendance as an Evidence in the Suit James Robert against Thomas Tetsworth - amounting to Ƚ6-14 Proc. Money.

Hugh Smith and his wife appointed guardians to Alexander Young, orphan child of Alexander Young, dec'd.

46-230 Charles Stevens app. Overseer of Road in room of Joseph Henderson.
Stephen Terry " " " " " " " Gilbert Strean.
Rob. Donalson " " " " " " " Gabriel Davis.

William Dunnagan's mark recorded.

David Hart and John Lea to examine the accounts of Josiah Dixon, Adm. of Estate of James McCall, dec'd, and make return thereof. (On the next page is their report that they find the "Accounts Just.")

"Moses Ridley a poor Debtor under Execution at the suit of William Chavis - plaintiff be summoned to show cause why he may not have the Benefit of the Insolvent Act."

Letters of Administration to Mary Brantley, widow and Adm'x of Lewis Brantley, dec'd. Bond: Ƚ 200. Bondsmen: John Brantley, Henry Braswell.

46-230' Marks recorded by James Armstrong, Gilbert Strean, Thomas Linley, Thomas Linley, Sr, William Thompson, & Enos Elmore.

Court of February 1761 continued -

46-230' William Morrow granted license to keep Ordinary at his dwelling.

47-231 Benjamin Guess petitions to build a Public Grist Mill on the land of Earl of Granville & waters of Sandy Creek. Earl of Granville's agents to be notified.

John Highett app. Overseer of Road in room of Benjamin Piggott.

Michael Murry's mark recorded.

Henry Braswell granted license to keep a Ferry on Cape Fear River where Richard Baswell formerly kept one.

Letters of Administration to Margaret Craig on the Estate of William Craig, dec'd. Bond: £ 200. She exhibits an Inventory of the Estate.

Letters of Administration to Lawrence Vanhook on the Estate of Aaron Vanhook, dec'd. Bond: £ 200.

47-231' George Reaves records his mark.

William Petty. Sr and Thomas Tucker app. Overseers of Road in the room of James Copland.
Samuel Parks app. Overseer in room of Thomas Cooper.(Should be Capper.)

"Ordered that Joseph Morgan & James Dochester be fined each £ 20 for not appearing agreeable to summons in the Suit David Lowe against Josias Wallace --"

"Ordered that the following persons be appointed to lay out a road... from County Line near Andrew Shepheard's to Henry Braswell's and thence to Johns(t)on County line - to wit : Richard Cheek, Joseph Evans, Sampson Williams, Valentine Braswell, William Yarborough, Joseph Mims, Robert Jones, Charles Brum, Randal Cheek, John Brooker, Henry Braswell, John Bohannon, Thomas Saymore, Richard Braswell, Wm. Braswell, Isaac Cooper, James Stringfield, & William Cone, and that Simpson Williams be appointed Overseer on the S Side of Haw River, and Richard Cheek app. Overseer on the N. Side of Haw River."

47-232 "John Richmond a prisoner under Execution at the Suit of John Richey (?)" swore that he was not worth 40 shillings - took benefit of Insolvents Act.

"Ordered that Solomon West. Hezekiah Collins, John West, Jr, Solomon Jones, Wm. Mills, John Mills, Robert Mills, Robert Jones, John O'Daniel, Wm O'Daniel, Thomas Lynch, Francis Wilkinson & Edward Baily, John Boid. & Thomas Lapsey, Michael Boyd, Jacob Raily & Daniel Sullivant with their Taxables work upon the road laid out by order of this Court from James Cantril's to Taylor's Road - also that the Inhabitants in the following Districts work on the said Road to wit- from Dolittle's on the Country line Creek to Lewis Odean's on Hoggans Creek, Thence to the head of Hogans Creek, thence to the head of the Country line --"

Court of February 1761 continued -

47-232 "John Dowel against John Jones, Original Attachment, Jos. Maddock bei summoned to declare what he has in his hands saith that there is nothing in his possession but what is under former process."

47-232'	Jacob Mason	vs	John Ross	Case
	David Mimms	"	Sampson Williams	"
48-233	Francis Day	"	James Moss	"
	Richard Holman	"	John Powell	Or. Attch.
48-233'	John Boyd, Jr	"	John Bickerstaff	" "
	Henry Whitsetts	"	Warwick Keasley (?)	" "
48-234	Thomas Anderson	"	Edward Williams	" "
	Hugh Linum (?)	"	Thomas Strean	" "
	Wm. Grace & Uxr.	"	Daniel Caine	Ass. & Batt
	David Lyles	"	Josiah Wallice	" " "
49-235	Josiah Wallice	"	David Lyles	Case
	William Kirkbey (?)	"	Robert Patterson	"
49-235'	John Hawkins	"	William Moore	"
49-236	James Graves	"	Absolom Looney	Debt
	James Couch	"	Jacob Huggins	Or. Attch.
49-236'	Robert Hastie	"	Jacob Jones	Case
	Charles Jones	"	Thomas Brooks	"
50-237	Hugh Smith	"	William Howlett	"
	Mary Montgomery	"	Samuel Moore	"
50-237'	Charles Jones	"	John White	Or. Attch.
	Thomas Bowman	"	Joseph Sutton	Case
	Hercules Ogle	"	Benjamin Bolin	Petition
50-238	Alexander Shane	"	Phillip Sitton	"
	" "	"	Thomas Sitton	"
50-238'	John Herring	"	Shadrick Jacob	"
	Zachariah Caddle	"	Barzaleel Brashear	"
	Andrew Hampton	"	James Daniel	"
51-239	Henry Lemon, Jr	"	William Wiley	Case
51-239'	Robert Jones, Jr	"	Josias Dixon, Esq	Petition
	William Draper, Assignee & Agent	"	William Hucker & Cornelius Rowe	"
51-240	Nathaniel Cary	"	Samuel Stuart	"
	John Dowell	"	John Jones	Or. Attch.
	Nathaniel Cary	"	Benjamin Cate	Debt
51-240'	" "	"	Joseph Sharp	"
	William Nunn	"	Robert Brashears	Petition
52-241	James Couch	"	Joseph Maddock	Case
	Thomas Anderson	"	Daniel Dean	Or. Attch.
	John Patterson	"	Wm. Baker, Sr	" "
	Jacob Mason	"	Thomas Donalson	Debt
52-241'	Dennis Wheeler	"	James Fruit	"

"Court adjourned till Court in Course."

52-242 Court began 3rd Tuesday (19th day) May 1761, in Childsburg.

"Ordered that the Sheriff make sale of the goods of Zachariah Routh, attached at the Suit of James Armstrong."

Deed from Wm. Churton to James Watson - 400 acres, proved.

Last will of James Alston, dec'd, proved. Letters issued to John Dawson, Phillip Alston, Solomon Alston, Jr, and "John Alston son of Solomon", Executors.

John Lambert's mark recorded.

52-242' Letters of Administration to Esther Boggs, Adm'x of Joseph Boggs, dec'd. Bond: £ 200. Bondsmen: John Wright, Lodowick Clap.

"Ordered that Letters of Administration be granted to Joseph Fooshee, Adm. of Charles Fooshee and Susannah his wife .."
Bond: £ 100. Bondsmen: Henry Brewer, William Marsh.

"Ordered that Haner, or Honor, Graw (?) or Grace (?) have letters of Administration on the Estate of William Graw, dec'd. Bond: £ 200."

Henry Wagoner app. Overseer of Road in room of Robert Davis.

Jacob Mason's mark recorded.

"following persons - Grand Jurors - to be fined for neglect - Wm Chambers, Andrew Linum, Solomon West, John West Jr, Thomas Lowe, James Collins, Henry Morris, Joseph Dolittle, Semore York, Hezekiah Collins, James Stewart, Samuel Paul, Wm Porter and John Stroud."

53-243 Robert Taylor appointed Constable in room of Cairnes Tinnen.
Jesse Brashear " " on the head of Haw River.
John Baldwin " " in the room of William Brezzer.

Letters of Administration granted to Elizabeth Harris, Adm'x of Thomas Harris, dec'd. Bond: £ 600. Bondsmen: James Bowie, Thomas King.

Edmund Fanning appointed "Prosecutor for the Crown."

"Ordered that a Road be laid out ... from the Courthouse to Pendergrasses Ford on Morgan's Creek and thence to Tucker's Road at Robert Patterson's Plantation by the following Jury to wit - William Griffin, William Bynum, James Rigsby, Robert Patterson, Thomas Durham, John Edwards, Gideon Kirksey, Christopher Kirksey, John King, Isaac Collins, John Collins & Henry Brewer, and that Isaac Collins & Robert Pendergrass be appointed Overseers thereof."

Court of May 1761 continued -

53-243' "The Grand Jury Impanelled & Sworn to wit - Thomas Stagg, Robert Wells, William Grimes, James Armstrong, Samuel Watt, Jeffrey Beck, John May, Peter Youngblood, Joseph Foshee, Henry Gold, Joseph King, William Marsh & Gibeon Kirksey."

John Graves Ordinary license renewed.

"Ordered that John Gray, Alex. Mabin, & George Allen, Esquires, do view the Flatt or Ferry boat at Giles Chapman's Ferry & make report thereof to next Court."

Andrew Caldwel appointed Constable in the room of Samuel Stuart.
Isaac Grisam " " " " " " Lodowick Clap.

53-244 "Mordecai Gwinn who was Security for John Pearson in the Suit brought by him against Michael Holt, Jr, came into Court & surrendered up the principle whereon Mordecai Gwinn & Benjamin Phillips came into Court and acknowledged themselves special bail in the suit aforesaid, for the aforesaid John Patterson." (Clerk's error).

"Jesse Breshear & Middleton Breshear Securities for John Pearsons in the Suit brought by John Powell against him came into Court & surrendered the principal, whereupon Peter Noey & Benjamin Phillips enters themselves Special Bail for the said John Pearson..."

"Ordered that Joseph King, Edward Smith, Henry Gold, John Bryant, Hosea Tapley, and his hands work on the Road from Robersons Mill to Cushy (?) Camp Branch under John Cate, Jr, Overseer."

"Thomas Roberson appointed Overseer of the Road from his house to James McCallister's & that the hands on the upper side of the road ... work ... under him."

James McCallister proved his attendance as a Juror at Halifax Superior Court.

53-244' William Reed, Thomas Lloyd and John McGee recommended as candidates for Sheriff of Orange County.

Deed from Zachariah Harlin to Thomas Fussell for 247 acres, proved by oath of Thomas Cate.

"Ordered that the Tythable Persons subject to work on Roads - Living in Childsburg work on the following District to wit - from Thomas Wiley's Creek called the Great Creek to Enoe River & from the North line of the said town to the several Roads leading to the said Enoe River being the South line of the said Town & that William Nunn be appointed Overseer thereof."

Court of May 1761 continued -

53-244' "Ordered that the following persons to wit Isaac Allen, Jonathan Allen, Solomon Debow, Leonard Hoff & Ephraim Gold do work on the road from the Country line to Hico (?) ford under James Dochester, Overseer --"

Samuel Wall appointed Overseer of Road from the place where Edward Smith formerly lived to John Boyd's on Haw River.

William Reed, Sheriff, protests that the County Prison is not secure.

54-245 Eight deeds proved (2 from Peter Youngblood & Magdalene his wife.)
54-245' " " " .
54-246 Six deeds proved.

	Hugh McGomery	vs	James Boyd	Debt
54-246'	Charles Jones	"	John White	Or. Attch.
	Hugh Smith	"	Michael Murry	Case
55-247	Sherrod Reynolds	"	John Clark	"
	Robert Jones, Jr	"	William Brown	Petition
55-247'	" " "	"	Margaret Boggan	"
	Reason Ricketts	"	William Barton	Debt
	" "	"	Timothy Lea	"
55-248	Mordecai Gwinn	"	Samuel Parks	Case
	John Wright	"	John Liles	Petition
	John Dowell	"	David Liles	"
	John Meherg	"	Richard Burton	"
55-248'	Mathew Lock	"	Hugh Smith	"
	Charles Basingdine	"	William Vornal	"
56-249	Hugh Foster	"	Jacob Armfield	"
	Gilbert Strean	"	Michael Waldrop, Jr	"
56-249'	Michael Holt, Jr. & Uxr	"	John Pearson	Case
	John McGowen	"	Joshua Stroud	T.V.A.
	John Wright	"	Josiah Wallice & James Morgan	Or. Attch.
	John Johnson	"	Josiah Wallice	" "
56-250	Luke Lea	"	Henry Reynolds, Jr	Petition
	Thomas Stagg	"	Charles Harris	"
	Nathaniel Cary	"	Benjamin Saxon	Case
56-250'	John Griggs	"	Hosea Tapley	"
	John Meherg & Ux'r	"	John Mitchell & Ux'r	"
	Thomas Stagg	"	Samuel Burton	"

"Court adjourned till Court in Course."

57-251 Court began 1st Tuesday (4th day) in August 1761, in Childsburg. Present: William Churton, Thomas Lloyd, Tyrie Harriss, Esquires.

Jacob Mason's Ordinary license renewed.

Court of August 1761 continued -

57-251 Letters of Administration to "Elizabeth Browning on Estate of her deceased husband Thomas Browning." Bond: £ 100. Bondsmen: James Bowie, Robert Patterson.

Letters of Administration to Ann Morgan on the "Estate of her deceased husband Henry Morgan". Bond: £ 100. Bondsmen: John Jones, John Marsha

57-251' James Cummings granted license to keep Tavern at his Dwelling in Childsburg. Securities: Jacob Mason & John Hallums.

"John Bohannon appointed Overseer of Road from Cape Fare River to White Oak, and Robert Jones from thence to the County line."

William Nunn's Ordinary license renewed.

Daniel Weldon, Att'y at Law,appointed Prosecutor for the Crown in Orange County.

"The Grand Jury Impanelled & Sworn to wit - Hugh Porter, Robert Taylor, John Taylor, John Douglas, Alexander Murahin (?), Nathaniel Walton, John Tinnen, James Hart, Francis Wilkinson, John Slater, Robert Patterson, Charles Johnson, Edward Stone, John Barbee, Jr, Isaac Collins, Alexander Nelson, Robert Marsh, William Rhodes & William Lea."

Ann Morgan, Adm'x of her deceased husband, proved an Inventory of his Estate. Sale to take place 28th August at Plantation where deceased formerly lived.

"Ordered that the Mill formerly Thomas Laxton & Son, Neil McCoy's, be a Public Mill agreeable to law --"

57-252 "Ordered that Thomas Wilson, Thos Wilson, Jr, William Maxwell, David Maxwell, Thomas Dobbins, John Fogerson, Andrew Fogerson, John Wright, Jonathan Allen, Gresham Allen, Isaac Allen, David Chambers, Leonard Hopson, James Bell, Robert Bell, Samuel Bell, George Bagby, Sr & Jr, Francis Wright, James Lea, Francis Carney, John Campbell, Stephen Serjant, William Serjant, John McFarland, James McFarland, Solomon Debow, & George Gold work the road from John Roberson's shop, by John Campbell's, thence by Stephen Serjant's unto the Great Road leading to Solomon Debow's and McCoy's Mill under the Inspection of William Lea, Overseer thereof.-"

"Ordered that Richard Womack, Jacob Womack, Abraham Womack, Josiah Adley, Robert McFarland, Andrew Evans, Frederick Kerlock, Robert Donalson, Hugh Barnet, William Barnet, William Chambers, Jr, Edward Chambers & John Hurley be appointed a Jury to lay out and open a road to begin where the road from the County line crosses the road leading from where John Pryor, Esq lives to Orange Court house, thence ... to .... Granville County line, and that Edward Chambers, Robert McFarland & Thomas Douglas be appointed Overseers."

Court of August 1761 continued -

57-252' William Reed, Esq., qualified as Sheriff of Orange County.

Last will of Richard Braswell proved by oath of Henry Braswell.

Letters of Adminstration to Sarah Crethers (no deceased named). Bond: £ 200. Bondsmen: James Tinnen, Charles Milligan.

Last will of Duncan Bohannon proved by oath of Joseph Brantley. Benjamin Bohannon qualified as Executor. Richard Bohannon relinquished his right as Executor.

58-253 Susannah Bohannon, widow of Duncan, relinquishes her right as Executrix.

Jury to lay out a Road "from the Court house to the red fields - Robert Cate, John King, Henry Morris, Henry Brewer, William Stroud, Jr, Wm. Long, Gideon Kirksey, Christian Kirksey, Hezekiah Collins, John Hunter, James Spratt, and John Crugs ? (Creegs ?) and ... Hezekiah Collins and James Stroud be appointed Overseers thereof."

John Alston, Exec. of James Alston, dec'd.returned an Inventory.

58-253' "Ordered that the Sheriff provide 24 staffs for Constables before the next Court ..."

John Campbell prays leave to build a Public Grist Mill on Haw River above the trading path - rejected - he appeals to Halifax Superior Court.

Marks recorded by Alexander Forgerson & James Hart.

Sheriff to sell personal Estate of Susannah Fooshe - 1st Tuesday in October, at Plantation of the deceased.

"Ordered that Joseph Fooshe do bring Hannah Fooshe the orphain child of Charles and Christian Foshe to the next Inferior Court held for this county to choose her a guardian."

"William Mebane and Jane his wife, Administrators of James Wade, dec'd, exhibited a further inventory of the said Estate..." (She was called "Jane the widow" in MINUTES for Nov. 1760.)

58-254 John Taylor & Francis Wilkinson enter themselves as Securities for William Daniel in the suit brought by Robert Tate against him.

Dorman Hinson app. Overseer of Road in room of Daniel Norris.

"Ordered that Wm. Mills, Sr, be appointed Overseer of the Road from James Allison, Esq's to Henderson's Creek, John Roberson from thence to John Boyd's, and George Adams from thence to the end."

Court of August 1761 continued -

58-254 "Anthony Stanford appointed Overseer of Road from James Burnhill's to the pine ford and the Ferry at Trollinger's on Haw River."

Alexander McCracken app. Overseer of Road in the room of John Douglas.

Letters Testamentary to John Slater, Executor of the last will of Mary Stafford, dec'd. Will proved by affirmation of Samuel Money, (Qu

58-254' Account of Sales of the Estate of Joshua Ambrose Smith returned by the Sheriff.

Aaron Harland taken into custody on account of his behavior in Court.

Honor Graw, widow and Adm'x of William Graw, dec'd, returned an Invento of the Estate.

John Slater, Exec. of Mary Stafford, dec'd, returned an Inventory.

Marks recorded by Joshua Griffin & Richard Parker.

59-255 "Michael Holt, Jr, is appointed Overseer of the Road from Pine Ford on Haw River to the fork of the Road westward, and from Trollinger's Ferry into said Road, Ordered that William Raney, John Pearson, Benjamin Phillips, Jesse Phillips, Jacob Holt, John Gant, Thomas Sharpe, Adam Trollinger, Henry Trollinger & John Powell lay out and open the new Road from the Ferry into said road ..."

William Reed, Sheriff, protests that the Goal is not sufficient.

"Francis Wilkinson appointed Overseer of the Road from Taylor's Ford to Stagg's Creek, and James Boid ? or Bird? from thence to where he dwells."

Benjamin Long app. Overseer of the Road in the room of Luke Roberson.

59-255' "William Reed the younger" qualified as "under Sheriff."

John Booth appointed Overseer of Road in the room of Samuel Parks. Thomas Parker appointed Overseer of the Road from Middle White Oak to County line.

John Wrightsman's mark recorded.

..."following persons to attend next Superior Court at Halifax 1st day of September next - as Jurymen - to wit -
Mark Morgan, John Alston, & Robert Little, as Grand Jury.
John Armstrong, John Stroud, Sr, & Gilbert Strayhorn, as Petit Jury.

Court of August 1761 continued -

59-256 "Ordered that Argulus Henderson, Simon Fooshe, Thomas Shields, John Stuart and his Tythables, William Marsh, Jr, Simon Poe, Jr, Stephen Poe, James Poe, Joseph Fooshe, Cornelius Roe, Wm. Tucker, Elnathan Davis, Charles Clanton, Benjamin Clanton, Robert Colley, Samuel Marsh, Wm McDaniel & his Tythables, Zachariah Martin, Jr, Roger Martin, Thomas North, John Brooks, John Crow, John Mullis, John Webster & Charles Webster, do work on the road from Haw River to Roberson's Ford, being Wm. Petty. Sr's District."

Robert Burnside's mark recorded.

Ordered that .."James Watson and William Reed do employ a proper person to repair the prison..."

59-256	Alex Torrington	vs	Wm & Alex. Spence	Or. Attch.
59-256'	Robert Hastie	"	Charles Jones	Case
	Hugh Smith	"	William Armstrong	"
60-257	Thomas Donalson	"	Samuel Parks	T.V.A.
	" "	"	Henry Porter, Esq, and James Thompson	" " "
60-257'	John Woods	"	Benjamin Phillips	" " "
	Hugh Smith	"	Micajah Wright	?
	Hugh McConnell	"	Peter Furley or(Turley)	Or. Attch.
60-258	Davis's Adm's	"	William Howlett	Case
	William Burgess	"	James Webb	"
	John Crawford	"	" "	"
60-258'	Nathaniel Cary	"	Benjamin Saxon	"
	John Stroud, Sr	"	Hugh McConnell	Petition
	William Nunn	"	" "	"
61-259	John Stubbs	"	James Aspey	Case
	David McKnight	"	Adam McConnell	Debt
	Edward Moore	"	William Nealey	Case
	William Grimes	"	William Stephens	"
61-259'	John Kelly	"	Waldrop, Sr & Hinckey	"
	" "	"	Michael Waldrop, Sr	"
	Reason Ricketts	"	Cammer	Debt
	Thomas Lowe	"	James Lindley	Case
61-260	James Ricketts	"	Bordon	Or. Attch.
	Wm. Mebane & Ux'r, Adms.	"	Powell & Stagg	Debt
	Thomas Brown	"	Joseph Sutton	Case
61-260'	Charles Jones	"	John White	Or. Attch.

"Court adjourned till Court in Course."

62-261 Court began 1st Tuesday of November 1761, at Courthouse at Childsburg.

62-261'	John Kelly	vs	Joshua Fincher	Debt
	Joshua Fincher	"	Hugh Smith	Case
	Leonard Claybourn	"	William Petty	Petition
	Adam Dixon	"	John Meherg	T.V.A.
62-262	Michael Boyle	"	Daniel Cain	Debt

Court of November 1761 continued -

62-262'	John Cox	vs	Thomas Capper	Case
63-263	John McComb	"	John Armstrong	Debt
	Hugh Dobbin	"	Jacob Roberson	Case
	John Kelly	"	James Benton	Or. Attch.
63-263'	David Knight	"	Samuel Fulton	Debt
	Nathaniel Harris, Jr	"	Moses Dossett	Or. Attch.
	Reason Ricketts	"	Josiah Watkins	Debt
63-264	Samuel Means	"	Thomas Holden	T.V.A.
	David Bradford	"	Michael Boyle	Case
	Benjamin Posey	"	Thomas Landrop	Or. Attch.
	John Collins	"	Thomas Gibson	Debt
63-264'	William Cummings, Esq	"	Joseph Trotter	Case
	" " "	"	Adam Butner	"

"Court adjourned till Court in Course."

Court began 1st Tuesday February 1762, at Courthouse at Childsburg.

64-265	Robert Boyd	vs	James & Nath'l Cary	Case
64-265'	James Armstrong	"	Zachariah Routh	Or. Attch.
64-266	Reason Ricketts	"	William Dugger	Debt
	John Meherg	"	Adam Dixon	T.A.B.
64-266'	Josiah Wallice	"	David Liles	T.V.A.
	David Liles	"	Josiah Wallice	Case
65-267	" "	"	" "	"
	Joseph Walker	"	William Kirby	"
65-267'	John Dowell	"	John Jones	Or. Attch.
65-268	James Couch	"	John McCormack	Case
	Reason Ricketts	"	William Barton?	Debt
65-268'	Jacob Mason & Wife	"	David Liles	T.V.A.
	" "	"	" "	Traver
66-269	William Pickett	"	William Willis	Case
	John Kelly	"	John Hinchey	Petition
66-269'	Reason Ricketts	"	Isaac Whitter?	Debt
66-270	" "	"	Charles Burnes	"
	William Cummings, Esq	"	Thomas ---ey (?)(torn)	Petition
66-270'	William Cummings, Esq	"	Benjamin Phillips	"
	William Gode	"	James Webb	Debt
67-271	John Kelly	"	James Williams	Case
	Richard Simpson	"	Joseph Little	"
	Reason Ricketts	"	Stephen Clayton	Debt
	Benjamin Williams	"	John May, Jr	Case
	Edmund Fanning	"	Thomas Sheppea (?)	Debt

"Court adjourned till Court in Course."

67-272 Court began 1st Tuesday in May 1762, at Courthouse at Childsburg.

	Jacob Mason	vs	John Woods	Case
67-272'	John Meherg	"	Adam Dixon	Petition
	Davis's Adm's.	"	William Howlett	Case
68-273	William Burgess	"	James Webb	"
	James Crawford	"	" "	"
68-273'	William Pickett	"	Richard Burton	Petition
	Thomas Fannin	"	Edward Kirksey	"
	John Meherg & Wife	"	John Mitchell & Wife	Case
68-274	Thomas Brooks & Wife	"	John Dowell & Wife	"
68-274'	John Norriss	"	Hugh Connell	Petition
	John Dowell	"	Terrance McMullin	Or. Attch.
69-275	John Hallum	"	Jessee Breashear	Case
	Jessee Breshear	"	John Hallum	T.A.B.
69-275'	William Cummings, Esq.	"	Conrod Lowe	Case
	Josiah England	"	Prichett Stone	Petition
69-276	Bowman's Adm.	"	Samuel Burton	Case
	Joshua Stroud	"	Nathan Howard	Petition
69-276'	Samuel Barker	"	John Armstrong	"
	John Spann	"	Dorman Hanson	"
70-277	John Mitchel	"	John Meherg	"
	Thomas Hart & Co.	"	Marshal Lovelatty	Case
70-277'	Wm. Martin ~~Assignee~~	"	William Webster	Petition
	William Webb	"	Eliz. Harris, Adm'x	Case
	Robert Lytle	"	Thomas Cate, Sr	"
70-278	John Dowell	"	Harris's Administrators	Case

"Court adjourned till Court in Course".

Addenda to this Volume.

Omitted from page 20-41'. Ann Leach (?) swears that Andrew Shepheard is the father of her child. Shepheard's Securities were Josias Dixon, John Gordon, Alexander Mebane, Esquires, and the Rev. Wm. Miller.

Court of January 1755. Justices presiding: James Dickey, John Patterson, Lawrence Thompson, John Pitman.

Court of March 1755. Justices presiding: Alexander Mebane, James Dickey, Josias Dixon, John Gordon, Andrew Mitchel, John Patterson, Lawrence Banckson, John Pryor, Joseph Boggs, James Allison.

Court of June 1755. Justices presiding: Alexander Mebane, John Pryor, Josias Dixon, Lawrence Banckson, James Dickey, John Pitman.

Court of September 1755. Justices presiding: James Dickey, Lawrence Thompson, John Pitman, John Patterson.

Here begins a new volume

AUGUST 1762 through AUGUST 1766

Pages are numbered 1 through 481

1 Court began 2nd Tuesday in August 1762 at Courthouse in Corbintown.

	Robert Jones,Jr	vs	Zachariah Martin	Case
	John Stubbs	"	Joseph Voss	Debt
2	David Knight	"	Samuel Fulton	"
	Thomas Bedford	"	James Terry	"
3	William Stroud, Sr	"	John Bolin	"
	Charles Cupple (Copley ?)	"	James Terry	Case
	Thomas Hart	"	William Gladden	"
	William Martin	"	William Webster	Petition
4	Peter Noey	"	Patrick Morris	Case
	John Giles Thomas	"	George Morris	Petition
5	William Long	"	Joseph Sharp	"
	John Dowell	"	Jane Gold	"
	Conn's Administrators	"	Joseph Dolittle	"
6	James Benton	"	Amos Whitehead	Case
	Thomas Fanning	"	Christian Kirksey	"
	John Dowell	"	Phillip Morriss	Or. Attch.
7	Benjamin Phillips	"	George Shepheard, Sr	Case
	James Cary, Jr	"	Nicholas Boyles	Petition
	" " "	"	Wm. Armstrong	"
8	Bohannon & Co.	"	Joseph Akin	Case
	Robert Waters & Co.	"	" "	"
	John Thrasher	"	Samuel Parks	"
9	Robert Witty	"	John Smith	"
	Thomas & Benj. Hart	"	George Lumpkin	Debt
	James Bowe (Bowie ?)	"	Samuel Watt	Case
10	John McGee, Esq	"	Lott Warren	Or. Attch.

"Court adjourned till Court in Course."

---

11 Court began 2nd Tuesday, November 1762 at Courthouse in Hillsborough.
* (Note the change in the name of the town. It was premature.)

	John Stroud	vs	John Woods	Case
	Robert Brashear	"	William Shallom	Debt
12	James Bowie	"	Luke Smith	Case
13	Edward Moseley	"	Thomas Dunlop	Petition
	John Stubbs	"	James Espey	Case
14	William Pickett	"	Richard Burton	Petition
	Adam Dixon	"	Charles Hubbard	Or. Attch.
15	Reason Ricketts	"	Elisha Teague	Debt
	" "	"	Needham Bryant	"

*(The name was not changed to Hillsborough until November 1766)

Court of November 1762 continued -

16	John Kelly	vs	Waldrop, Sr & Hinchie	Case
	Adam McConnel	"	Espay & Wiley	"
17	Jacob Jones	"	James Cox	Debt
	John Kelley	"	James Benton	Or. Attch.
18	Benjamin Posey	"	Thomas Lambiss (?)	" "
	James Bohannon	"	Reason Ricketts	Case
19	Benjamin Miller	"	Jacob Mason	Debt
	John McGown	"	Joshua Stroud	T.V.A.
20	John Davis	"	Isaac Gaddis	Case
	John Powell	"	David Phillips	Petition
21	John Wright	"	Zachariah Wood	Petition
	Wade's Administrators	"	Samuel Burton	Case
22	John Esdale	"	George Ingle (?)	"
	Stephen Merritt	"	Isaac Cooper	T.V.A.
	Joseph King	"	John McCarver	Petition
23	William Long	"	Joseph Sharp	"
	William Yarborough	"	Richard Womack	Debt
	Robert Hastie	"	George Ingle	Case
24	Mordecai Gwinn	"	Plunkett Ballard	"
	Hugh Kelly	"	Valentine Braswell	"
	John McGee, Esq	"	Lott Warren	Or. Attch.

"Court adjourned till Court in Course."

---

25 Court began 1st Tuesday (3rd day) of May 1763 at Corbintown.

Edmund Fanning, Esq, qualified as Register for the County of Orange.

Francis Nash, Esq. qualified as Clerk of Court for Orange County.

Robert Cate, Sr and Thomas Langley, Sr to be exempt from taxes.

Enos Elliman filed an Inventory of the Estate of John Collins, dec'd. Proved by the affirmation of the said Enos Elliman.

Robert Woody filed an Inventory of his father's Estate.

26 Judy Stag appointed Aministratrix of her late husband (his name not stated). Bond: £ 200. Bondsmen: Edmund Fanning, Lawrence Thompson, Esq's.

Judy Stag has leave to keep an Ordinary.

Adminstrators of Robert Woody, dec'd have leave to hold sale. "Wm. McPharson & John Piles appointed (ap) Praisers".

Richard Henderson, Att'y at Law, qualifies.

Court of May 1763 continued -

26 "Ordered that Jeremiah Hadley be appointed Overseer in the room of Edward Teague on the Cape Fare Road from Terril's Creek to the Fork of the Road this side of Zachariah Martin's, Jr.

County Surveyor is to lay out an acre "the property of Francis Dossett on the N Side of Rocky River & one on S Side to erect a Water Grist Mill..."

Richard Cook appointed Overseer of Road in room of John Bohannon.

Robert Cate's mark recorded.

27 James McGoing (McGowan ?) granted license to keep Tavern. His Securities: Gilbert Strayhorn & James Hunter.

Thomas Lockheart granted license to keep Tavern. His Securities: Samuel Farmer & Hugh Smith.

Inventory of Samuel Crawford's Estate filed by Christopher Husten, Adm.

Robert Woodie accuses Thomas Thompson of giving him a counterfeit 40 shilling bill.

Nicholas Colbertson, Evidence in the Suit - Davis vs Gaddis - showed sufficient cause for his not attending.

Grand Jury sworn: Solomon Debow, Jacob Womack, George Sallings, William Hallams, John Cate, George Hobson, Jr, Semore York, William Willson, Wm. Rhodes, Moses Teague, Thomas Douglas, Robert Donalson, Robert Patterson & John Armstrong.

28 Gideon Marr, Gentleman, to practise law.

Thomas Hart, Tyrie Harris & Lawrence Thompson recommended as candidates for Sheriff of Orange County.

John Lea to have liberty to erect a Water Grist Mill on Rich Creek.

"Stephen Johnson and Ann Johnston (spelled both ways) came into open Court and chose James Visseth (?) their Guardian, and William Burford and Wm. Luten, Sr enter themselves as Security ...."

William Gee is appointed Constable in the room of George Smith.

Stephen Merritt granted license to keep Tavern. Securities: William Few, James Bowie.

Inventory of the Estate of John Burney, dec'd recorded.

Court of May 1763 continued -

29 "Joseph King appointed Overseer of Road from Flatt River at Roberson's Mill to Bush Camp in the room of John Cate."

Road Jury named for "Road to be opened from Hart's Road by Saxon's (L?) Mill... to ... the road from Runnels Cabbins"..."John Graves, Henry Runnolds, John Fuller Lane, James McDaniel, John Lay, William Grimes, Dudley Reynolds, Thomas Barnett, James Calburton, John Walker, Patrick Porter, Richard Lane, Christopher Husten, Joseph Dolittle, and David Stephens."

"James Hunter appointed Overseer of Road from Stinking Quarter to the Country Line in the room of James York".
"John Hornedy appointed Overseer of Road called Cape Fare Road from Jeremiah Hadley's to the fork of the Road where Simon Hadley did live."
"Benjamin Gest app. Overseer of Road whereof James Martin was late Overseer
"John Johnson app. Overseer of Road from a black oak above his house to Jeremiah Hadley's place in the room of Brumley Barnes."

Henry Hays appointed Constable in the room of James Nichols.
Laughlin Campbell " " " " " " Richard Smith.
John King " " " " " " James Murray.
30 William Black " " " " " " William Maines.

"Abraham Fulkerson appointed Overseer of Road in room of Stephen Terry on the Road from N. Hico towards Colonel Terry's Ferry."

"Ordered that a road from Peter Nowey's to William Wiley's be laid out & opened..... following to lay out the same .... John McComb, Walter Murry, Alex. Mebane, Jr, Robert Irwin, John Butler, John Armstrong, Paul Harmon, Peter Nowie, John Whitman, John Oliver, John Hopkins & John Barker."

Road to be opened from Island Ford on Haw River to Childsburg... by Joseph Kirk, Wm. Copeland, Sr, John Ricketts, Joseph Copeland, Nathaniel Milton, Benjamin Clemens, Robert Patterson, John Edwards, John Bracey, James Haygood, Christopher Kirksey, William Griffin, Wm. Long, James Craig, Wm. Bynum, James Ballard and Wm. Salley.

James Bird paid £ 4,1sh for his attendance as Juryman at last Halifax Superior Court.

"Elijah Cain appointed Constable in the room of James Cellers."

"William Barney ? appointed Overseer of Road from John Ambres (?) to Childsburg in the room of Henry Waggoner.
31 John Anderson app. Overseer of Road in the room of John Hendrix.
William Rankin " " " " " " " John Camp.
John Fuller Lane " " " " " " " Benjamin Carter.
Garland Terry app. " " " whereof Benjamin Carter was formerly.
Edward Stone " " Cape Fare Road from John Patterson's to Childsburgh in the room of William Cox.
John Barbey app. Overseer of the Road leading from Cape Fare, from Trice's Bridge to John Patterson's in the room of William Cox."

Court of May 1763 continued -

31 "Ordered that Charles Chavis (son of Hannah Chavis) 3 years old October next be bound to William Mebane... to learn the art of a shoemaker."

Hugh Smith granted license to keep Tavern at Stinking Quarter. Bondsmen: John Sample & William Mebane.

Robert Hunter granted license to keep Tavern at his Dwelling House on Haw River. Bondsmen: John Sample & William Mebane.

William Luten paid for his attendance as Juror at Halifax Court.
32 Samuel Burton " " " " " " " " " .

"Ordered that Charity Rigsby daughter of Tabitha Rigsby, 9 years old in April last be bound unto William Stroud, Sr till she arrives to the age of 18 years."

"Ordered that Moses Wallace an Infant of the age of fifteen years the son of John Wallace deceased be bound to Robert Tinning agreeable to law."

Two deeds proved.

"Pompey, a negro boy belonging to Charles Johnson is adjudged to 10 years" (of age).

Three deeds proved.
33 Three deeds proved.

"Ordered that George Minor son of James Minor aged 14 years be bound to James Few until he arrives to the age of 21 years."

John Powell appointed Constable in the room of John McDaniel.

"Ordered that the following persons work on the Road whereof Daniel Duncan is Overseer, to wit, William Bustard, Jacob Roberson, Thomas Whitton, John Oakes, Daniel Smith, Isaac Allen, Wm. Chambers, Sr, Adam Lackey, Jonathan Allen, Francis Wright, Daniel Duncan, Leonard Huff & Alexander Roberson."

"Ordered that the following persons work on the Road whereof Solomon Debow is Overseer, to wit, John McFarland, Stephen Serjant, Thomas Serjant, Joseph Barnett, Thomas Barnett, James Cavenaugh, Ephraim Gold & Humphrey Barnett."

34 John Dowell's Ordinary license renewed. Six deeds proved.

Michael Synott revokes his Power of Attorney given to Edward McVey, dated 6 Nov 1761.

William Neal appointed Constable in the room of John King.

Court of May 1763 continued -

35 "Ordered that John Brantley's District begin at the mouth of Beaver Creek, from thence to the head of said Creek, from thence to Johns-(t)on's line, along the said line to Cumberland line where it falls in with Deep River & from the mouth of Bush Creek up the said creek to Collins's ford, and from the mouth of Arons Creek up the said creek, and from thence a direct line to Deep River."

"Ordered that John Patterson Esquire's District be from the mouth of Beaver Creek the upper side to Johns(t)on's line including the whole to the branches of Eno and New Hope (Creeks)."

"Ordered that Thomas Lloyd's District be from the mouth of Bush Creek up the said creek, to Collins's Ford, and up the Haw River to the mouth of Cain Creek, from thence up the said creek to a branch called Mabry Fork, up the said branch to the head, thence to the head of New Hope and thence down to the mouth of Bush Creek."

"Ordered that Andrew Mitchel's District begin where the Cape Fare Road crosses New Hope, thence up the said Road where it falls in with the Road that leads from Rowan to Halifax, thence to where the said Road falls in with Woody's Road, all of the lower side of Haw River thence down the said Road to the mouth of Caine Creek."

"Ordered that all other Districts stand as they formerly were."

"Ordered that Robert Marsh, Elijah Caine & John Boyd, Constables, summon the Taxables within the District of John Brantley."

36	Philip Gee	Constable	in	District	of Thomas Lloyd.
	George Herndon	"	"	"	" John Patterson, Esq.
	John Craig	"	"	"	" Andrew Mitchell, Esq.
	Henry McCoy	"	"	"	" William Lea, Esq.
	Mark London	"	"	"	" David Hart, Esq.
	James Nicholson	"	"	"	" " " "
	John Powell	"	"	"	" John McGee, Esq.
	Richard Wood	"	"	"	" Alexander Mebane, Esq.
	David Knight	"	"	"	" James Allison, Esq.
	John Keedle	"	"	"	" John Pryor, Esq.
	Thomas James	"	"	"	" Tyrie Harris, Esq.
	John Taylor	"	"	"	" Lawrence Thompson, Esq.

37 Deed of Mortgage registered - from John Hinchey to Reason Ricketts.

Robert Pryor claims that William Lytle gave him two counterfiet bills.

Nathan, a negro boy belonging to Gilbert Strayhorn, judged 10 yrs old.
Rachel, a negro girl " " " " , " 9 " " .

Hugh McConnell fined 10 shillings for profanely swearing in Court.

Court of May 1763 continued -

38 Richard Clements appointed Constable in the room of Samuel Burton.
John Boyd " " " " " " James Hagges.

	John Dowell	vs	Joseph Sharp	Case
39	Reason Ricketts	"	Arthur Paine	Debt
	James Watson	"	Bazel Brashear	Case
40	Plunkett Ballard	"	Jacob Mason	"
	Thomas Hart	"	William Gladden	"
41	Stephen Merritt	"	Isaac Cooper	T A B
	Sarah Hales	"	Robert Thompson	Debt
42	John Morris	"	Hosea Tapley	"
	Barnaby Cabe	"	William Few	Case
43	John Clark	"	George Morris	"
	Richard Simpson	"	Samuel Watt	"
44	William Yarborough	"	Richard Womack	Debt
	Sharpless & Bradley	"	Timothy Terrell	Case
45	Semore York	"	Lott Warren	Or. Attach.
	Adam Loving	"	James Minnis	Case
46	Edmund Fanning	"	George Lumpkin	Petition
	Robert Taylor, Assignee	"	Thomas Wiley	"
47	Thomas Hart	"	Thomas Whitehead	Case
	Benjamin Phillips	"	Joseph Richardson	"
	Stephen Merritt	"	Amos Whitehead	"
48	John McGowen & Uxr	"	John Stroud	T A B
	Jacob Mason	"	Thomas Page	Case
	Barnaby Cabe	"	Phillip Jackson	"
	Thomas Humphries & Uxr	"	John Dowell	"
49	John Scott & Uxr	"	" "	T A B

"Court adjourned till Court in Course."

---

50 Page 50 is blank.

51 Court began 2nd day of August 1763.

John Railey & John Talbert recommended to be exempt from taxes.

"Sarah, daughter of John Scott, to be bound unto Andrew Caddell (or Cadlwell ?)" until she is 18 years old.

George Flynn appointed Overseer of Road in room of Robert Donalson.
Thomas Linley, Jr. " " " " " " " William Hallams.

Thomas Willson, Sr. appointed Constable in the room of Henry McCoy.

52 Phillip Gee's mark recorded.

Court of August 1763 continued -

52 William Nunn granted license to keep Tavern at his Dwelling in Childsburgh. Securities: Abner Nash, Francis Nash.

James Saunders has liberty to build a Water Grist Mill on Little Creek, a branch of Dan River, he having land on both sides.

Elizabeth Johnson granted letters of Administration on the Estate of John Johnson, dec'd. Bond: £ 200. Bondsmen: James & Joshua (H)Adley.

Christopher Husten, Adm. of James Crafford, dec'd, files an account of sa

"Ordered that the following persons (to wit) Peter Nowey, John McCombs, Lodwick Clap, John Oliver (?), Jacob Brown, Jacob ?oots, Ludwick Albright Elias Powell, John Powell, John Shady, Barnett Troxler, & John Smith... lay open a Road ... from Peter Noe's to William Willey's & report ..."

Mourning Milton, daughter of Robert Milton, dec'd, to be committed to the care of Mr. Robert Cate, Junior. Bond: £ 50. Bondsman: Thomas Cate.

53 Grand Jury: Richard Holeman, foreman, Thomas Thompson, Gilbert Strayhorn John Lawson, Joseph Gold, James Wilkinson, David Vanhook, John Hunter, James Craig, William Burney, Christopher Kirksey, John Salling, John Edwards, Edward Grisham & Gilbert Davey.

Ralph Williams, Constable, appointed to attend the Jury.

The following 8 Justices return their lists of Taxables: John Pryor, Thomas Lloyd, John Brantley, James Allison, Tyrie Harris, Alexander Mebane, Francis Nash & John McGee, Esquires.

Justices presiding on this day were: Thomas Lloyd, Andrew Mitchell, James Allison, John Patterson, William Lea, Esquires.

"Ordered that James Cummings be Keeper of the Public Standard of this County."

"Ordered that the following persons to wit Robert Bumpass, Samuel Bumpass Jonas Parker, Thomas Striplen, John Bumpass, John Bridges, Gabriel Davey, Samuel Yarborough, Thomas King, John Lawson, John Byars, George Flynn, John Tabor, John Thompson & John Payne - lay open a road ... from where Striplin's Path turns out of the old road to the County line near John Parks & that John Bumpass be Overseer thereof."

54 "Ordered that William Miles, John Boyd, Charles Phillips, Solomon West, Ralph Shaw, David Knight, Edmund Bailey, Hezekiah Collins, Charles Philli Walter Thetford & Isaiah Thetford, work on the road leading to the Plantation of John West, Sr, under the Direction of Samuel Parker, Overse

Court of August 1763 continued -

54 "Ordered that William Rankin, John Satterfield, James Sattercield, Jr, Bidwell Satterfield, Hosea Tapley, John Camp, Henry Ford, Edward Moore, David Vanhook, Thomas Flynn, Henry Gold, Joseph King, John Allen Tharp, Samuel Fulton, Elijah Eastwood, Benjamin Tharpe, & Jacob Garnett... lay open a road ... from the end of the Hico (Vanhook's) to the Country line - opposite to the Tarborough Road in Granville County & that all the inhabitants on Flatt River, Deep Creek, South Fork & Napper Reeds from James Bolling's upward assist in keeping the said road in repair ... under John Satterfield, Overseer."

William Laughlin appointed Overseer of Road in the room of Henry Halliday.

William Lea, Lawrence Thompson, John Patterson & Andrew Mitchell, Esquires, return their lists of Taxables.

55 "Ordered that the following persons, to wit, Wm. Smith, John McMillion, Wm. Wear (?), David Hicks, Isaac Middlebrooks, James Tinsley, Charles Crawford, John Roberts, David Roper, Samuel Paul, Alexander Montgomery, & Patrick Porter... lay open a road ... from Hogan's Creek... between Round Hill & Wm. Waters, thence down to the Roun (?) Oak Road near Alex. Montgomery's Sr under the direction of Wm. Ware, Overseer."...

"Ordered that John Booth be appointed Guardian to Gilly Booth aged 16 years, & Joseph Booth aged 14 years, until they arrive of age ..." Bond: L 200. Bondsmen: Edward Trice, Thomas Capper.

"Ordered that the following persons (to wit) be appointed Jurors to lay out a Road ... from Johnsons Line near Edward Herring's spring to the Cape Fare Road, near the place where James Trice formerly lived... Edward Herring, Edward Sorrell, Benjamin Blake, Tignal Jones, Nathaniel Jones, Christopher Barbee, Henry Beasley, Benjamin Saxon, Samuel Saxon, Richard Hopson, Nathaniel Almond, Samuel Parks, John Booth, Dred Bennett, William Dorom? (Durham ?), George Herndon, John Trice, James Acock, & Joseph Barbee & that Christopher Barbee be app. Overseer...."

"John Gouge, son of John Gouge, dec'd, aged 17 years, came into open Court and chose Thomas Hines for his Guardian...." Bond: L 500. Bondsmen: Robert Abercrombie, Hugh Wood.

56 Alexander Mebane, Esq, granted license to keep Ordinary at his Dwelling house. Bondsmen: John McGee, Esq., James Allison, Esq.

Hugh Sloss granted license to keep Ordinary at his dwelling house. Bondsmen: Alex. Mebane, Charles Adams.

Jacob Mason granted license to keep Ordinary. Bondsmen: John Powell, John Stroud.

Court of August 1763 continued -

56 "Ordered that the suit Adam Moffitt vs Michael Holt, Jr be continued at the Plaintiff's cost & that a Dedimus Potestatum issue to Amhurst County to George Stoval & James Dilliard, Esq to take the doposition of Ellinor Morris."

Thomas Hart, Gentleman, qualified as Sheriff of Orange County. Bondsmen: Tyrie Harris, Esq, Nathaniel Hart, David Hart, Benjamin Hart & Robert Wells

Abraham Penn & William Penn qualified as Under Sheriffs.

Philip Jackson's Ordinary license renewed. Bondsmen: Thomas Hart, Francis Nash.

57 Thomas Barnes recommended to be tax exempt.

Thomas Clarke (Overseer) fined 6d damages for failing to keep his road in repair.

Adminstrator of Thomas Stag to sell perishable part of his estate.

57 Elizabeth Conner proved her attendance in the Suit Davis vs Stone.
Peggy Conner " " " " " " " " " .

John Pryor, Esq, granted license to keep Tavern. Security: Francis Nash.

58 James Curry appointed Overseer of Road in the room of Benjamin Long.

"Thomas Hines to take into care and manage the Estate of John Gouge, son of John Gouge, dec'd."

"Ordered that the following persons to wit, Benjamin Davis, John Whaler, Jacob Whitehead, Annanias Allen, Wm. Brooks, John Craw, Miles Goforth, Joseph Sutton, Wm. Satterfield, James Satterfield, Thomas Willson, Sr, Patrick Mullen & John Railey be recommended to the next assembly as proper persons to be exempt from paying public Taxes."

"Ordered that John Barbee be appointed Overseer of the Road from New Hope Bridge to Widow Hopson's in the room of John Trice."

"Ordered that Henry Cobb be appointed Overseer of the Lower Town Road from the Country Line to John Cantril's & that all the hands on the waters of the Country Line assist...."

Grand Jurors to attend next Superior Court at Halifax:
Lawrence Vanhook, Tyrie Harris, Robert Lytle.

Petit Jurors to attend Superior Court at Halifax:
James Armstrong, William Barney, George Lumpkin.

Court of August 1763 continued -

59 Thomas Webb to be paid for 4 days attendance at Halifax Superior Court "and riding ninety miles" - £ 1-14-6 Proclamation Money.

Michael Holt, Jr & Michael Holt, Sr, Lodowick Clap & David Lowe "appointed to lay out, value, & condemn 1 acre of land belonging to Henry Eustice McCullock lying on the Trading Path ford of Haw River, Also an other acre on the opposite side of the said River the property of Robert Nugent, & that the said McCullock have liberty to erect a Water Grist Mill --".

The King vs George Foutz - Foutz is "bound to keep the peace towards his wife & all others" ... Securities: Thomas Hart, James Cummings.

60 Samuel Benton & Al ?.. vs Bazel Brashears Case.
Brashear took the Insolvent Debtor oath & was released.

"Derwin Elwick, sworn as Garnishee of the Estate of Nicholas Pendrake, saith he hath no effects."

"John Oliver, sworn as Garnishee of the Estate of Nicholas Pundrick saith he hath 5 shillings & 7 pence in his hands" -

"Thomas Fuller, sworn as Garnishee of the Estate of Nicholas Pendrake saith he hath no effects."

Hugh Montgomery vs James Hall, Bail - Sciere Facias.

Thomas Lapsley appointed Overseer of Road in the room of Cairns Tinnen.

61 David Lawson & Alexander Shaw proved their attendance in the Suit Nash vs Fanning, Esq.

Jeremiah Piggott, Administrator of Thomas Berry, dec'd, filed Accounts.

"Ordered that Oldham Hightower be appointed Overseer of the Road in the room of Elijah Cain, beginning at Isaac Collins to John Pitts Plantation & that all the hands in the fork of Haw River & New Hope River are to assist... "

"Dempsey Rolls appointed Overseer of Road in the room of Elijah Cain, & that all the hands within six miles assist in keeping the same in repair."

"John Johnson vs Joseph Sharpe, Jr. The Bail surrendered the principle whereon the Sherriff is ordered to take him into custody."

David Stroud vs Bryant McBridge brought to Salisbury Superior Court, defendant appeared and took the oath of Insolvent Debtors, discharged.

62 John Dowell appointed Overseer of Road in the room of William Comb.

"Ordered that Francis Nash collect all the documents & writings belonging to the Clerks since the Commencement of this County, & record them in Books bought for that purpose ...."

Court of August 1763 continued -

62 Waller (or Walter) Ashmore & James Ashmore to be added to Capt. McGee's list of Taxables.

Richard Parker, Esq, presents his commission as Captain of Foot in the Regiment of Orange.

Court adjourned for half an hour - Justices present: Francis Nash, William Lea, Robert Patterson.

63 "Raichel Riley allowed 19 sh & 9d Proclamation Money as a witness for Stone against Davis."

William Dunnagan posts bond "to keep the Peace towards Wm. Churton, Esq & all others His Majesty's subjects till the Court 1st Tuesday in November next." Bondsmen: James Bowie & Wm. Barney.

"Ordered that William Few have liberty to open a Bridle way at his own Expense the nearest & most convenient way from his Plantation where he now keeps Tavern to his Mill on Enoe River.

"Court adjourned till tomorrow morning - met - present: Francis Nash, William Churton, William Lea, Esquires."

Edward Wolf to be added to Mr. Francis Nash's list of Taxables.

Thomas King's Ordinary license renewed. Bondsmen: James Bowie, James Trice

Thomas Webb appointed Administrator of the Estate of Elizabeth Harris, dec'd. Bond: £ 100. Bondsman: Samuel Burton.

64 "Ordered that all the causes shall stand continued whereon two Rules have been taken this Court."

Marks recorded by Frederick Brown, John Coble, George Coble & Peter Spoon.

	William Cummings, Esq	vs	Joseph Trotter	Case
	Hugh Smith	"	Nathan Carter	"
65	Stephen Collins	"	James Webb	Debt
66	James Elliott	"	Joseph Dolittle	Case
	Reason Ricketts	"	Stephen Clayton	Debt
67	Daniel McDaniel	"	Giles Chapman	Case
	John Dowell	"	Thomas Wiley	"
68	George Watkins	"	David Hambre	Petition
	Thomas Erskine	"	Peter Craven	"
69	Wm. Cummings, Esq.	"	Conn's Administrators	Case
	Thomas Hart, Esq.	"	James Bowie	"
70	Thomas Flynn	"	Edward Moore	Debt
71	Francis Nash	"	Edmund Fanning	Case
72	Benjamin Phillips	"	George Shepheardson	"

Court of August 1763 continued -

72	Thomas Erskine	vs	John Warren	Debt
	James Cary, Jr.	"	Joseph Dolittle	"
73	Robert Hastie	"	George Ingle	Case
	Andrew Campbell	"	Andrew Bailey, Esq.	"
74	James Bowie	"	Samuel Watt	"
	Francis Nash	"	John Tabor, Sr	Petition
	William Crockett	"	John Spradling	"
	Richard Hanson	"	Joel Blackwell	Case
75	Joseph Preston Parker	"	James Meherg	"
	John Adams	"	Samuel Burton	S. Facias
76	Isaac Gray	"	Robert Whitton	Case
77	Thomas Tabb	"	Robert Stubblefield	"
78	Thomas Rainey	"	John Robertson	"
	Jennings Executors	"	James Webb	"
79	Buchannon & Co.	"	" "	Debt
	Zachariah Woods	"	Webster William	Case
80	David Miers	"	Absolom McDonald	Petition
	Abner Nash, Esq.	"	Thomas Littlejohn	"
	John Sample	"	Bazel Brashear	"
81	James Hunter	"	Edward Bull	"
	William Journey	"	Hugh Quynn	"
	Andrew Cochrane & Co.	"	John Daniel	"
82	" " " "	"	" "	"
	George Lumpkin	"	Thomas Spradling	"
83	Jacob Mason	"	Christian Shy	"
	Wm Mash, Assignee, Etc	"	Robert Lepper, Jr	"
	Mary Conn's Admin's.	"	Joseph Dolittle	"
84	David Knight	"	Benjamin Cate, Sr	"
	Robert Jones, Jr	"	Samuel Burton	"
	John Giles Thomas	"	Hugh Quynn	Debt
85	James Bowie	"	Samuel Stewart	Case
	Richard Tyass (?)	"	Micajah Pickett	"
	Thomas Webb	"	" "	"
86	Henry Simmon (or Lemmon)	"	Phillip Helesveston	"
	Thomas Green	"	John Dowell	T A B
	William Robinson	"	Thomas Willson, Jr	Case
	Gideoh Marr	"	Plunkett Ballard, Esq	T A B
87	Robert Patterson	"	William Ursury	T A B
	Jacob Black	"	Hugh Quinn	Debt
	Robert Barnett, Assignee	"	Samuel Barnett	Case
88	William Reaves	"	Francis Desern	"
	John Dowell	"	John Scott & Ux'r	T A B
	Cochrane & Co	"	Stephen Jett (?)	Case
	George Lumpkin	"	Robert Barnett	"
89	" "	"	Joseph Dolittle	"
	James Bowie	"	William Martin	"
	John Johnston	"	Joseph Sharpe, Jr	"
	John Cox	"	Stephen Maret	"

Court of August 1763 continued -

	Plaintiff		Defendant	
90	John Camp	vs	William Maret	Case
	Nathaniel Austin	"	George Ellmore	"
	William Tabb	"	William Gibbons	"
	Abraham Miles	"	Robert Barnett	Debt
91	Richard Finch	"	Alexander Going	T A B
	John Kighler	"	John Tabor	T A B
	Andrew Campbell	"	Nicholas Pendrake	Or. Att.
	Luke Robertson	"	Robert Hawkins	T A B
92	Samuel Ricketts	"	John Pompey	Case
	Benjamin Phillips	"	Daniel Higdon	T A B
	William Thompson	"	William Brashwell	T A B
	Robert Patterson	"	William Ursury	T A B
93	James Robinson	"	Gideon Marr	Case
	Thos Humphries & Ux'r	"	James Ramage	"
	John Cox	"	William Callahan	Or. Att.
	Francis Nash	"	William Pittman	" "
94	" "	"	Robert Perkins	" "
	Thomas Hart, Esq	"	James Espey	Debt
	" " "	"	Samuel Watt	"
95	" " "	"	Thomas Wiley	"
	Abner Nash, Esq	"	Frederick Friley ?	"
	" " "	"	Samuel Stewart	"
96	Thomas Hart	"	John Graves	Case

"Court adjourned till Court in Course."

97 Court began 1st Tuesday in November (1st day) 1763, Childsburg.

Justices present: Tyrie Harris, Thomas Lloyd, William Lea.

"Ordered that John Satterfield be appointed Overseer of the Road leading from Widow Vanhook's to Tarborough to wit from Rankins to the Dry Branch" "Jacob Garrard appointed Overseer from the Dry Branch to the head of Gibson's Creek" .... "Robert Thompson appointed Overseer from the head of Gibson's Creek to the Granville County line."

Elias Powell app. Overseer of Road in the room of Michael Holt, Jr.

98 Robert Woodie, Adm. of Estate of John Woodie, dec'd, filed an Inventory.

William Castleberry granted leave to erect a Water Grist Mill on Boling' Creek.

"Ordered that those deeds executed by the Securities of the late Sheriff & Deputy Sheriffs be not admitted to probate."

"Ordered that the probate of a deed from Micajah Pickett to (blank) be reversed."

Court of November 1763 continued -

98 "Ordered that Wm. Thompson, Daniel Norris, Thomas Beal, Charles Saxon, James Kindrake, Wm. Sisson (?), Samuel Temples, John Davis, Thomas Dowdy, William Dowdie, George Williams, & Dorman Hinson ... lay open a road .... from Bear Creek to Cumberland line ...."

Micajah Barbee, William Barbee & Betty Barbee chose Joseph Barbee as their Guardian. Bond: £ 200. Bondsmen: Thomas Hart, Esq & John Barbee.

Manning Barbee chose John Barbee as his Guardian. Bond £ 150. Bondsmen: Benjamin Hart, Joseph Barbee.

99 "Ordered that the Sheriff make sale of Effects of James Bowie which was attached to satisfy Ralph McNair, Michael Waldrop & Thomas King.

Thomas Hart recommended to be tax exempt.

"Ordered that the road leading from the Red Fields to Johnston line be dropped."

Mathew Hubbard granted license to keep Tavern at his Dwelling. Bondsmen: Abraham Miles, James Blackley.

Paul Harmon produced Naturalization papers.

100 The perishable Estate of John Johnston, dec'd, to be sold.
Inventory of " " " " " Filed.

Robert Burton is jailed on the accusation of Richard Simpson, that he stole Simpson's mare. To be tried at Halifax Supreior Court.

Grand Jury sworn: "James Hart, Nathaniel Walton, Daniel McDaniel, Joseph Dunnagan, Solomon West, John West, John Robinson, John Thrasher, Jacob Holt, Midleton Brashears, Abraham Nelson, Abraham Miles, John Pitts, Robert Samuel Brashears, James Minnis, Mathew Couch & Jacob Withrow ...."

"Ordered that Rachel Tumbleston a poor orphain be bound an apprentice to Mary Stubblefiels to learn the art & calling of a Seamstress."

Isabella Doyle resigns her Administration of the Estate of Martin Doyle. Martin Doyle app. Administrator. Bond: £ 100. Bondsmen: James Tinning, John Johnston.

101 Inventory of Estate of Martin Doyle, dec'd, filed. Perishable Estate to be sold "25th day of this Instant."

Samuel Allen granted license to keep Tavern. Bondsmen: John Woods, Robert Hunter.

John Meherg's Ordinary license renewed. Bondsmen: Thomas Webb, Thomas Hines.

Court of November 1763 continued -

101 "Ordered that Christian Hynes wife of James Hines have the Guardianship (of) John, Mary, James, Charity & Sarah Alstons of James Alston deceased, She having given bond with Robert Abercromby, John Patterson, William Reaves (?) & Thomas Webster in the sum of £ 3,000 proclamation money ...."

William Johnston, Merchant, has leave to turn the road ...

"Ordered that Henry Ivey, natural son of Oliver Ivey, aged 11 years next May be bound .... to Joseph Hencock ... trade of saddler."

102 There is no page numbered 102.

103 "Ordered that the persons under William Ware's Jurisdiction work on the road whereof he is Overseer - viz - David Hive ? (Hier?) William Hier?, Isaac Middlebrook, Evans Hatterly, George Hatterly, Samuel Hatterly, Nathaniel Russell, John Thomas, Gray Bynum, Andrew McMillion, John McMillion, Samuel Paul, John Wood, John Gown (?), David Roper, Alexander Montgomery, John Roberts, Charles Crawford & James Tinsley."

Mathew Mehaffy granted license to keep Tavern at his dwelling.
Sureties: John Ramsey & Joseph Kellet or Kettel.

In the suit James Netherly vs James Espey - Alexander Mebane called as a witness for Plaintiff failed to appear. And in the same suit Mary Long called as witness for the Plaintiff failed to appear.

In suit #27 Adam Mehafty vs Michael Holt, Jr, Adam Campbell called as a witness for the Plaintiff, failed to appear.

Col. John Gray, Mark Morgan & William Luten, Sr. are appointed to divide the Estate of James Alston, dec'd.

104 Robert Baker appointed Overseer of Road in the room of John Craig.
Samuel Money " " " " " " " " John Slater.

"... Road to be laid out from Coxes Mill to Collinses Road & the following lay it out .... Isaac Varnum, Harmon Cox, Nicholas Barker, John Cox,* Wm. Cox, Jr, William Moffit, Daniel Brown & Jeffry Beck (or Beek or Buk)."

John Graves granted license to keep Tavern.
Securities: Michael Holt, John Powell.

William Hallums appointed a Constable.

John Howlett, a poor orphan, to be bound unto Edward Hardin till he is 21 years old. Shoemaker.

105 Thomas Hart & Francis Nash appointed to employ workmen to set up a Stockade 10 feet high around the prison.

* Wm. Cox, Sr, and Thomas Cox.

Court of November 1763 continued -

105 Estate of Susannah Fooshe dec'd to be divided into five equal shares. Five negroes belonging to the Estate to be sold.

"Frederick Nall (or Natt) by reason of his great age & Infirmitys" recommended to be tax exempt.

Nathan Hampton, a witness for Joseph Sharp & wife against James Scarlett, failed to appear.

106 Thomas Harrison takes benefit of Insolvent Debtors Act.

	James Pritchett	vs	John Borden	Or. Attch.	
107	James Nethery	"	James Espey & Others	Debt	
	Adam Moffit	"	Michael Holt, Jr	Case	
108	John Meherg	"	Samuel Burton	"	
	James Webb	"	Harris's Adm's	"	
	John Alston	"	Richard Muldin	Petition	
109	Thomas Fanning	"	Christopher Kirksey	Case	
110	Joseph Dolittle	"	Boggs' Administrators	"	
	Joseph Sharpe & Ux'r	"	James Scarlett	"	
	Richard Sprugg	"	James Yancey	"	
111	Mordecai Gwinn	"	Plunkett Ballard, Esq	"	
	Samuel Allen	"	James Boyd	"	
	Harmon Husband	"	" "	Debt	
112	Thomas Hart, Esq	"	John Graves	Case	
	Robert Hastie & Co.	"	Esther Roberston	"	
	" " " "	"	John Robinson	"	
113	" " " "	"	William Stephens	Petition	
	John Shelton	"	Richard Womack	"	
114	William Lankford	"	Edward Moore	"	on note
	Hastie Buchannon & Co	"	John Kirksey	Debt	
	McCawl Lytle & Co	"	Darbey Handley	"	
115	" " " "	"	Isaac Middlebrooks	"	
	George Lumpkin	"	William McMillion	"	
	" "	"	Thomas Harrison	"	
116	" "	"	George Whitton	"	
	" "	"	William Going	"	
	" "	"	Wyatt Stubblefield	"	
117	John Bynum	"	William Stephens	"	
	" "	"	David Stephens	"	
	McCawl Lytle & Co	"	Syth Stubblefield	"	
118	John Wimbush & Co	"	Thomas Willson, Jr	Petition	
	James Bowie	"	Christopher Vandergraft	"	
	Andrew Cochrane & Co	"	Robert Marsh	"	
	" " " "	"	Simon Foshea	"	
119	Thomas Hart	"	John Carragan	Debt	
	John Dowell	"	Andrew Campbell	Case	
	Joseph Wells	"	Hugh Smith	"	

Court of November 1763 continued -

120	Andrew Norwood	vs	Jacob Mason	Case
	James Minnis	"	Nathaniel Astin	Debt
	John Jones	"	George Lumpkin	Case
	Buchannon Spiers & Co	"	Hosea Tapley	Debt
121	Bowman Spiers & Co	"	John Rogers	Petition
	" " " "	"	Jacob Mason	Case
	Thomas Lowe, Assignee	"	Andrew Campbell	"
122	Micajah Pickett	"	Richard Burton	"
	John Meherg	"	Thomas Wiley	Petition
	John Allen	"	William Hallams	Case
	James Bowie	"	James Pompey	"
123	Francis Nash	"	William Armstrong	"
	Phillip Gee & Co	"	Richard Strayhorn	"
	James Lesslye	"	Alexander Going	"
124	William Mabene	"	Martin Mehaffy	"
	Jacob Mason	"	Thomas Brooks	"
	Reason Ricketts	"	James Bowie	Case
	Thomas King	"	Edward Stone, Sr	"
125	John Dowell	"	Joseph Sharpe, Sr	"
	Adam Dixon	"	Alexander Clarke	Petition
	Middleton Brashears	"	Peter Shearman	"
126	" "	"	Thomas Lovelatty, Sr	"
	" "	"	Robert Brashears	"
127	James Bowie	"	James Trice	"
	Middleton Brashears	"	Ralph Shaw, Sr	"
	" "	"	William Runnals	"
128	John Brown	"	Moses Riddle	"
	" "	"	Edward Chapple	Attachment
	Henry Morris	"	James Patterson and Amos Whitehead	Case
129	Josias Dixon	"	James Bowie	"
	Thomas Hart	"	John Dennis	Debt
	Samuel Chapman	"	Henry Morriss	Case
130	Thomas Lockheart & Co	"	Hugh Quinn	"
	Thomas Hart	"	Gideon Lincicum	Debt
	Benjamin Croker	"	" "	Case
131	Thomas Hart	"	William Cox	"
	Thomas Webb	"	Thomas Whitehead, Jr	"
	William Johnston	"	" " "	"
	John Meherg	"	" " "	"
132	William Few	"	James Espey	"
	James Bowie	"	William Cox	"
	Phillip Jackson	"	Robert Reed	Attachment
	Croker & Nash	"	Edward Stone, Sr	"
133	Thomas Hart	"	Henry Reynolds	Debt
	Middleton Brashears	"	Henry Mims	"
	" "	"	John Lovelatty	"
134	" "	"	Marshal Lovelatty	"
	" "	"	David Knight	"

Court of November 1763 continued -

135	Middleton Brashears	vs	Christopher Vandergraft	Debt
	Ralph McNair	"	James Bowie	Or. Attach.
136	Michael Waldrope	"	" "	" "
	Thomas King	"	" "	" "
137	Abner Nash, Esq	"	Edward Sweeten	Debt
	" " , "	"	George Glover	"
	" " , "	"	Wm Davis (or Davie)	"
138	" " , "	"	Venerius Turner	"
	" " , Assignee	"	James Bohannon	"
	" " , Esq	"	John Smith	"
139	" " , "	"	John Clarke	"
	" " , "	"	Thomas Harrison	"
	" " , "	"	John Tillefarrs (?)	"
140	" " , "	"	Joseph Richardson	"
	" " , "	"	James Espay	"
141	Thomas Hart	"	Moses Hollis	"
	Clement Reed, Esq	"	George Morriss	"
	" " , "	"	James Espey	"
142	" " , "	"	Isaac Cooper	"
	William Stokes	"	George Lumpkin	"
	Abner Nash, Esq	"	Samuel Burton	"
143	Francis Nash, Esq	"	Thomas James and David Knight	"
	" " , "	"	George Flynn	"
144	Francis Nash, Esq	"	Thomas Littlejohn	"
	" " , "	"	Walter Ashmore	"
	Abner Nash, Esq	"	" "	"

145 "Court adjourned till Court in Course."

146 Court began 7th day of February 1764, at Childsburg.

Justices Present: Tyrie Harris, Alexander Mebane, Richard Parker.

"Ordered that a Road known as Harmon Husband's leading from Bear Creek to Cumberland line be cleared out & kept in repair across Deep River, at William Thompson's, & that Wm. Thompson be Overseer of said Road from Cumberland line to Bear Creek with the hands on the S Side of said creek from John Mills's and from Harmon Husbands Plantation on the N side of said Creek & also the hands on the S side of the said creek to Cumberland line -- also Robert Watkins is appointed Overseer from Bear Creek to Low Creek -- & George Adam Salling is appointed Overseer from Low (Love's ?) Creek to Cox's Road, & Harmon Husbands is appointed Overseer to Sandy Creek."

William Reed appointed Overseer of the Road from the head of Collins's Road to the main Waters of Flat Creek - and Isaac Varnon Overseer from thence to Cox's Mill.

Court of February 1764 continued -

147 "In the Suit Railey against Bowie - Gideon Lincicum, William Dunnagan, Reason Ricketts & Joseph Dunnagan who being summoned as Garnishees being called saith they have nothing."

"In the Suit Nethery against Espey - Mary Long appeared in Court & qualified that she was never summoned as a witness in the said suit on which the fine nisi was remitted."

Letters of Administration granted on Goods & Chattels of William Lesslie, dec'd, to John Wiley. Bond: £ 100. Bondsmen: William Wiley, Andrew Findley.

"In the Suit Cochrane & Co. against William Roberts the Bail surrendered the principle, & was ordered into custody."

Nathan Howard says he was never summoned as a witness in the Suit, Espay against Scarlett.

"Ordered that Joseph Bowring (Boaring ?) be appointed Overseer of the Road from North Hico to head of Enoe, & John Thompson from thence to town."

Last will of William Forbus proved by oath of John Wilice (or Willis).

Letters of Administration granted to William Wiley on Estate of Arthur Parr, dec'd. Bond: £ 100. Bondsmen: John Wiley, Andrew Findley.

148 "Ordered that Robert Bumpass, John Bumpass, Jonas Parker, Samuel Bumpass, Gabrile Davie ?, Thomas King, John Bridges, John Bain, Peter Black, James Satterfield, John Satterfield, George Colley, John Trap, John Thompson, George Flynn, William Jay, James Blackley, John Thomas, Samuel Yarborough, John Carrington, Samuel Fulton, Thomas Pearsons & Robert Pryor or any 12 of them .... lay open a road .... from where Striplands path turns out of the old road to the Country line - near Jonas Parker's, & that William Byas be app. Overseer thereof...."

Alexander Mebane excused from fine for not appearing in the Suit Nethery vs Espey.

Joseph Barbee enters himself as bail for William Roberts in the Suit Cochrane & Co against Roberts.

John Pryor, John McGee & Robert Lytle, Esquires, to attend next Superior Court at Halifax as Grand Jurors - and Michael Holt, John Graves & John King as Petit Jurors.

149 "Ordered that Hugh Smith's be recorded a Publick Mill."

Court of February 1764 continued -

149 "Ordered that a road from Isaac Lowe's mill to Alexander Mebane's mill and from thence to Woody's Ferry on Haw River be opened ... by the following jurors ... James Anderson, David Anderson, Francis Wilkinson, Thomas Lapsey, James McGown, Thomas Cate, Sr, Thomas Cate, Jr, Robert Cate, Robert Tinnen, George Allen, & Cairnes Tinnen..."

Samuel Torringtine app. Constable in the room of William Hullams.

Vachel Clarke app. Overseer of the Road "from Robert Cellars up to the old Fields."

James Cheek appointed Overseer of the Road "whereof William Barney ? was formerly with the same hands."
"James McGown appointed Overseer of Road whereof Henry Willson was formerly."

Joseph Brittain granted license to keep Ordinary at his dwelling. Securities: Benjamin Rhodes, Gideon Lincium.

150 "George Poplen bail for Richard Mauldin at the Suit of Andrew Shepheard delivered him up in open Court - ordered that the Sheriff take him into custody."

"Ordered that William Byars be appointed Overseer of the Road from Deep Creek to where Stripland's path turns out of the Old Road, thence along the new Road to the Country line, near Jonas Parker's & that the hands of the following persons open & maintain the same (to wit) Robert Bumpass, Jonas Parker, Samuel Parker, John Day, John Bumpass, John Trap, John Hamlet, George Cauley, Samuel Yarborough, John Bridges, Thomas Bridges & John Sowell."

"Ordered that a road from Lindley's Mill to John Armstrong's Mill be laid out ....., & from thence to the Country line & that the Jury formerly appointed make report of their proceedings to the next Court."

John Armstrong (Haw River) granted license to keep Tavern at his dwelling house.

"Samuel Stewart being summoned as a Garnishee of the Estate of James Bowie ... saith he hath nothing."

Nathaniel Harris Jr, appointed Overseer of Road in the room of George Law(s).

Samuel Allen appointed Overseer of the Road from Alexander Mebane's to Haw River.

151 William Brashwell granted license to keep a Tavern at his Dwelling. Bondsmen: William Mebane, John Kirk.

Court of February 1764 continued -

151 Grand Jury charged: Solomon Debow, Ephraim Gold, Henry Fuller, John Dunnagan, Thomas Blake, James Clarke, Jonathan Fincher, Daniel McDaniel, Joseph Allison, Jacob Womack, Joseph Dolittle, John Carrington, Archibald Bowling, John Stroud, Sr, & Phillemon Gresham.

	Edmund Fanning	vs	James Saunders	Debt
	" "	"	Edward Camp	"
152	" "	"	Christian Shy	"
	" "	"	Daniel Allen	"
	George Lumpkin	"	Benjamin Garrot & Benjamin King	"
153	" "	"	Nathaniel Fields	"
	" "	"	John Spradling	"
154	" "	"	Charles Harrison	"

"Court adjourned till Court in Course."

---

155 is blank.

156 Court began 1st day (Tuesday) of May 1764 - Childsburg.

Justices present: James Allison, John Sample, John Oliver.

Commissions as Justices of the Peace issued to

John Pryor	Richard Parker	Joseph Barbee
Lawrence Thompson	Tyrie Harris	Robert Lytle
John Patterson	David Hart	James Terry
James Allison	Francis Nash	John Oliver
Andrew Mitchell	Thomas Hart	Thomas Hines
John McGee	John King	John Sample
Thomas Lloyd	John Brantley	Enoch Spinks
William Lea *	Richard Simpson	John Lea.

* The Clerk omitted William Lea's surname, but he is the only Justice named William. See 244, 406, 439, 449.

John Sample & John Oliver qualified as Justices & "took their seats on the bench."

Deed of Sale from John Pugh to Even Pugh of Hampshire County in Va. for his right to a certain tract of land in the aforesaid County on North River a branch of Great Capon - bounded by Henry Batten's line & William Horner's line - Entered by John Pugh in Lord Fairfax's office about 1753.

157 Nicholas Butts appointed Overseer of Road in the room of Martin Loye.
John Armstrong " " " " " " " " Richard Smith.
Richard Henderson " " " " " " " John Hornaday.

Court of May 1764 continued -

157 "Samuel Smith appointed Overseer of Road whereof William Copeland was formerly - to wit - from Braswell's Ordinary to James Cellars."
"James Cellars appointed Overseer of Road whereof William Copeland was formerly - to wit - from James Cellars to William Thomas's old line."

"Joshua Eason appointed Overseer of Road whereof John Price was formerly to wit from William Thomas's to New Hope."
"James Craig appointed Overseer of Road whereof John Price was formerly to wit from New Hope to the Country line."

158 John Auldrige appointed Overseer of Road in the room of John Allison.
Joseph Kirk " " " " " " " " Jeremiah Hallady.
Nathan Almond " " " " " " " " John Booth.
Andrew Warwick " " " " " " " " Thomas Kilgore.
Owen Reed " " " " " " " " John Batown (?).
James Taylor " " " " " " " " John Tinning.
Barney Clapp " " " " " " " " John Fuller.
Jacob Boon " " " " " " " " John Powell.

William Rainey appointed Constable in the room of William Blackwood.

Court met next morning with John Pryor, Tyrie Harris & Lawrence Thompson, Esquires, presiding.

159 Letters of Administration granted to Elizabeth Wood on the Estate of James Wood, dec'd. Bondsmen: John Oliver, John Powell.

David Castleberry recommended to be tax-exempt- also John May.

Thomas Cate appointed Overseer of Road in the room of James Tinning.

George Johnston appointed Constable in the room of Laughlin Campbell.

Robert Lytle & Enoch Spinks qualified as Justices of the Peace.

Lodowick Clap, Adm. of Peter Boon, dec'd, filed a settlement.

(In ADMINISTRATIONS OF ORANGE COUNTY, N. C. pages 50-54, Boon seems to be called "Pastor". His widow was Mary Boon. This book is in the State Archives in Raleigh, N. C.)

160 Martin Mehafty appointed Overseer of Road in the room of John Green.

Grand Jury Sworn - Solomon Debow, foreman, Henry Fuller, William Marsh, John Allison, John Marsh, John Tinning, John Woods, Burgess Harrison, Charles Stephens, John Powell, Patrick Porter, William Hargis, Robert Taylor, William Wilbourn & Samuel Farmer.

James Lindley, Joseph McLester, & John Carter appointed to divide the Estate of John Woodie, dec'd... Robert Woodie, Administrator.

Court of May 1764 continued -

160 James Few to be paid Ł 10 Proclamation Money "for curing William Willice when he was in Goal, of a wound, occationed by shooting him in taking of him, &."

"John Hughlett, an orphan child of John Hughlett, dec'd," to be bound to James Acock until he is 21 years old.

James Terry qualified as a Justice of the Peace.

161 William Ursury granted license to keep a Tavern at his Dwelling. Bondsmen: John Tabor, Benjamin Long.

William Stroud, Jr appointed Constable in the room of Phillip Gee.
James Graves " " for the Deep River District.

"Ordered that Mary Pulliam a daughter of William Pulliam, dec'd, be bound to John Graves - until 18 - she being now 12 years old."

Thomas Lockhearts Ordinary license renewed.
Bondsmen: Samuel Farmer, John Blackwood.

Charles Adams to be fined for not appearing as a Petit Juror.

Election for Sheriff: David Hart 10 votes, Wm. Nunn 7, Ralph McNair 6 votes. (These candidates were selected by the Justices, who sent three names to the Governor, who chose the Sheriff.)

William Kennady recommended to be tax exempt.

"John Jones an orphan child of Sarah Jones be bound apprentice to Phillip Mathews" ... till he is 21.

Christopher Smith app. Overseer of Road in the room of Robert Willie.
James England " " " " " " " " Thomas Clarke.
Nathaniel Harris " " " " " " " " George Laws.

163 Estate of Mathew Hubbard - Hosea Tapley has part of it. Ordered to be so

"Christopher Vandegraft being summoned & sworn to declare what part of the Estate of James Bowie he hath in his hands, saith he hath nothing."

Letters of Administration to Mathew Lard ? (Law ?) and Cairnes Tinnen on the Estate of James Brown, dec'd. Bond: Ł 500. Bondsmen: John Meherg, Lawrence Thompson.

William Mebane granted license to keep Tavern at his dwelling. Bondsmen: Edmund Fanning, John Sample.

"Thomas Goforth came into open Court & delivered up Miles Goforth for whom he was Bail at the Suit of Robert Motherel."

Court of May 1764 continued -

163 Richard Barney granted leave to keep a "public Ferry over Haw River at the place called the red Fields."

164 John Dowell's Ordinary license renewed.

Letters of Administration on the Estate of John Alberd, dec'd, granted to Jane Alberd. Bond: £ 100. Bondsmen: Wm. Means (?), James McGowen.

Robert Woodie, Adm. of the Estate of John Woodie, returned an account.

"Robert Kilgore, Sr, & Andrew Bankson enters themselves Special Bail for Miles Goforth at the Suit of Robert Motherel."

Tobias Clap's mark recorded.

Letters of Administration granted to Richard Parker and Patience Brooker on the Estate of Patience Brooker, dec'd. Bond: £ 500. Bondsmen: Thomas Hart, Joseph Barbee.

165 Deposition of John McMaith taken in the suit of John McDaniel against Giles Chapman.

John Mullain appointed Constable in the room of Mark London.

166 Letters Testamentary granted to Jannett Allison & Robert Ray... on the Estate of William Brown, dec'd. (Wm Brown's will recorded in the Book A page 31, no Executors named.)

Presiding on this day of Court: Thomas Lloyd, Tyrie Harris, Richard Parker, Enoch Spinks, Esquires.

Bill of Sale from Benjamin Rhodes to William Pickett for stock ... dated 16 May 1764. Witness: William Rhodes.

	John Boyd	vs	Robert Brashears	Petition
167	John Esdale	"	George Ingle	Case
	John Meherg	"	Samuel Barton	"
168	Samuel Burton	"	John Woods	Debt
	John Dowell	"	Harriss's Admin's.	Sec Facias
	John Pierce	"	Thomas Wiley	Case
169	Peter Noey	"	Patrick Morris	"
	John Meherg	"	Jacob Mason	Petition
170	Buchannon & Co.	"	Joseph Akin	Case
	Thomas Erskine	"	Vanhook's Exec's	"
	William Carlisle	"	Benjamin Phillips	F.A.B.
171	William Morgan	"	" "	Case
	Samuel Allen	"	James Boyd	"
172	John Carson	"	William Luten, Sr.	"
	Epaphroditus Benton & Ux'r.	"	Mordecai Sutherland	T.A.B.

Court of May 1764 continued -

173	John Woods	vs	Jacob Mason	Case
	Peter Terry	"	George Lumpkin	"
174	Robert Hastie & Co	"	William Almond	"
	John McMaith	"	Hugh Smith	"
175	Robert Witty	"	John Smith	T.A.B.
	John Thompson	"	Isaiah Watkins	Case
176	John Dowell	"	Andrew Norwood	"
	John Dunnagan	"	William Whorton	"
	Reuben Roberts	"	Humphrey Barnett & Ux'r	"
177	Robert Hastie & Co	"	Joseph Akin	"
	William Brackett	"	William Armstrong	"
178	Henry Walker & Co	"	Samuel Burton	"
	Thomas Raney	"	John Robinson	"
179	Isaac Raney	"	Jeremiah Duckworth	"
	George Lumpkin	"	William Williams	"
	Derring Manning	"	Micajah Pickett	"
180	Robert Jones, Esq	"	Reuben Roberts	"
	Isaac Gray	"	Robert Barnett	Attachment
181	James Lindley	"	Vachel Clarke	Petition
	William Wiley	"	Jeremiah Duckworth	"
182	Hugh McGarrock	"	George Finley & Al.	"
	Thomas Hart	"	William Barton	Attach.
183	Anthony Hampton	"	Benjamin Phillips	Case
	Stephen Marett	"	Amos Whitehead	"
	John McGowen & Ux'r	"	John Stroud	T.A.B.
184	Jacob Mason	"	Thomas Page	T.A.B.
	George Lumpkin	"	Frederick Fitzgarrand & Al.	Case
185	Thomas Moore	"	John Going	"
	Thomas Humphries & Ux.	"	John Dowell	T.A.B.
186	Reason Whitehead	"	Thomas Pledger	Petition
	Josiah Mitchell	"	Owen Reed	Case
	John Fish	"	Thomas Green	Petition
187	Bathena Perkins, Exec.	"	John Lovelatty	"
	George Watkins	"	Peter Craven	"
188	John Sample	"	Bazel Brashears	"
	John White	"	John Couch	Case
	Henry Lemon	"	Phillip Hilviston	"
189	Thomas Green	"	John Dowell	T.A.B.
	Joseph Landrum	"	Walter Ashmore	Case
190	McCaul, Lytle & Co	"	Alexander Going	Debt
	" " " "	"	Moses Hollis	"
	" " " "	"	William Garrett	"
191	Richard Bullard	"	Samuel Barnett	"
	George Lumpkin	"	Robert Barnett	Case
192	James Bowie	"	William Martin	"
	John Camp	"	William Camp	"
193	Richard Finch	"	Alexander Going	T.A.B.
	Robert Hastie & Co	"	Jacob Robinson, Jr	Case
	Andrew Cochrane & Co	"	William Marsh	Petition

Court of May 1764 continued -

194	Francis Nash	vs	William Armstrong	Case
	John Dowell	"	Daniel Handley	"
195	John Wood	"	William Nelson	Petition
	Conrod Strader	"	Nicholas Burndrake	Or. Attch.
196	James Fruit	"	" "	" "
	John Brown	"	Edward Chapple	Case
197	Edward Chapple	"	John Brown	"
	Bethena Perkins	"	Larkin Pearpont	"
	Thomas Williams	"	George Lumpkin	Debt
198	Samuel Watt	"	Larkin Pearpont	Case
	John Calwill	"	" "	Debt
	John Bynum	"	Wyatt Stubblefield	Case
199	Robert Waters & Co	"	George Lumpkin	Debt
	Robert Williams	"	" "	"
	Thomas Bauldin	"	" "	"
200	Buchannon Bowman & Co	"	" "	"
	Richard Holden	"	Richard Hill, & Al.	Case
	Thomas Page	"	Neal McCallister	"
201	Daniel Handley	"	John Dowell	T.A.B.
	John Swillivant	"	Henry Fuller	T.A.B.
	Richard Lyon	"	Edward Bull	Petition
202	Stephen Jett	"	Phillip Jackson	Case
	Roger Adkinson & Co	"	Thomas Thompson	"
203	Walker & Nusum	"	Samuel Smith	Petition
	Joseph Parish	"	John Pilkinton	Case
	Phillip Jackson	"	William Barney	"
204	" "	"	Baswell Thompson	"
	John Graves	"	Hugh Smith	Petition
	William Fry	"	Joshua Eason	Case
205	John Bickerstaff	"	Thomas Holden	"
	John Lambert	"	John Brooks	Petition
206	Thomas Capper	"	John Cox	Case
	George Flynn	"	Samuel Vanhook	"
	William Williams	"	John Caven (?)	Debt
207	" " , Esq	"	Bazell Brashears	"
	James Young & Co	"	Joseph Sharpe, Jr	Or. Attch.
	John Daley	"	George Lumpkin	Debt
	Thomas Hart	"	William Wiley	"
208	John Williams, Esq	"	Joseph Sharpe, Jr	Or. Attch.
	Thomas King	"	Nathaniel Wm. Banks	Petition
209	Christmass Ray	"	Thomas King	Case
	John Graves	"	Nicholas Bundrake	Or. Attch.
	Thomas Hart	"	Stephen Cantril	Debt
210	Judith Terrill	"	Alexander Mebane	T.A.B.
	" "	"	Robert Tinning	T.A.B.
	" "	"	John Stroud	T.A.B.
211	William Dunman (?)	"	John Lambert	Case
	Galloway & Co	"	Joseph Burchfield	Debt
	" " "	"	John Burchfield	"

Court of May 1764 continued -

212	Robert Abercromby	vs	John Meherg	Case
	William Bridgett	"	Samuel Moore	"
	John Camp	"	James Saunders	"
	Hugh Irwin	"	James Anderson & Al (?)	Petition
213	Richard Hanson	"	Charles Stephens	Case
	David Steel	"	Thomas Brooks	T.A.B.
	James Benton	"	Thomas Nelson	Petition
	William Ursury	"	William McDaniel	Debt
214	Luke Robertson	"	Wm. & Robert Hawkins	Case
	John Marshal	"	Joshua Eason	Petition
	Robert Motherel	"	Giles Goforth	Case
215	Thomas Karr (?)	"	Hosea Tapley	"
	James Young & Co	"	John Dennice	"
	David Castleberry	"	John Cox	"
216	Patrick Porter	"	Benjamin Phillips	Petition
	Nathaniel Hart	"	Patrick Parker	Case
	Croker & Co	"	Peter Terry	"
217	William Banks	"	Nathaniel Harris	"
	Robert Abercromby	"	William Baker	Debt
	Nash & McNair	"	Joseph Burchfield	"
218	William Nunn	"	George Chapman	"
	Thomas Hart	"	Richard Pilkinton	"
	John Williams, Esq	"	Richard Tyers	"
219	Edmund Fanning, Esq	"	John Swillivant	"
	John Dowell	"	John Dunnagan	"

"Court adjourned till Court in Course."

220 Court began 1st Tuesday (7th day) of August 1764, at Childsburg.

Justices present: Thomas Lloyd, Tyrie Harris, John Patterson, Lawrence Thompson.

John Harrington & John Whealer - to be tax-exempt.

Stephen Poe appointed Overseer of Road in room of William Petty
James Moon " " " " " " " Charles Davis.

"Ordered that Naomi Fisher an Orphan, Base born Daughter of Samuel Sell, be bound to John Dennis until she arrives to the age of 18 years- she being now 8 years & 3 months old."

221 "Ordered that Tydence (?) Lane, Thomas Albred, Herman Cox, Adam Mofit, William Wilbourne, Jr, Semore York, Henry York, Edward Wilbourne, Wm. Home Isaac Kirnes (?), John Hayes, Wm. Norton, John Springer, Jr, James Martin, Edward Cowan & Jacob Polk.... lay out a road, from the county line between Rowan & Orange, crossing Sandy Creek, about 2 miles above Guess's Mill, thence into the best & most convenient Road leading to Cape Fare...."

Court of August 1764 continued -

221 Grand Jury - called & sworn - John Powell, foreman, Joseph Britain, George Hopson, Isaac Cantril, Jacob Womack, James Curry, Elias Powel, John Conner, Hugh Dobbin, Michael Dixon, Hugh Barnett, Samuel Barnett, William Miles, Thomas Cate, Edward Smith & Alexander Toringtine.

The Estate of James Alston, dec'd, to be divided agreeable to the Last Will - on Sept 20th next- by Thomas Lloyd, Tyrie Harris, John Gray, Mark Morgan & William Luten, Sr.

"Ordered that Mary Chance an orphan daughter of John Chance, dec'd, aged 6 years, be bound to James Bauldin" till she is 18.

222 Patrick Porter bound to keep the Peace "with his wife Susannah Porter and others ...." for one year.

Alexander Mebane's Ordinary license renewed.

Jane Albread, Adm'x of John Albred, dec'd, returns an Inventory.

Robert Ray & Jane Allison, Adm's of Estate of William Brown, dec'd, returned an Account of Sales of said Estate.

William Mebane lost a bond given by Joseph George to the Estate of Charles Fooshe - for £ 132-8-0, dated about 15 Dec 1763.

(Page numbers 221 & 222 are repeated.)

221A Estate of John Woodie, dec'd divided.

Adm's of Thomas Berry return a further Inventory.

John Wiley, Adm of Estate of Wm Lesslie, returns an Inventory.

James Allison, Esq. granted license to keep a Tavern at his dwelling.

James Jones (son of John) to be tax exempt.

"Samuel Williams an orphan son of Mathew Williams dec'd to be bound to James Ross until 21 ... he being 14 years old ... calling of a weaver."

222A "Ezekiel Chance - aged 14 years - orphan of John Chance, dec'd, be bound to John Ross until 21.... Art of a weaver..."

Joseph Allison granted license to keep Ordinary at his dwelling. Securities: James McCallister, William Ray.

William Nunn qualified as Sheriff. Ten bondsmen named.

Joseph Richardson appointed Overseer of Road in the room of Wm. Laughlin.
David McCorgan (?) " " " " " " " " Thomas Lindle

Court of August 1764 continued -

222A "On motion of John Graves praying for an order for a mill on Wolf Island ordered that the following persons - to wit- Christopher Hustens, John Fuller Lane, Richard Lea, John Lea, Joseph Dolittle, William Grayhame, Nathaniel Runnolds, Henry Runnolds, John Graves, Venereas Turner, Richard Lane, James McDonald, John Cimbro, John Bryant and Charles Boling..examine the fitness for a mill at the aforesaid place...."

223 "Ordered that Richard Simpson, Alexander West, David Hart, John Powell, Elias Powell, Peter Noey, Michael Holt, Jr, Nicholas Holt, Thomas Rich, John Robinson, Jessee Oldham, Robert Wells, & Hugh Porter...lay out a road...from Hart's Road to Haw River Mill - from thence to Jno. Powell's & from thence to Lindley's Road leading to Cape Fare..."

Joseph Sloss's Ordinary license renewed. Bondsmen: Jno. Armstrong, Francis Nash.

James Anderson appointed Overseer of Road in room of John Anderson.

"Ordered that Windsor Pierce (?), Jeffrey Beek (Buk ?), Christopher Monday, John Needham, John Williamson, & John Needham-James Pittman, James Graves, Ralph Hinwolt, & Charles Strange, Solomon Morgan & John Purslay, Peter Fucannon, and William Searcy, Henry Smith, Adam Andress, John Garner, John Lawrence & Jno Rhodes...meet and lay out a Road ... from Rowan line opposite Frazier's Road to the best & nearest Road leading to Cross Creek..."

224 "Ordered that the following Jury... Samuel Cox, Thomas Cox, Elisha Cadsal (?), Christopher Husay, Solomon Cox, John Cox, jr, William Wierman, Francis Chaney, Joseph Comber, John Hodgins, Robert Hodgins, Stephen Husay, Hercules Ogle, & John Trammel, meet and lay out a road ... from the south side of Deep River to Rowan line to Cross Creek ... and report ..." Christopher Husay to be Overseer from county line of Rowan to Richland Creek, and John Lawrence Overseer from Richard Creek to Cumberland line.

William Nunn, Sheriff, complains about the Prison.

Albright Reynard to be tax exempt.

Road jury - Thomas Cate son of Robert, Isaac Cantril, John Edwards Sr, Rob't Tinning, James Tinning, Charles Milican, Joshua Wittie, James Ball, Jr, Wm. Stroud, John Buckner & James Collins to lay out a Road to Tinnings Mill - from thence to Crow's ford & from thence to Cape Fare Road - and make report to next Court.

225 Letters of Adminstration granted to Edmund Fanning and Francis Nash of the Estate of William Reed, dec'd. Bond £ 500. Bondsmen: Thomas Lloyd, Esq, & Zachariah Martin.

Court of August 1764 continued -

225 "Court adjourned till tomorrow morning at 8 O'clock."
Justices presiding: Richard Parker, Robert Lytle, James Allison, John Brantley.

Elizabeth Johnston, Adm'x of John Johnston, dec'd, returns an account of debts paid by her.

Last will of William Long, proved by oaths of Charles Johns(t)on and David Craig, Executors, and David Mitchell. (The Clerk's writing in Orange Will Book A is so hard to read that OLDS read this name as SAWNEY, and I read it as YOUNG, but LONG is correct, as later entires in the MINUTES show. R.H.S.)

"Ordered that the Road from Hodges Ford to Copeland's Island on Haw River be opened & repaired ... by ... William Riddle, Thomas Holdon, James Holdon, Richard Kirk, Richard Holdon, Cary Minter, William Gamblin, George Wooter, James Brantley, John Shepheard & Benjamin Braswell, & William Riddle be appointed Overseer thereof...."

226 "James Bird app. Overseer of the Road whereof James Hunter was formerly."

Caleb Noe, John Wright, Drury Cumbo & Isaac Cooper committed to jail "for various felonies and misdemeanors", to be tried at Halifax Superior Court.

Reason Whitehead fined ₤ 5 & costs for attempting to rescue some prisoners from Goal.

"Ordered that the money taken from Isaac Cooper and William White who stand committed to Halifax Superior Court be lodged in the Clerk's office until further orders. "

Moses Dossett committed to Goal - accused of passing counterfiet bills.

227 James Mulkey and John White committed to Goal.

"Court adjourned till tomorrow morning, at 8 o'clock."
Court met, presiding: Thomas Lloyd, Tyrie Harris, Richard Parker, David Hart, John Patterson, Esquires.

"Nicholas Scott, brought before the Court on Committment of David Hart, Esq, who being examined is ordered to be acquitted on paying fees-"

Letters of Administration on Estate of Robert Barnett, dec'd, granted to Samuel Watt. Bond: ₤ 100. Bondsmen: David Hart, Esq, Daniel McCollum.

William White brought before the Court and examined, sent back to Goal.

Court of August 1764 continued -

228 William Mebane accused of passing counterfiet money, committed to stand trial at Halifax Superior Court.

Lewis Holwell found guilty of stealing a hog from Warham Glen. Recieved 40 lashes on his bare back.

"Court adjourned till tomorrow morning, at 8 o'clock."
Met, presiding: Thomas Lloyd, Tyrie Harris, Richard Parker, Enoch Spink Esquires.

229 "Ordered that an order made in February for laying out a road from Stripland's Path to the Country line be renewed with the following alteration - to wit - Phillip Pryor & Henry Ledbetter added to list of Jurors."

"Ordered that Thomas Stripland be appointed Constable in the lower part of this county."

Tyrie Harris, James Watson & John Sample to attend next Superior Court at Halifax as Grand Jurors, and John Wood, George Lumpkin, & James Allison as Petit Jurors.

Three shillings levied on "every taxable person in this county" for expenses of building the new Goal, etc.

"Ordered that a Dedimus Potestatum issue to Granville to take the Deposition of John Glover, Jr, David Mitchell & William Thrower in the suit brought by Hugh Montgomery against James Hall."

230 "Ordered that a Dedimus Potestatum issue to Lunenburg County in Va. to take the deposition of Benjamin Whitehead in the Suit brought by Buchannon & Co. against Hosea Tapley."

"Ordered that the Bail in the Suit brought by George Lumpkin against Robert Barnett be Discharged, the Defendant being dead."

"Ordered that John Dowell who was summoned as a Garnishee in the Suit John Stubbs against James Espay be Discharged he having made it appear that he hath no effects of the said Espey in his hands."

Sheriff is ordered to pay John Dowell £ 25 proclamation money for buildi a stockade around the Goal.

"Ordered that the Taxable Persons in Town work only on the Road within the limits of the same."

"Ordered that a summons issue to John Armstrong to lay before the next succeeding Court the last Will & Testament of Joseph Armstrong, dec'd."

Court of August 1764 continued -

230 Sheriff ordered to summon a Guard to serve both day and night while the prisoners are in the Jail. Sheriff to hire a wagon and a Guard to convey the prisoners to Halifax.

231 Richard Parker returns an Inventory of the Estate of Patience Booker, deceased.

William Dunnagan appointed Overseer of Road in room of Joseph Brittain.

Robert Howell's mark recorded.

	Robert Lytle	vs	Alexander Going	Case
	Middleton Brashears	"	Ralph Shaw	"
	" "	"	" "	"
232	William Murrow	"	John Boyd & Joseph Fuller	Petition
	Alexander Going	"	William Going	"
233	" "	"	Edmund Fanling (?)	"
	Gabriel Penn	"	John Williams & Al ?	Debt
	Joseph Chilton	"	Jacob Herrendon	Petition
234	Wyatt Satterfield	"	John Cox	"
	Solomon Gross	"	Lawrence Rambo	Case
	Isaac Taylor	"	Enoch Lewis	Trespass, Etc.
235	John Meherg	"	William Mebane	Case
	William Mebane	"	John Meherg	Petition
	Luke Waldrop	"	" "	Case
	Mathew Brown	"	John Dowell	"
236	Alex. Fuller & Ux'r	"	" "	T.A.B.
	" " " "	"	" "	Case
	Adam Dixon	"	William Childers	"
237	Peter Perkins	"	Nathaniel Austin	
	Thomas Hart	"	John Cate, Jr.	Petition
238	John Dowell	"	Thomas Cate, Sr.	"
	Anthony Steel	"	David Hembrie & Al.	Debt
	Daniel Swilivant	"	John Slater	T.A.B.
239	William Jordon	"	John Armstrong	Case
	Robert Thompson	"	George Bagbey	Petition
	Edward Kirksey	"	James Ayliot	Case
240	Anthony Warwick	"	James Terrell	"
	Edmund Fanning, Asg.	"	John Williard	"
	Nathaniel Austin	"	William Austin	"
241	William Barney	"	Nathaniel Austin	"
	William Whorton	"	John Dunnagan	"
	Buckannon & Co.	"	William Petty, Sr.	"
242	Peter Copeland	"	William Mebane	"
	James Young & Co.	"	Benjmain Cane	"
	James Way	"	John Dennis	Debt
243	Thomas Hart	"	William Pickett (or u)	"
	" "	"	Richard Webb & Wm. Phillips	"
	" "	"	Wm. Shepheard & Wm. Bailey	"
	" "	"	William Luten, Sr.	"

"Court adjourned till Court in Course."

244 Court began 1st Tuesday in November - 6th day - 1764 "at the Court house in Hillsborough".
Present: Tyrie Harris, Wm. Lea, John Lea & Thomas Hart, Esquires.

"Ordered that Daniel Smith be appointed Overseer of the Road from N. Hico to Col. Terry's Ferry in the room of Stephen Terry."

Sheriff is to pay Mr. James Watson ₤ 34 for his extra services as Clerk of the Inferior Court of Orange County.

"Ordered that William Mebane, Jr be appointed Overseer of the Road from County line between Rowan & Orange County crossing Sandy Creek about 2 miles above Guest's Mill."

Grand Jury sworn: William Few, foreman, Benjamin Forrester, James Railey, James McDaniel, John Wood, Joseph Kirk, Archibald Bowling, Richard Holdman, James Trice, Samuel Paul, Abraham Shelton, James McCallister, Gilbert Strayhorn, Henry Reynolds & John Stroud.

245 "Ordered that John Graves' Mill on Wolf Island be recorded a Publick Mill."

"Christopher Eustin by Edmund Fanning, Esq his Attorney, comes into Court and offers Samuel Paul & John Walker Securities for his due & legal administration on the Estate of James Crawford, Deceased."

Harmon Husband is granted letters of administration on the Estate of John Beverley, deceased. Bond: ₤ 200.
Bondsmen: Thomas Stubbs, Laughlin Campbell.

"Ordered that John Martial & Harmon Husbands be appointed Guardians to the orphan children of John Beverly, deceased."

Court adjourned for one hour.
Met with Tyrie Harris, Wm & John Lea, & Lawrence Thompson, Esquires.

"Ordered that the road called Stewart's road be discontinued."

"Court adjourned till tomorrow morning, 8 o'clock."
Met, present: Wm. Lea, Thomas Hart & John Lea, Esquires.

Edward Smith appointed Overseer of the Road whereof Joseph King was former

246 "Ordered that a Dedimus Potestatum issue to King William County in Virgini to take the deposition of Solomon Hughstuff in the suit brought by Christmass Ray against Thomas King."

The will of Joel Brooks was proved by the affirmation of William Brown, Charles Keys and Charles Stout, Quakers, Executor, Joseph Wells, Jr.

Alexander Underwood appointed Overseer of Road in room of John Hyatt.

Court of November 1764 continued -

246 Aaron Harland granted license to build a Water Grist Mill on Rocky River just above John Brantley's line & that Reuben Landrum, Charles Saxton, Samuel Temples & John Brantley, Jr view an acre of land & lay it off for that purpose.

"Phillip Jackson & Stephen Marritt who were Bail for James Couch at the Suit of Reason Ricketts came into Court & delivers him up, Ordered that he stand committed-"

Letters of Administration on the Estate of Andrew Mishelly (?) deceased granted to James Fossett. Bond: ₤ 100. Securities: James Cunnimgham & David Fossett.

247 Stephen Marit's Ordinary license renewed. Bondsmen: William Johnston & Robert Abercromby.

James Ryann granted license to keep Tavern at his dwelling. Bondsmen: James McGowen, Peter Perkins.

John Pryor, Esq's Ordinary license renewed. Bondsman: Francis Nash.

Robert Wells & William Grimes, Bail for Charles Phillips in the Suit against him by John Tomlin, delivered him up.

William Carlisle app. Overseer of Road whereof Elias Powell was formerly.

Court adjourned for one hour.
Met, present: Tyrie Harris, John Pryor, Richard Parker, Esquires.

Solomon Alston returns an account of the Estate of James Alston, deceased. Sales ₤ 197-18-2.

Charles Johnston and David Craig returned an Inventory of the Estate of David Long. (This should be William Long, but the Clerk wrote David).

248 "Ordered that a Road be laid out ... to Granville line near David Embry's old place from Hugh Barnetts, that leads to Rosters Ferry by the following Jury to wit - Robert McFarland, Jr, Rob't McFarland, Sr, William Hawkins, Hugh Barnett, William Chambers, Burges Harrelson, Paul Harrelson, William Barnett, J. Harley, John Long, John Douglass & Moses Walker & that the same Jury lay out A Nother (another) Road from that near Mayo's & Lawrence Rambo's to Hico near John Pryor's, Esq & that the following hands assist in opening the said roads to wit - William Miles, Thomas Barnett, Henry Willice, Giles Tuckey ? or Tinkey ?, James Cavanaugh, Benjamin Long, Edward Nash, Robert Harrilson, Robert Barnett, Thomas Mullin, David Embrie, John Tabor, Timothy Tony ?, Samuel McMurry, Robert McFarland, Sr, Silvester Stokes, Robert McFarland Jr, Silvester Stokes Jr, Moses Walker, William Hawkins, John Hurtley, Walter Butler, William Barnett, John Lusk, John Long, Thomas Douglass, John Douglass, James Byass, Josias Olday, Jacob Womack,

Court of November 1764 continued -

248 Hugh Barnett, Paul Harrelson, Paul Ham, Burges Harrelson, Garrett Guttery, Edward Chambers, Michael Cockburne & Wm. Chambers, Jr, and that Burges Harrelson be appointed Overseer of the Road leading from Mayo's to Hico ford and that Thomas Douglass be Overseer of that part leading to Granville line."

"Court adjourned till tomorrow morning, 8 o'clock."
Court met, present: John Pryor, Francis Nash, Richard Parker, Esq's.

Elizabeth Johnston, Adm'x. of John Johnson, dec'd, returned an account of 20 shillings against the Estate, which was allowed.

249 Abner Nash to erect a Public Grist Mill on Enoe River on the Mill lot in Childsburg belonging to the said Nash. Col. John Gray, Thomas Hart, Esq, Enoch Lewis and William Nunn, Esq are appointed to lay off and value an acre of Hon. Francis Corbin's land for the mill.

"Ordered that Flower Swift be appointed Overseer of the Road from Daniel McCullom's on Hogans Creek to the County line on Dann River at the Sarrow Town ford- & that all the hands on Dann River from the mouth of Wooley Island Creek to Sallaw Town & those residing on Wolf Island Creek are ordered to work on the said Road."

Deed from Peter Ream & Mary his wife to John Forest for 202 acres of land - proved by oath of Michael Holt, Jr.

Samuel Watt, Administrator, returned an Inventory of the Estate of Robert Barnett, deceased.

Receipt from Henry Eustace McCullock to Malachi Fogleman for £ 34 proved by oath of Michael Holt, Jr and recorded.

Thomas Douglass granted license to keep Ordinary at his dwelling.
Bondsmen: John Armstrong, William Ursury.

250 "Thomas Hart, late Sheriff" ordered to pay Barnaby Cabe £ 4-10 sh. for guarding prisoners down to Halifax Superior Court.

Edmund Fanning and Francis Nash, Administrators of Estate of William Reed, dec'd, returned an Inventory. Sale to be held 20 December next.

"Ordered that a Road be laid out ... from Lewis Green's ford on Dann River to Boyd's Mill on Haw River by the following Jury to wit - Joseph Pain, Phillip Prator, Richard Simpson, Jesse Oldham, William Porter, Hugh Porter, William Millier, Joseph Prichett, James Prichett, James Starratt & William Boyd..."

John M Williams appointed Overseer of Road from Alexander Mebane's Mill to Trollinger's ford on Haw River.

Court of November 1764 continued -

250 William Carlisle appointed Overseer of Road from Trollinger's Ferry to Rowan County Road.

251 "Ordered that the Sheriff pay Francis Nash, Esq £ 12 for his Extraordinary services as Clerk of the County ..."

"Court adjourned till tomorrow morning."
Court met, present: Tyrie Harris, Richard Parker, Thomas Hart, Esq's.

Phillip Jackson's Ordinary license renewed. Security: Francis Nash.

Harmon Husband returned an Inventory of the Estate of John Beverley, dec'd.

"N. C. Orange County, This day came William Bridgett before me John Sample one of his Majesty's Justices for the County aforesaid and made oath that he wronged James Allison in speaking so rough of him concerning his killing of a hog that was none of his own.
signed William Sample. Sworn before John Sample."

	Daniel McDaniel	vs	Giles Chapman	Case
252	Thomas Lowe	"	James Lindley	"
	Andrew Shepheard	"	Richard Mauldin	"
253	William Grimes	"	William Stephens	Case
	Roger Adkinson	"	James Terry	"
	Thomas Webb	"	William Armstrong	"
254	John Woods	"	James Trice	"
	Robert Thompson	"	Sarah Hayles	"
255	Andrew Campbell	"	Christian Morris	"
	Isaac Ramsey	"	Jeremiah Duckworth	"
	Thomas Cresap	"	James Martin	Petition
256	Hugh Montgomery	"	James Hall	Case
	Thomas Cresap	"	William Shepheard	"
	John Scott & Ux'r	"	John Dowell	T.A.B.
257	Reason Ricketts	"	James Bowie	Case
	William Journey	"	Hugh Quinn	Petition
258	John McLeroy	"	Benjamin Saxon	Debt
	Thomas Hart	"	Phillip Jackson	Case
	William Nunn	"	William Humphries	"
259	Joshua Haughton	"	William Luten, Sr	"
	David Castleberry	"	William Browning	Or. Attch.
	Croker & Co.	"	Thomas Cate, Sr.	Petition
	Thomas Dobbin	"	Andrew McMillion	Or. Attch.
260	Hamilton & Co.	"	George Ring (K?)	Case
	John Williams, Jr.	"	Middleton Brashears	Or. Attch.
	Phillip Williams	"	John Tomlin & Ux'r	Case
	Benjamin Bohannon	"	Joseph Kirk	"
261	William Nunn	"	Nathaniel Austin	Or. Attch.
	John McMillion	"	John Thomas	" "
	Adam Salling	"	George Hobson, Jr	Debt

Court of November 1764 continued -

262	John Williams, Esq	vs	Richard Tyers	Debt
	" " "	"	Wm. Cannon Childers	"
	" " "	"	William Thompson	"
263	Thomas Hart	"	Lancelott Armstrong	"
	" "	"	Alexander Ritchey	"
	" "	"	William Weatherspoon	"
264	Abner Nash	"	Benjamin Rhodes and William Pickett	"
	John Giles Thomas	"	Hugh Quinn	"
265	Andrew Cochrane & Co	"	Stephen Jett	Case
	James Bowie	"	James Pomfrey	"
	William Mebane	"	Martin Mehaffy	"
266	Reason Ricketts	"	James Bowie	"
	Robert Langley	"	Hugh Quinn	"
	John Fuller Lane	"	Patrick Porter	"
267	Richard Holden	"	Richard Hill & Al (?)	"
	Thomas Page	"	Neal McCallister, Sr	"
268	Phillip Jackson	"	William Barney	"
	" "	"	Baswell Thompson	"
	John Camp	"	James Saunders	"
269	Thomas Carr	"	Hosea Tapley	"
	Croker & Co.	"	Peter Terry	"
270	James McCraw	"	John Kirksey, Jr	Petition
	Ralph Shaw	"	Middleton Brashears	Case
	" "	"	" "	T.A.B.
271	Cochrane & Co.	"	John Graves, Jr	Petition
	Micajah Pickett	"	John Alston	Case
	John Ross	"	William Burney	Or Attch
	Wyatt Stubblefield	"	John Cox	Petition
272	Michael Willson	"	Elisha Eastwood	Case
	Reason Ricketts	"	James Couch	"
	Nathaniel Austin	"	William Barney	"
273	Owen Reed	"	Thomas Brooks	"
	Robert Taylor, Assignee	"	James Bowie	"
274	Joshua Hawkins (2 cases)	"	Lawrence Rambo	"
	Robert Jackson's Exec's	"	Joseph Stewart	"
	William Nunn	"	Zachariah Martin	"
275	Thomas Dobbins	"	Patrick Porter	"
	Phillip Jackson	"	Baswell Thompson	Petition
	William Stokes & Co	"	Henry Willice	"
	James Way	"	James Davis	Case
276	John Scott	"	John Scott & Ux'r	T.A.B.
	Thomas Hart	"	Phillip Jackson	Case
	Joshua Haughton	"	William Luten, Sr.	"
277	David Castleberry	"	William Browning	Or. Attch

"Court adjourned till Court in Course."

Court of February 1765

278 Court began at Courthouse in Childsburg the 2nd Tuesday (12th day) of February 1765.
Present: Thomas Lloyd, John McGee, Thomas Hart, Esquires.

James Cummings granted license to keep Tavern "at his dwelling house in this Town". Bondsmen: Thomas Hart, Phillip Jackson.

279 to 300 Here follow twenty-one and a half pages of bonds for various Sheriffs and other county officers, dating from 1759 through August 1767, which contain no new names or information.

300 "Ordered that Michael Holt have leave to erect a Water Grist Mill on his land on the Alamanchey River & that the same be recorded a Public Mill."

Cattle marks recorded by Joshua Hadley & James Ross.

Grand Jury sworn: Benjamin Long (foreman), Henry Fuller, John Lawson, Daniel McDaniel, Thomas Bailiff, Barnaby Cabe, John Latty, John Miles, David Steel, George Tate, Edward Willson, Peter Noe, Robert Carson, & Enoch Bradley.

Gideon Kirksey granted leave to build a water grist mill on Haw River at the Seven Islands.

John Dowell's Ordinary license renewed.
Bondsmen: John Dennis, John Stroud.

"Ordered that Isaac Beverley, an Orphain child of John Beverley, aged about 11 years, be bound to Joshua Hadley until he arrive to the age of 21 years, who is to receive the sum of £ 12 above his freedom dues."

301 Court adjourned for one hour.
Court met, present: Tyrie Harris, Richard Simpson, Thomas Hines, Esq's.

No business, "Court adjourned till tomorrow morning."
Court met, present: John McGee, Richard Simpson, Robert Lytle, Esq's.

William Braxton's cattle mark recorded.

William Gibson appointed Overseer of Road whereof Robert Baker was formerly.

302 Joseph Wells returned an Inventory of the Estate of Joell Brooks, deceased.

"Richard Berry who was summoned at the instance of James Collins to give an account of what part of the Estate of James Fogerson he had in his hands, saith he hath nothing but an old wigg."

Court of February 1765 continued -

302 Samuel Blair appointed Overseer of Road in room of John Adam Salling.

"Ordered that Ruth Chance an orphan daughter of John Chance, deceased, about 12 years of age be bound unto John Patten until she arrives to the age of 18 years."

Harmon Husband returned an Inventory of the Estate of John Beverley, dec'd.

Three orphan children of John Beverley are bound out -
John Beverley bound to Harmon Husband till 21 years old.
Jesse Beverley bound to William Moffitt-"weaver"-till 21.
Hannah Beverley bound to John Fruit till she is 18 years old.

303 "Mary Terrill. widow and relict of Timothy Terrill. deceased, exhibited his last will, and was appointed Executrix."

"John Piles an Executor of Timothy Terrell, dec'd, came into open Court and relinquishes his right of administration."

"Thomas Hines & John Sample, Esq's returns a Certificate setting forth that James Hall who was imprisoned at the Suit of Hugh Montgomery & Francis Nash, appeared before them and took the benefit of the Act of Assembly made for the Relief of Insolvent Debtors."

Elinor Butts granted Letters of Administration on the Estate of Nicholas Butts, dec'd. Bond: £ 100. Bondsmen: John Holt, Daniel McDaniel.

John Latty appointed Overseer of Road in room of Samuel Money.

Cattle marks recorded by Benjamin Coleman, Richard Castleberry, & Mordecai Southerland.

John Alexander recommended to be tax-exempt.

304 James Clarke appointed Constable in the room of James Latta.

Tavern Rates listed.

Marks recorded by Richard Right & Herman Husband.

305 "Thomas Trice Exhibits on Oath an Account against the Orphans of James Alston, Deceased, which is accordingly admitted."

"Ordered that a Mill built by Francis Cypart on New Hope be recorded a Publick Mill."

Phillip Cellar granted Letters of Administration on the Estate of George Cellars, dec'd. Bond: £ 100.

Court of February 1765 continued -

305 "Abraham Nelson being summoned as a Guarnishee in Sundry attachments laid in his hands at Instance of Sundry persons saith that he hath the Ballance that is due on a Bond to Thomas Nelson in the hands of Gilbert Strayhorn but doth not know the sum."

"Court adjourned till tomorrow morning."
Court met, present: Thomas Hart, Richard Parker, Thomas Hines, John Lea, Esquires.

"Ordered that James Cummings deliver up to William Reed the Standard and take his receipt for the same which he is to lodge in the Clerk's office."

"William Shepheard who stands imprisoned at the suit of Thomas Cresap, gives up to the Court a schedule of his Estate" and petitions as an Insolvent Debtor.

306 "Mark London, Robert Saunders & Charles Abercromby, Deputy Sheriffs under Thomas Hart, Esq. late Sheriff, came into Court and made oath that the number of Insolvents as returned by them - amounting to 292 for the year 1762 and 296 for the year 1763 was just and true which is accordingly allowed in settlement for the County and Parish Taxes."

Marks recorded by James Cellars, Stephen Lloyd and Henry Rudolph, Bartholonew Bunch (?) and Thomas Green.

Edward Young appointed Constable in the room of James Terry, Esq.

John Stroud recommended to be tax exempt.

307 "Court adjourned till Monday."
Court met, present: Tyrie Harris, Thomas Hines, Francis Nash, Esq's.

"Deed of Sale from Jesse Hollingsworth to Herman Husband for 225 acres- dated 9 Sept 1764, was proved in open Court by the acknowledgement of the said deed before George Catto ? (Calto ?) & Joseph Griffin, & that certificate under the hand and seal of Francis Key, Clerk of Cecil County, Md., was received as legal proof."

"William Shepheard now in Goal" returns the following schedule of his Estate to be sold for the benefit of Thomas Capper, Esq..." (Is this an error by the Clerk? Thomas Cresap sued Shepheard.)

..."following to serve as Grand Jurors at Halifax Court - John McGee, Esq, Joseph Barbee & Abraham Miles, and as Petit Jurors: John Meherg, William Grimes & Jno Dowell."

308 "Ordered that Robert Graves be appointed Graves (Constable is meant) in the room of James Graves." (See page 161.)

Court of February 1765 continued -

308 The King vs James Hall, Indictment - Issue of Traverse.
Abner Nash, Attorney for defendant.

309 "Court adjourned till tomorrow morning at 8 o'clock."
Court met, present: Tyrie Harris, Thomas Hart and Thomas Lloyd, Esq's.

"John Williard exhibits an account against the County for Burying Arthur Parr and Robert Burton and for keeping the Goal a short time amounting to £ 5-11-4 which is allowed. Ordered that the Sheriff pay the same."

"William Shepheard returns a further account of his Estate, viz't -
In the hands of Mark London £ 1-2-6
" " " " Joseph Thrasher -8-
" " " " James Saunders 2-10-."

William Shepheard took the Insolvent Debtors oath.

Mathew Brown vs John Dowell - Debt
Plea: "Nil Debit" - released on appeal.
Bondsmen: John Wood, Sr, David Steel.

310 Nathaniel Hart granted license to keep a Tavern at his dwelling.
Bondsmen: Edmund Fanning, Thomas Hart.

"Ordered that the mill built by Nathaniel Hart on Hosley's (?) Creek be recorded a Public Mill."

"Ordered that the Sheriff pay Nash & McNair £ 3-12-8 on account of George Foutz assigned to them."

"Ordered that the Sheriff be allowed 10 shillings for his extraordinary services in removing the effects of Bazil Brashear."

"Sheriff to pay Robert Reed £ 5-12-6 for his Extraordinary services done for this County."

311 Cattle marks recorded by Henry Fuller, John Craig & Archibald Bowling.

Jury reports on acre of land laid off for a mill site for Aaron Harland. (Exact lines given.)

"Ordered that George Black, Gresham Allen, Isaac Fitzwood (?), Jacob Robinson, Sr, Phillip Phillips & Hugh Dobbin work on the Road whereof Daniel Duncan (is Overseer) besides those that formerly worked under him." (See page 33.)

"Ordered that Richard Clements Mill on New Hope be recorded a Publick Mill."

Court of February 1765 continued -

311 "Ordered that John Powell, Michael Holt, Sr & Jr, Peter Island, John Holt, Elias Powell, John Piles, Hugh Laughlin, Peter Noey, John Graves, David Phillips & William Phillips lay out a Road ... from the mouth
312 of Reedy Fork on Haw River ... and that John Powell be appointed Overseer of the said Road."

Cattle marks recorded by George Rigsby, John Shaddy, Ludwick Albright & Charles Johnston.

	Thomas Webb	vs	Richard Burton	Case
	Adam Lawrence	"	Peter Shearman	"
313	Robert Dunlap	"	John Thrasher	Petition
	George Boyd	"	Joseph Dolittle	Case
314	Walter Ashmore	"	William Wallice	"
	Richard Burton	"	John Meherg	"
	Joseph Richardson	"	Benjamin Phillips	"
315	Thomas King	"	William Collins	Or. Attch.
	Gideon Marr	"	Plunkett Ballard	T.A.B.
	John Dowell	"	John Scott ' Ux'r	T.A.B.
316	Andrew Cochrane & Co.	"	Stephen Jett	Case
	Thomas Brooks	"	John Dowell & Ux'r	T.A.B.
317	Benjamin Phillips	"	Daniel Higden	T.A.B.
	James Robinson	"	Gideon Marr	Case
	John Cox	"	William Callahan	Or. Attch.
318	Robert Hastie & Co.	"	Easther Robinson	Case
	John Dowell	"	Andrew Campbell	"
319	James Minnis	"	Nathaniel Austin	Debt
	John Jones	"	George Lumpkin	Case
	Buchannon Spiers & Co.	"	Hosea Tapley	Debt
320	Bowman " " "	"	John Rogers	Petition
	" " " "	"	John Day	"
321	James Lesslie	"	Alexander Going	Case
	Thomas King	"	Edward Stone, Sr	"
	John Dowell	"	Joseph Sharpe, Jr	"
322	Benjamin Crooker & Co.	"	Gideon Lincicum	"
	Middleton Brashears	"	Ralph Shaw, Jr.	"
323	William Few	"	James Espey	"
	Richard Parker	"	John Clarke	"
	John Wyatt	"	Bynum Stubblefield	"
324	John Swillivant	"	Henry Fuller	T.A.B.
	Thomas Capper	"	John Cox	Case
	James Young & Co.	"	Joseph Sharpe, Jr	Or.Attch.
325	John Dailey	"	George Lumpkin	Debt
	Christopher Ray	"	Thomas King	Case
326	Judeth Terrell	"	Alexander Mebane	T.A.B.
	" "	"	Owin Reed	T.A.B.
	" "	"	Robert Tinning	T.A.B.
327	" "	"	John Stroud, Jr	T.A.B.
	Richard Hanson	"	Charles Stephens	Case
	William Ursury	"	William McDaniel	Debt

Court of February 1765 continued -

328	Nathaniel Hart	vs	Patrick Porter	Case
	Henry Morris	"	William Fry	Or. Attach.
	John Cate, Sr	"	Mathew Hubbard	" "
329	James Bowie	"	Young Pitts & Al (?)	Petition
	Nathaniel Hart	"	Jacob Green & Al (?)	Case
330	Drury Hawkins	"	Joshua Hawkins	"
	Mary Redman, Adm'x	"	John Mills	"
	Ralph Shaw	"	Middleton Brashears	"
	" "	"	" "	T.A.B.
331	Gilchrist & Co.	"	William Nealey	Case
	William Ursury	"	David Embree	"
	" "	"	Joshua Hawkins	Debt
332	Peter Howe, Esq	"	William Gibbons	Case
	Mathew Axum	"	John Arrington	"
333	Epaphroditus Benton & Ux'r	"	Mordecai Southerland	T.A.B.
	Phillip Taylor	"	James Roberts, Jr	Debt
	Peter Watkins	"	Francis Posey	Case
334	Mathew Brown	"	John Dowell	"
	Alexander Fuller & Ux'r	"	" "	T.A.B.
	Samuel Farmer	"	Abraham Hales ? (States?)	Case
335	Anthony Street	"	David Embree & Al.	Debt
	Edward Kirksey	"	James Elliott	Traver
	Anthony Warrick	"	James Terrell	Case
336	William Thompson	"	Elijah Cane	"
	James Young & Co.	"	Benjamin Caine	"
337	Nathan Carter	"	Hugh Smith	"
	John Camp	"	" "	"
	Thomas Levvitt?, Assignee	"	Joseph Hawkins	"
338	John Dowell	"	Daniel Handley	"
	John Hogan	"	Nathaniel Austin	Or. Attch.
	Joshua Haughton	"	William Luten, Sr	Case
339	David Castleberry	"	William Browning	Or Attch
	Croker & Co.	"	Thomas Cate, Sr	Petition
	Benjamin Bohannon	"	Joseph Kirk	Case
340	John Williams, Esq	"	Walter Ashmore	Or Attch
	Wade & Stokes	"	Joseph Cooker	" "
	William Reed	"	James Terrill	" "
	John Williard	"	" "	" "
	" "	"	Hope Taylor	" "
	Hugh Smith	"	Thomas Raborn	Case
341	Jesse Amberson	"	Benjamin Thompson	T.A.B.
	William Gilbert	"	William Jameson	Petition
	Robert Jennings	"	Mary Redmond, Adm'x	"
342	John Williams	"	Joseph Dolittle	Debt
	Francis Nash	"	Francis Carney	Case
	" "	"	Thomas Camp	"
343	Ed. Fanning & Fr. Nash	"	Samuel Watt	"
	Edmund Fanning and Francis Nash, Adm's	"	John Dowell (4 suits)	Debt

Court of February 1765 continued -

344	Ed. Fanning & Fr. Nash, Adm's	vs	Mary Redman, Adm'x	Peititon
345	Francis Nash	"	John Warren	"
	Abner Nash	"	Valentine Brashwell	Case
	Nash & McNair	"	John Camp	Petition
346	Thomas Hart	"	Benjamin Saxon	Or Attch
	John Meherg	"	John Dowel & Al	Petition
	Nash & McNair	"	William Saunders	Case
347	" " "	"	Benj. Allen Tharpe	"
	" " "	"	Mark London	Petition
	William Nunn	"	John Webster	"
	Henry Hastings	"	Christian Shy	Case
348	Nash & McNair	"	Jacob Herrendon	Or Attch
	James Minnis	"	Frederick Nall or Natt	Case
	Thomas Langdon	"	Larkin Pearpont	"
	Michael Synnot	"	William Baker, Sr	"
349	Thomas Hart, Esq	"	John Edwards	"
	James Young & Co.	"	John Williard	"
	Joseph Sharpe, Sr	"	John Dennise	Debt
350	Nathaniel Edwards	"	Howell Brewer	Petition
	Andrew Norwood	"	Samuel Hill	Case
	Michael Synnott	"	Barnaby Baker	Petition
	Richard Grove	"	John Armstrong	"
351	John Williams, Esq	"	Samuel Watt	Case
	Phillip Jackson	"	William Brashwell	Or Attch
352	George Parmor	"	Samuel Faar ?	Case
	William Phillips	"	Thomas Winberry	Or Attch
	Nathaniel Rice	"	James Collins	" "
	Edward Stapler	"	William Wiley	Debt

353 "Court adjourned till Court in Course."

---

354 is blank.

Court began 2nd Tuesday in May 1765 at Courthouse in Childsburg.

355 Elias Powell appointed Constable in room of Jacob Boon.
William Millwee ? " " " " " William Rainey.
William McCear " " " " " Henry Hayes.

"Ordered that John Graves & Barnett Trocks have leave to build a mill on waters of Great Allimance on the land of the said Trocks."

Letters of Administration on the Estate of Margaret Nelson, granted to David Nelson. Bond: £ 140. Bondsmen: David Craig, George Nelson.

William Nunn granted license "to keep a Tavern in this Town."

Sarah Horton granted Letters of Adm. on Estate of William Horton, dec'd. Bond: £ 300. Bondsmen: Wm. Johnston, Wm. Burford.

Court of May 1765 continued -

356 Letters of Adm. to James Acock on the Estate of William Acock, dec'd. Bond: £ 300. Bondsmen: Benjamin Blake, ... Williams.

Abraham Hilton appointed Constable in the room of Barnard Clapp.

Phillip Hartso has leave to build a Water Grist Mill on Rocky River about one mile above Captain Martin's.

Nicholas Copeland to be tax-exempt.

James Rigsby app. Overseer of Road whereof James Cellars was formerly.

"Ordered that Jannett Caldwell and James Freeland have letters Testamentary on the Estate of Andrew Caldwell, deceased."

Letters of Administration on the Estate of Hugh Laughlin, dec'd, granted to Mary Laughlin. Bond: £ 3,000. Bondsmen: John Oliver, Wm. Laughlin.

357 Richard Clemens appointed Constable for the ensuing year.
James Hunter " " in the room of Benjamin Guest.
Wm. Laughlin " " for the District of Cain Creek.

John Oliver granted license to keep Tavern at his dwelling.
William Wiley " " " " " " " " .
Peter Noey " " " " " " " " .

The Court recommend ... William Nunn, John Patterson & Thomas Lloyd, Esquires, as candidates for Sheriff of Orange County.

William Nealey appointed Overseer of Road in room of John Satterfield.

John Moore appointed Constable in the room of William Neill.

Jeremiah Piggott who was appointed Executor of the last will of Joell Brooks, refused to serve.

358 The last will of Hugh Laughlin was proved in open Court by William Payne, William Laughlin & John Lambert. (Recorded A39)

Mary Henson (aged 5 years) daughter of Benjamin Henson, bound to Adam Trollinger, until she is 18 years of age.

Thomas Hart, Esq, late Sheriff, by his Goaler exhibits in open Court the following accounts against the County to wit-
for William Willice's committment & charges whilst in Goal -
also Price Willice, Charles Gunter, John Posten, & William Runnolds.
Total £ 18-15-4.

Shadrick Morrice is committed for trial at Halifax Superior Court.

Court of May 1765 continued -

358 William McMath app. Overseer of Road from Allamance to Lindley's Mill.

James Morrow appointed Constable in the room of Mullington Blalock.
Joshua Stroud, " " " " " " John Craig.

359 Road Jury reports they have laid out the new road to Granville.
David Halleyburton appointed Overseer of said road from Mayo to Granville line.

Thomas Breeaze appointed Constable in the room of Ralph Williams.

Sackfield Brewer	appointed	Overseer	of	Road	in	room	of Thomas Cate.
James Ball	"	"	"	"	"	"	" Thomas Cate, Sr.
Timothy Murphy	"	"	"	"	"	"	" John Moore.
John Morrow	"	"	"	"	"	"	" John Cantril.
Samuel Bumpass	"	"	"	"	from Deep Creek to the County line.		

Alexander Ritchey granted license to keep Tavern at his dwelling.

360 Abraham Miles appointed Overseer of the Road from Thomas Hart's old place to Runnolds Cabbins.

William Graves an orphan son of John Graves, dec'd, (aged 9 years) bound to Richard Wood, blacksmith.

William Hargas mark recorded.

Windsor Pierce appointed Constable in the room of John Carson.

"Court adjourned till tomorrow morning."
Court met. Present: Thomas Lloyd, John Lea & Enoch Spinks, Esquries.

Augustine Hightower to serve as Constable in ensuing year in the room of William Stroud, Jr.

John Thomas (aged 8) son of John Thomas, dec'd, bound to John Camp, till 21.

John Dunnagan appointed Constable in the room of William Rea.

Arthur Mangum appointed Overseer of the Road in the room of Robert Thompson on the road that leads to Tarborough.

361 "Ordered that the following Jurors to wit Henry Brewer, Vachel Clarke, Oliver Brewer, Isaac Collins, John Price, John Edwards, William Marsh, Richard Copeland, Aaron Horton, Joseph Kirk, Micajah Fike ?, Hercules Anderson, John Fike & Charles Landrum ... lay out a Road .... from Wm Johnston's Store on Little River to Henry Brewer's ford on Haw River & that Vachel Clarke be app. Overseer of said Road on the North Side of Haw River & William Marsh on the South side."

Court of May 1765 continued -

361 Charles Johnston & David Craig, Adm's of Estate of William Long, dec'd, returned an Inventory of said Estate.

Robert Kilgore, Sr to be tax-exempt.

George Foultz proved an account against the County of £ 1-13-.

Charles Saxon appointed Overseer of Road in the room of Howell Brewer.
Enos Elliman " " " " " " " " Joseph Aldridge.
Joseph Henderson " " " " " " " " John Fuller Lane.

Marks recorded by Peter Dear & John Oliver.

362 "Ordered that a Road be laid out ... from the ford at the Red Fields into the Western Road at Little River by Mr. Johnston's by the following Jury to wit - Robert Patterson, James Rigsby, Robert Pendergrass, Luke Bynum, Thomas Durham, John Edwards, William Castleberry, Solomon Draper, William Rhodes, Thomas Forrist, William Forrist, Benjamin Forrist & Edward Gresham ... and report ..."

"Ordered that a Road be laid out the best & most convenient way from the Old Cape Fare Road nigh Zacharaih Martin's on Rocky River unto Cape Fare Road commonly called Harman Husbands Road-"(no Jury named).

"William Wiley, Adm of Arthur Parr, dec'd, returns an account of sundry debts paid for the said Estate which is allowed."

William Wiley, Adm of Estate of William Forbus, dec'd, returns an account of Debts paid by him for said Estate which is allowed.

William Couch appointed Overseer of Road in the room of James Craig.

"Ordered that the Road from Finley's Road into Allison's Road be continued the best and most convenient way by the following Jury to wit - Richard Simpson, Jessee Oldham, Robert Wells, Solomon West, John West, John Robertson, George Finley & William Porter, James Starratt, Hugh Porter, Joseph Pritchett & Samuel Means - & that William Porter & Robert Wells be Overseers of the said Road."

363 "Ordered that a Road be laid out ... from William Braswell's ferry on Cape Fare to Hamilton's Store on Crabtree Creek by the following Jury to wit - David Chapman, Richard Cheek, Burwell Williams, Joseph Aven ?, Robert Jones, Drury Mims, John Tally, Henry Day, Valentine Braswell, William Ashley, Samuel Lehman, Thomas Seamore & Henry Braswell - "

John Woods appointed Overseer of Road in room of James England.

Thomas Brown appointed Constable in the room of William Hart.
John Smith " " " " " " John Mullin.

Court of May 1765 continued -

363 "Ordered that the Clerk direct the Warrants for taking the List of Taxables to the several Magistrates as was directed last year."

"Ordered that the part of David Hart's District which is on the waters of Haw River be taken by Richard Simpson, Esq."

John Dowell to receive £ 1-16- "for his extra services done for this County."

"Ordered that Thomas Hart, Esq take the list of Taxable persons in the following district to wit - from Town along the Trading Road to Haw River, crossing the said River at the mouth of Sandy Creek, from thence to George Salling's on Rocky River down the same to Cape Fare Road & along said Road to County line."

364 "Ordered that Tyrie Harris, Thomas Lloyd, Thomas Hart, John King, John Patterson & Francis Nash, Esquires, also James Watson, James Few & Joseph Maddock (Gentlemen), meet at the Court House on Whitson Monday next to consult & determine on a plan for building a Public Goal, & that they advertise the letting of the same to the lowest bidder.

"Ordered that William Lea, Zachariah Lea, Peter Bankson, Robert Kilgore, Sr, Joseph Sarratt, Niel McCoy, James Lea, John Bratcher & John Lea ... lay out a road, from Pinson's Path nigh Thomas Runnolds, from thence into Synnot's Road nigh the meeting house ..."

Marks recorded by John Howell & Thomas Beal.

	Josiah Mitchell	vs	Owen Reed	Case
365	John Wimbush & Co	"	Fred. Fitzgerald & Al	"
	Jacob Black	"	Hugh Quinn	Debt
	Thomas Lowe, Assignee	"	Andrew Campbell	Case
366	Henry Morrice	"	James Patterson & Al	"
	Joseph Parish	"	John Pilkinton	"
367	John Bickerstaff	"	Thomas Holden	"
	John Williams, Esq	"	Joseph Sharpe, Jr	Or Attch
368	Robert Abercrombie	"	John Meherg	Case
	Thomas King	"	Benjamin Bohannon	"
	Nicholas Cooke	"	Edward Roberts	"
369	Jacob Mason	"	Robert Brashears	Petition
	Peter Johnston	"	Phillip Dossett	Case
	Adam Dixon	"	William Childers	"
	Samuel Farmer	"	Abraham States	Debt
370	Peter Perkins	"	Nathaniel Austin	"
	Francis Nash	"	Benjamin Long & Al	"
	Peter Copeland	"	William Mebane	Case
371	John Dowell	"	Daniel Handley	"
	John Camp	"	Hugh Smith	"

Court of May 1765 continued -

372	Michael Sullivant & Ux'r	vs	Joseph Sloss	T.A.B.
	John Dowell	"	Henry Trollinger	Petition
	William Nunn, Esq	"	William Humphries	Case
	John McMillion	"	John Thomas	Or Attch
373	Valentine Braswell	"	Mary Morris & Al	" "
	Nathaniel Austin	"	William Barney	Sciere Facias
	Joseph Duncan, Sr	"	John Dunnagan	T.A.B.
374	Zachariah Martin	"	Daniel Norris	Petition
	Gordon and Boyd	"	Hugh Dobbins	"
	John Williams, Esq	"	David Phillips	"
375	" " "	"	Alexander Going	Case
	Joseph Aken	"	" "	"
	Francis Nash	"	Thomas Camp, Sr	"
376	" "	"	Samuel Fulton	Petition
	" "	"	John Smith	Case
	James Young & Co.	"	Joseph Stewart	"
377	Nash & McNair	"	Alexander Mahone	Petition
	" " "	"	James Nicholson	Case
	" " "	"	John Warren	"
378	Henry Hastings	"	Christian Shy	"
	Patrick Rutherford	"	Andrew McBroom	"
	John Kelley	"	Henry & Thos Nelson	Or Attch
	Thomas Hart, Esq	"	Hugh Porter	Petition
379	William Johnston	"	Thomas Nelson	Or Attch
	John Powell	"	Amos Whitehead	" "
	George Lumpkin	"	Thomas Harrison	" "
	James Saunders	"	" "	" "
380	Robert Jones, Esq	"	James Herndon	Case
	John Pankey (?) & Co.	"	John Brassfield	Or Attch
	William Few	"	James Espey	Sciere Facias
381	Derrick Manning	"	Micajah Pickett	" "
	John Thompson	"	Isaiah Watkins	" "
	Benjamin Crooker	"	Gideon Linicum	" "
383	John Wimbush & Co	"	Moses Hollis	" "
	Anthony Hampton	"	Benjamin Phillips	" "
	Thomas Moore	"	John Going	" "
383	Wither & Co.	"	Samuel Burton	" "
	John Dowell	"	Joseph Sharpe	" "
384	Derwin Elwick	"	Nicholas Pundrake	Or Attch
	William Few	"	Christian Shy	" "
	Micahel Killinger	"	John Dowell	Petition
	Edward Moore	"	John Camp	"
385	Hugh Smith	"	" "	Case
	John Meherg	"	Noel Johnston	Petition
	William Armstrong	"	Thomas Whitton	"
386	James Young & Co	"	John Camp	Case
	John Brooks	"	John Webster	T.A.B.
	Hugh Smith	"	David Lowe & Al	Case

Court of May 1765 continued -

387	Thomas Hynes, Esq	vs	Phillip Jackson	Petition
	William Nunn, Esq	"	Hugh Smith	"
	Nash & McNair	"	Benjamin Hart	"
	James Ryan	"	Robert McConnal	"
388	Thomas King	"	James Wileston	"
	Peter Copeland, Esq	"	William Ketor ?	"
389	Isaac Middlebrooks	"	Michael Boyle & Al	"
	Joseph Preston Parker	"	John Meherg	Case
	Abner Nash, Esq	"	Alexander Going	Petition
	" " "	"	John Brown	"
390	John Lam(p)bert	"	John Brooks	"
*	Barnaby Clapp, Assignee &	"	Christian Shy	"
391	Robert Maxwell & Co	"	William Ware	Case
	John Ward	"	Thomas Shiels	Petition
	John Dowell	"	John McVey	"
392	John Dowell	"	Samuel Fulton	"
	" "	"	Isaac Holden	"
	" "	"	James Minnis	Case
	" "	"	George Smith	"
393	Phillip Jackson	"	Gabriel White	"
	James Elliott	"	William Marsh, Jr	Petition
	Joseph Brantley	"	John Bohannon	Case
394	Wm. Brantley, Assignee	"	" "	"
	John Jackson	"	Robert (Ferguson) Fogerson	Petition
	Edward Sorrell	"	James Trice	Case
395	Benjamin Drummond	"	Valentine Braswell	"
	Jeremiah Piggott	"	John Armstrong	Petition
	John Armstrong	"	Richard Lyon & Co.	Debt
	Richard Leigh	"	John McMillion	Or Attch
396	James Young & Co.	"	James Ryan	Petition
	William Johnston	"	Charles Johnston	Or Attch
	Wm Hamilton & Co.	"	Robert Marsh	Debt
	" " " "	"	John Brooks	"
397	" " " "	"	Benjamin Clanton	"
	" " " "	"	John Cortner ? or S?	"
398	Derwin Elwick's Exec's	"	John Boyd	"
	" " "	"	Michael Beaver	"
	" " "	"	John Phillips	"
399	" " "	"	John McQuery and Henry Mullin	"
	" " "	"	Henry Mullin and John McQuery	"
	" " "	"	John Sitton	"
400	" " "	"	Joseph Harvey	"
	James Young	"	Nathan Whitton	"
	" "	"	Francis Cozart	"

*
390 Thomas Hart, Esq. " James Hagan Petition

Court of May 1765 continued -

401	James Young	vs	Samuel Hicks	Debt
	Robert Carmichael & Co.	"	David Embree and Jacob Womack	"
	Wm. Hamilton & Co.	"	Elijah Eastwood	"
402	James Young & Co.	"	Abraham & John Dennis	"
	Adam Dixon	"	John Collins	"
	Thomas Pervice ?	"	Thomas Collins	"
403	John Dowell	"	Henry Brasewell and Elijah Cain	"
	Jacob Womack	"	John Armstrong (D. River ?)	Debt
	John Williams, Esq	"	James Elliott	Debt
	" " "	"	Alexander Clarke	"
404	" " "	"	Robert Lumpkin	"
	John Meherg	"	Abraham Dennis	"
	" "	"	John Dennis	"

"Court adjourned till Court in Course."

---

405 Court began 2nd Tuesday in August, 13th day, 1765, Childsburg.

Present: Tyrie Harris, Thomas Hart, John Lea, Lawrence Thompson & John Oliver, Esquires.

Richard Camp appointed Overseer of Road in room of James Moon.

"Ordered that the Sheriff pay John Dowell £ 1-17- for his keeping Shadrick Morriss 37 days who made his Escape out of this Goal.".. and "15 shillings for summoning a Guard over William Willice."

Major, a negro boy belonging to James McCallester judged to be 12 years old.

James Pocock, Adm. of Estate of William Acock, dec'd, returns an Inventory of the Estate.

Elijah Beverley (aged 3 years) son of John Beverley, dec'd, bound to Henry Doyle .. "to learn the trade and occupation of a weaver."

John Murrow appointed Overseer of Road in room of John Cantril.

406 Tyrie Harris, William Lea, John Oliver, John Sample and Lawrence Thompson, Esquires, return their lists of Taxables.

Lawrence Thompson who was Bail for William Burch at the suit of Elwick's Exec's, came into Court & delivered him up. Ordered that he stand committed."

Court of August 1765 continued -

406 William Nunn, Francis Nash, Robert Lytle & Enoch Lewis appointed to lay off an acre of land on Enoe River for Abner Nash, Esq, instead of "them formerly appointed". (See 249, November Court).

James Horton appointed Overseer of Road in room of William Dunnagan.

"Court adjourned till tomorrow morning 8 o'clock."
Court met. Present: Richard Simpson, Tyrie Harriss, Andrew Mitchell, Esq's

Joshua Hadley appointed Overseer of Road in room of Joseph Kirk.

"The last will of Daniel Norris, dec'd, proved by oath of John Thompson. Letters Testamentary issued to Martha Norris & Thomas Beal. (Recorded in Book A page 37.)

Elinor Butts, Adm'x of Estate of Nicholas Butts, dec'd returns an Account of Debts against said Estate.

407 David Nelson, Adm. of Estate of Margaret Nelson, dec'd returns an Inventory.

Cattle marks recorded by Daniel Winter, Benjamin Cock.

Daniel Brown appointed Overseer of new Road from Old Cape Fare Road to Harmon Husband's Road.

William Dorum (Durham ?) & Edward Hopson are Bail for James Beazley in the suit by Hamilton & Co. against him.

Nicholas Trip appointed Overseer of Road in room of David Morgan.
Stephen Jones & John Barton appointed Overseer of Road in room of Powell Glass.
Henry Welsh appointed Overseer of Road in room of Christopher Smith.

Peter Noey Petitions about a road near his home.

408 Thomas Leach appointed Overseer of Road in room of James Boyd.

Elizabeth Woods, Adm'x of James Woods, returns an Account.

Samuel Vanhook app. Constable in the room of Thomas Wilson, Sr.

"Ordered that Richard Wright, Ebenezar Harris, John Field, Herman Husband, Thomas Pugh, Laughlin Campbell, James Hunter, William Ward, Benjamin Phillips, Jeremiah Field, Jessee Pugh, Joseph York & Peter Inlan ? ... lay out a Road beginning at the County line at the Plantation of John Hannah, from thence ..... to Harmon's Road ."

Court of August 1765 continued -

408 "Stephen Herndon, orphan son of Lucy Herndon, aged 11 years" is to be bound to Stephen Poe to learn the art and Mystery of a cooper."

Daniel McCullum appointed Overseer of Road in room of Benjamin King.

"Joice ? or Joie ? Goodrum an Orphain son of Thomas Goodrum, dec'd, aged 9 years, is bound unto Thomas Willson till he arrive to the age of 21 years."

The Perishable Estate of William Horton, dec'd, to be sold 3rd Friday in September.

Perishable Estate of Andrew Caldwell, dec'd, to be sold on 1st Friday in September.

409 "Ordered that Nathaniel Milton, Luke Bynum, Robert Cellars, James Cellars, Christopher Kirksey, Anson Milton, Robert Patterson, William Griffin, Vachel Clarke, James Rigsby, Thomas Durham, John Price, James Hogwood, Isaac Kirksey & John Gunter, lay out a Road ... from the Redfields ford on Haw River to New Hope Chapel ... and report ..."

James Cavanough to be tax-exempt.

Samuel Allen granted license to keep Tavern at his dwelling. Securities: John Sample, John McGee.

"Robert Patterson & Richard Woods who was Bail in the Suit brought by Robert Jackson against James Minnis ... delivers him up.."

"Court adjourned till tomorrow morning, 8 o'clock."
Court met. Present: Thomas Lloyd, Thomas Hart, John Pryor, Esquires.

Benjamin Phillips' mark recorded.

James Allay appointed Constable in the room of James Fletcher.

"The Sheriff returns a Pannel of the Grand Jury to wit - William Thompson (foreman), Gilbert Strayhorn, Archibald Bowlin, Lawrence Vanhook, Benjamin Long, Vachel Clarke, Robert Wittie, James Minnis, John Cantril, Barnaby Cabe, James Pratt, Joseph Cantril, John Price, Warham Glenn & James Crow, who having received their charge withdrew."

410 Charles Adams appointed Overseer of Road in room of George Sharpe.

"Robert Jackson against Joseph Stewart - Bail surrenders the principle- James Crow & Thomas Raborn enters themselves special Bail."

Thomas Lockheart granted license to keep a Tavern at his dwelling.

Court of August 1765 continued -

410 Elwick's Exec's against Robert Brashears - John Hogan who was Bail surrenders him.

Joseph Sloss's Tavern license renewed.

James Armstrong appointed Overseer of the Road called Jamestown Road in room of John Slaters.

George Mill appointed Overseer of the Road called Lowe's Road from Slaters Branch to the Trading Path.

Court adjourned. Met next morning. Present: Thomas Lloyd, John Lea, Thomas Hines, Esquires.

"Easther Robinson, who was committed to the Public Goal at the Suit of Hastie & Co., came into open Court & took the oath for the Relief of Insolvent Debtors," and was discharged.

Robert Abercrombie, William Luten, Sr & John Patterson, Esq to attend next Superior Court at Halifax as Grand Jurors.

Richard Parker, Thomas Webb & Thomas Lapsie to attend next Superior Court at Halifax as Petit Jurors.

411 John Meherg against William Mebane Suit

412 David Kenady to be tax-exempt.

James McGown appointed Overseer of Road in room of James Mason.
Phillip Jackson app. " " " " " " John Dowell.

"Thomas Hart, Esq, late Sheriff came into Court & delivered a list of Supernumerary Taxables for the year 1762 amounting to 35 in number."

"Ordered that Francis Nash, Tyrie Harris & Thomas Lloyd, Esq's, settle with the late Sheriff for the County Tax on Saturday the 24th day of this Instant & report thereof to the next Court."

Commissioners appointed for building Goal, if Thomas Hart, Esq the Undertaker shall have finished the same before the next Court, are to appoint a day for examining the work...

413 "Ordered that the Sheriff pay John Foutz 9 shillings 6 pence for mending & making Irons for the Goal."

William Nunn, Esq, produced his commission as Sheriff for Orange.

414 Cattle marks recorded by Enoch Lewis, John Handley, John Logue, Michael Sting, William Ruddock, Christopher Hussey, (or Hufsey ?) William Wilburne, Lawrence Rambo, Ruth Rambo, Lawrence Rambo, Jr, Ann Smith, John Currey.

Court of August 1765 continued -

414 "Joseph Brittain being prosecuted by Tyrie Harris, Esq (for saying that the said Harriss had acted partially in his office as a Magistrate, or words to that effect), came into Court & confessed that he had no Reason for the aforesaid aspersion, that what he said was nothing more than the Effects of Passion that he was sorry for it and Humbly Begged Mr. Harris Pardon, etc ..."

	Thomas Whitton	vs	Samuel Watt	Case
415	William Tabb	"	William Gibbons	"
	John Keighler	"	John Tabor	T.A.B.
416	William Thompson	"	William Braswell	T.A.B.
	Hastie, Buchannon & Co.	"	Richard Prewitt, Jr	Debt
	Thomas Erskine	"	John Bumpass	"
417	Joseph Wells	"	Hugh Smith	Case
	Micajah Pickett	"	Richard Burton	"
418	Jacob Mason	"	Thomas Brooks	"
	William Few	"	Barnaby Cabe	Petition
	Robert Witty	"	James McGown	"
419	John Railey	"	James Bowie	Or Attch
	William Bridgett	"	Samuel Moore	Case
	Henry Morris	"	William Fry	Or Attch
420	John Miller, Adm, Etc	"	Richard Robinson	Petition
	William Ursury	"	David Embrie	Case
	Nicholas Cooke	"	Edward Robert	"
421	George Neatherly (or H?)	"	Robert Lumpkin	"
	John Meherg	"	William Mebane	"
422	William Way	"	John Dennice	"
	Nash & McNair	"	James Nicholson	"
	Thomas Hart, Esq	"	Adam Dixon	"
423	William Johnston	"	Charles Jordon (?)	Or Attch
	Joseph Keys	"	James Phillips & Al	Debt
	" "	"	" " " "	"
424	Michael Willson	"	Elijah Eastwood	Case
	William Stokes	"	Isaac Grey	"
	Francis Nash	"	Edward Camp	"
425	John Roberts	"	Joseph Hawkins	"
	Abner Nash, Esq	"	Joshua Hawkins	"
	James Gordon & Co.	"	William Grayham	"
	William Hamilton & Co.	"	George Flynn	"
426	Nash & McNair	"	Henry Reynolds	Petition
	Edmund Fanning	"	Jessee Moore	"
	John Phillip Clapp	"	John Shy	Case
	Mary Humphries	"	Jane McGown	T.A.B.
427	Robert Jones, Esq	"	James Herndon	Debt
	Michael White	"	William Gibbins	Case
	David Aren ? or Drew ?	"	Charles Adams	"
	Richard Henderson, Esq	"	John Maroon	"
428	Wm. Hamilton & Co.	"	Simon Fooshea	Petition
	" " " "	"	Cary Minter (it says Cary Martin in text of report)."	

Court of August 1765 continued -

429	John Brooks	vs	Reuben Landrum & Al	Debt
	Empson Bromfield	"	Isaac Lowe & Ux'r	Case
	Benjamin Allen Tharpe	"	James Griffin	Debt
430	Wm. Hamilton & Co.	"	Jones ? Patterson	Case
	" " " "	"	Burwell Williams	Petition
	" " " "	"	James Beazley	Case
	John Salling	"	Joshua Hadley	T.V.A.
431	Elwick's Executors	"	Robert Brashears	Case
	William Johnston	"	Jonathan Hardin	Debt
	William Browning	"	David Castleberry	Case
432	John Meherg	"	Phillip Dossett, Sr	"
	Robert Thompston	"	John Springer ? and Joseph Walter	"
	Hosea Tapley	"	Thomas Erskine	Or Attch
	Wm. Stokes & Co.	"	Henry Willace	Debt
433	Stokes & Wade	"	Jonathan Allen	"
	William Johnston	"	Robert Smith	"
	Wm. Cannon Childers	"	John Vaughn	"
434	Edmund Fanning, Esq	"	George Miller	"
	" "	"	Isaac Gray	"
	William Nunn, Esq	"	John Webster	"
435	Nash & McNair	"	Andrew Banckston	"
	" " "	"	Lawrence Banckston, Sr	"
	Francis Nash, Esq	"	" "	"
436	" " "	"	" " , Jr	"
	" " "	"	George McGowan	"
437	" " "	"	Joseph King	"
	Peter Copeland	"	Sherwood Runnalds	"
	Nash & McNair	"	John Warren	"
	" " "	"	Joseph Trotter	"
438	James Young & Co.	"	Francis Day	"

"Court adjourned till Court in Course."

---

439 Court began 2nd Tuesday, 12th day, November 1765. Childsburg.

Present: Tyrie Harris, Thomas Lloyd, Thomas Hart, Lawrence Thompson, William Lea, John Lea, John Patterson, John McGee, Esquires.

Thomas Farrow, accused of passing counterfiet Virginia bills, "acquitted, on paying Fees, etc."

Robert Harlin (Hillard, later) brought into Court by John Allen Tharp his Security, acquitted. Accused of stealing a horse from Wm. Jay, Sr.

Nash and McNair	against	James Nicholson	Case

440 "Court adjourned till Court in Course."

Court of February 1766

441 Court began 2nd Tuesday, 13th day, February 1766, Childsburg.

Present: John Pryor, Tyrie Harris, David Hart, Thomas Hart, Richard Simpson, Richard Parker, Robert Lytle, John Lea, Esquires.

The only entry for this Court:
"Ordered that Richard Parker, Robert Abercrombie, & Joseph Barbee be summoned to attend the next Superior Court as Grand Jurors. And that John Graves, Epaphroditus Gould & Nathaniel Harris, Jr be summoned as Petit Jurors."

"Court adjourned till Court in Course."

442 is blank.

443 Court began 2nd Tuesday, 13th day, May 1766, Childsburg.

Present: the same eight Justices as at February Court.

Charles Milliken appointed Overseer of Road in room of James Ball.
Charles Francis " " " " " " " James Elliott.

Joseph Allison appointed Constable in room of James McCallister.
Jacob Railey " " " " " Thomas Breeze.

"James Freeland comes into open Court & relinquishes his right of Executorship on the Estate of Andrew Caldwell, deceased."

Robert Graves, old & infirm, excused from paying taxes.

Archibald Bowland appointed Overseer of Road in room of James Craig.

444 "Ordered that the Sheriff pay to John Dowell £ 1-12-8 Proc. for Repaving the Old Goal."

George Stanley appointed Constable in the room of James Clarke.
John King " " " " " " John Moore.
Ralph Williams " " " " " " John Woods.
George Findley " " " " " " George Miller.
Wm. Hightower " " " " " " Austin Hightower.
James Rutledge " " " " " " George Johnston.

Edmund Fanning's cattle mark recorded.

Jacob Gregg appointed Administrator of the Estate of William Gregg, dec'd. Bond: £ 500.

John Hunter's Ordinary license renewed.
445 John Dowell's " " " .

Court of May 1766 continued -

445 William Graden appointed Constable in the room of Richard Cate.
John York " " " " " " James Hunter.

Thomas Lowe appointed Overseer in the room of John Barton.

"An Inventory of the Estate of Andrew Caldwell, dec'd, was returned by Archibald & Janet McCallister (late Janet Caldwell) Adm's of said Estate.

Recommended to the Governor as candidates for Sheriff of Orange - "Tyrie Harris, Thomas Lloyd & Thomas Hart, Esquires who had an equal number of votes to wit 8 each."

"Court adjourned till tomorrow morning, 8 o'clock."
Court met. Present: Thomas Lloyd, Thomas Hart, David Hart, John Lea, Esquires.

Grace Maritt & James Scarlett granted Letters of Administration on the Estate of Stephen Maritt, dec'd. Bond £ 250.
Bondsmen: Stephen Scarlett, John Johnston.

446 James Talbert appointed Overseer of Road in room of James Anderson.
Hugh Dobbin " " " " " " " Daniel Smith.

John Bell appointed Overseer of Road in room of Timothy Murphy.
Thomas Stubbs " " " " " " " James Taylor.
John Cantril " " " " " " " William Laughlin.
William Murrow " " " " " " " Joseph Richardson.

"Ordered that the Districts laid off for the several Magistrates (last year) for their receiving their lists of Taxables continue as they were & that Orders issue to the several Constables etc."

"Ordered that Mary Rigsby (a base-born Female Child of Tabitha Rigsby) aged 8 years, be bound unto John Campbell & his wife, Mary, till she arrives to the age of 18 years - etc."

James Robinson returned to Jail for trial at Halifax "on Suspicion of having murdered a certain Charles Seal."

447 William Massey committed for trial at Halifax "on suspicion of having stolen sundry horses."

Jacob Pearson appointed Overseer of Road in room of John Woods.
James Paul " " " " " " " John Grubbs.

James Alley granted license to keep Tavern at his dwelling.

Last will of James Roney, dec'd, proved by oath of Mary Sample. Letters Testamantary to John Sample. (This is probably Raney, see below.)

Court of May 1766 continued -

447 Samuel King & Elizabeth King appointed Guardians to Ann Rainey an orphan daughter of James Rainey, dec'd, aged 12 years, till she is 18 years of age.

448 Andrew Hilbreath (?) appointed Constable in room of William Miller.
William Cowley " " " " " William Gibson.

"On report of Thomas Lloyd, James Watson, & Francis Nash, who were appointed Commissioners by the Court with sundry others for the Examining the Sufficiency of a new Goal built by Thomas Hart, Esq it is ordered by the Court that the said Goal be Received by the Court from the said Thomas Hart & that his Bond for Building according to contract be Nul & Void."

"Court adjourned till Court in Course."

---

449 Court began 2nd Tuesday, 12th day, August 1766 in Childsburg.

Present: Tyrie Harris, Thomas Lloyd, Lawrence Thompson, John Lea, John McGee, Jno. Oliver, & John Sample, Esquires.

William Lea, Thomas Hart, Thomas Lloyd, Tyrie Harris, Lawrence Thompson, John Sample, Esquires & James Terry return their "lists of Taxables for the present year."

John Holt's Ordinary license renewed.

James Carragan appointed Overseer of Road in room of Thomas Lynch.
Samuel Vanhook " " " " " " " George Lea.

450 Thomas Alred and Samuel Barker appointed Overseers of the Road "from the Country line where it crosses Sandy Creek to Coxe's Road that leads towards Cape Fare."

William Cox appointed Overseer of Road in room of Flower Swift.
William Teague " " " " " " " Joseph Hadley.
John Ramsey " " " " " " " Samuel Dark, dec'd.
James McGown " " " " from Enoe River to Alex. Mebane's.

James Thomas to be tax-exempt.

James Aycock, Adm. of Estate of Wm. Aycock, dec'd, proved an account against the Estate.

Last will of Thomas Mills, dec'd, proved by oath of Lewis Barton and Joseph Patterson.

Court of August 1766 continued -

450 Lawrence Rambo's list of Taxables (six in number) entered.

451 George Holt appointed Overseer of Road in room of Edward Trollinger.

William Brooks, Sr to be tax-exempt.

Last will of Hugh Tinning ? proved by affirmation of Thomas Lindley, Jr, and letters of Administration issued to Samuel Stewart.

Isaac Edwards, Esq qualified to practise as Attorney in Orange.

"The Sheriff returns a Pannel of the Grand Jury - to wit-
James Freeland (Foreman), Barney Clapp, George Whitton, George Robinson, William Few, Nathaniel Walton, Elijah Eastwood, Nathan Milton. Solomon Terrill, James Collins, Vachel Clarke. William Copeland, John Fuller Lane, Abraham Miles, Barney Cabe, and John May."

James Wilkinson appointed Overseer of Road in room of James Horton.

Martha Weldon (8 years old) an orphan daughter of Mary Weldon, & David Weldon (4 years old) son of the said Mary Weldon, to be bound to William Thompson, "agreeable to law".

"Ordered that Mary Neblet, daughter of Tilman Neblet, dec'd, aged 11 years, be bound unto John Odeneal, until he arrives to the age of 21 years".

452 "Letters of Administration granted to Elizabeth Hollingsworth on the goods and chattels of Valentine Hollingsworth, dec'd."

"Ordered that Joseph Tate an orphain child of Robert Tate, dec'd, aged 11 years, be bound unto David Linch, till he arrives to the age of 21 years."

"Ordered that James Tate, orphain son of Robert Tate, dec'd," be bound to Solomon West. till 21 years old.

"Thomas Rainburne who was Security for Joseph Stewart Adsum. (at the Suit of) Jackson's Executors, brings him into open Court and surrenders him up - whereupon - Elijah Cain & John Stewart enters themselves Special Bail."

"Jacob Grig, Adm. of Estate of William Grigg, dec'd, returns an Inventory of said Estate."

John Bohannon appointed Constable in room of John Boyd.

George Keark appointed Overseer of the Road from Robinson's Creek into the Road near Hodge's Ford.

John Trousdale granted "license to keep License" (Tavern is intended ?).

Court of August 1766 continued -

452 "Ordered that James Lanckston have liberty to build & erect a Water Grist on Flat River at Cedar Island."

"Ordered that George Harlin be appointed Overseer of the Road from Bear Creek at Norris's to Deep River Ford in the room of Dorman Hinson."

453 James Kirby appointed Overseer of Road in room of James Rigsby.

Henry Welsh appointed Overseer of the Road"called Harmon's Road, from Bear Creek to Lowe's Creek, in the room of Christopher Smith."

John Graves Ordinary license renewed.

Ordered that John Ritenour be appointed Guardian to Peter Harmon and Paul Harmon, orphans of Paul Harmon, dec'd. Bond: ₤ 150. Bondsmen: John Oliver, John Graves.

The last will of Charles Sinklin, dec'd, proved by oath of Joseph McLester & James Ferris. Amos Evans relinquished his right of Executorship. Ann Sinclin appointed Executrix. (Recorded A 45).

Gilly Forsyth swears that Richard Henderson is the father of her child. His bondsmen: John Lea and William Lea. Bond: ₤ 50. Henderson is to appear at next Superior Court.

"In the suit Waters & Co. vs Bengerman (?) the Bail came into Court & surrendered up the princip<u>le</u> whereupon Thomas Stanton enters himself Special Bail."

454 Mary Terrell returns an Inventory of the Estate of Timothy Terrell, dec'd

Margaret Caldwell, daughter of Andrew Caldwell, dec'd, chose Archibald McCallister, her step-father, as her Guardian. Bond: ₤ 150.

"In the suit Benjamin Nicholson against James Minnis, Joseph Glasson his Security comes into Court & delivers him up & he is ordered into custody."

Court adjourned for half an hour.
Court met, present: John Pryor, Thomas Lloyd, John Brantley, and John Sample, Justices.

John Brantley, Richard Parker & Enoch Spinks, Esqs, return their lists of Taxables.

Andrew Cowan to be tax-exempt.

Edward Moore appointed Overseer of Road in room of William Reed.

Court of August 1766 continued -

455 "On motion of John Williams, Esq it is ordered by the Court that John Holt and Daniel McDaniel, the former Securities for Elinor Butts (for her Administration of her deceased husband's Estate) be discharged of their Securityship on her entering into Bond with Jacob Albright and Martin Lloyd Securitys." (Was LOY intended?)

Letters of Administration granted to Mary Cummings and Thomas Hart on the Estate of James Cummings, dec'd. Bond ₤ 150. Bondsmen: David Hart, Edmund Fanning.

Edmund Fanning, Esq. qualified as Public Register for Orange. Bondsmen: Thomas Hart & Richard Henderson, Esquires.

Henry Trollinger's Grist Mill on the upper Ford of Haw River to be a Public Mill.

James Forsyth, Esq presented his Commission as Attorney.

William Seal (aged 10 years) orphan son of Charles Seal, dec'd, to be bound to John Douglas.

456 Letters of Administration on the Estate of Thomas Wiley, dec'd, granted to William Wiley. Bond: ₤ 500. Bondsmen: Wm. Reed & Joseph Reed.

James Roney (aged 14 years) an orphan son of James Roney, dec'd, to be bound to Frederick Albert Black.

"Ordered that William King Brown (aged 6) .... son of Sarah Brown, be bound to Daniel Booth."

George Blaik (Black ?) an infirm old man to be tax-exempt.

Court adjourned for one hour.
Court met, present: Richard Parker, James Allison & Thomas Hines, Esq.'s.
John Patterson, Esq returns his list of Taxables for the present year.
John Oliver, Esq returns his list of Taxables.

457 "In the suit Vincent Tollock vs Nicholas Durning, the Bail surrendered the principle, Ordered that he stands committed."

The Estate of James Alston, dec'd, to be divided "on Tuesday 19th of this month" by John Gray, Mark Morgan, Thomas Lloyd, Tyrie Harris & William Luten, Sr.

Thomas Moore appointed Overseer of Road in room of Samuel Blair.

John McGee, Thomas Hines, Richard Simpson & James Allison, Esq's, return their lists of Taxables.

Moses Watkins stole a drawing knife from John Woods. He gets 10 lashes on his bare back at the public whipping post.

Court of August 1766 continued -

457 Court adjourned "till tomorrow morning- 8 o'clock".
Court met. Present: John Pryor, Richard Parker, John McGee, Richard Simpson, Esquires.

458 Tyrie Harris, Esq, qualified as High Sheriff for Orange County.
Bond: £ 1,000. Bondsmen: Thomas Hart, Richard Simpson.

John Dowell allowed £ 13-11 sh. for feeding William Massey, James Robinson, John Ward, Moses Watkins & Bazzel Brashears while they were in Goal awaiting trial.

Benjamin Forrist granted Letters of Administration on the Estate of John Manen, dec'd. Bond: £ 250.
Bondsmen: Phillip Johnston, Phillip Dosset, Sr.

David Mashburn granted license to keep Tavern at his dwelling.

Court adjourned for half an hour.
Court met, present: John Patterson, Lawrence Thompson, John McGee, John Oliver, Esquires.

459 Jonathan Sell to be tax-exempt.

John Ward accused of stealing two deer skins from John Kelly - found guilty - to get 20 lashes at Public Whipping Post.

Robert Holloway accused of having marked three of Robert Tate's hogs with his own marks, not guilty.

Benjamin Marit an orphan son of Stephen Marit, dec'd chose James Scarlet as his Guardian.

Court adjourned till tomorrow morning at 8 o'clock.
Court met, present: John Pryor, Francis Nash, Richard Parker, Esquires.

460 John Pryor, Esq. returns his list of Taxables.

James Gregory appointed Constable in room of James Allen.

William Reed appointed Guardian to Andrew Corban Reed, orphan of Wm. Reed, dec'd. Bondsmen: Barnaby Cabe, William Few.

"James Freeland appointed Guardian to Margaret Elizabeth Simon and William Caldwell orphains of Andrew Caldwell, dec'd." (No punctuation.)
Bond: £ 1,000. Bondsmen: Alexander Mebane, Sr, John Butler.

Thomas Hart, Esq. late Sheriff's accounts settled.

"Ordered that Francis Nash, Edmund Fanning and James Watson, Esq's be appointed to lay out the Prison bounds and report."

Court of August 1766 continued -

460 "In the Suit Elwick's Executors vs Hugh Smith & William Raney, they give for their Securities James Lindley, James Doho (?), John Holt and Barnaby Clap."

461 William Few granted license to keep Tavern at his dwelling.
Bondsmen: Nathaniel Walton & James Taylor

"In the Suit Wm. Few vs Barnaby Cabe - John Hogan & Enoch Bradley enters themselves Special Bail."

Court adjourned till tomorrow morning - 8 o'clock.
Court met, present: Thos. Lloyd, Thos Hart, Thos. Hines, Esquires.

Phillip Jackson's Ordinary license renewed.
Alexander Mebane's " " " .

Thomas Hart's mark recorded.

Thomas, Henry and William Campbell convicted of having stolen and killed a hog belonging to Barnaby Cabe - each received 10 lashes on his bare back.

Creed Childers granted license to keep Tavern at his dwelling.

	Thomas Beford	vs	James Terry	Case
	Francis Day	"	Michael Synnot	"
	Charles Cupples	"	James Terry	"
462	John Bynum	"	William Stephens	"
	" "	"	David Stephens	"
	William Banks	"	Nathaniel Harris	"
463	Drury Hawkins	"	Joshua Hawkins	"
	Jacob Mason	"	Robert Brashears	Petition
464	William Stroud	"	Joseph Collins	Case
	Peter Perkins	"	Nathaniel Austin	Debt
	Andrew Lynum	"	Alexander Fogerson	Case
466	Thomas Dobbins	"	Patrick Porter	"
	John Scott	"	John Dowell & Ux'r	T.A.B.
	Michael Swillivant & Ux'r	"	Joseph Sloss	T.A.B.
467	Hamilton & Co.	"	George King	Case
	Phillip Jackson	"	Bazel Thompson & Al.	Sc. Facias
468	" "	"	William Barney	" "
	John Williams, Esq	"	Alexander Going	Case
	Jeremiah Piggott	"	John Armstrong	Petition
469	Epsom Bromfield	"	Isaac Lowe & Ux'r	Case
	William Johnston	"	John Coleman	Or Attch.
	John Handley	"	Archibald Bohannon	" "
470	John Wimbush & Co.	"	James York & Al.	Petition
	Francis Nash, Esq	"	John Scott	"
	Abner Nash, Esq	"	William Garrett & Al	"

Court of August 1766 continued -

471	Hamilton & Co.	vs	James Rigsby	Case
	" " "	"	David Griffin	"
	" " "	"	Jesse George	Petition
	" " "	"	Joseph Fooshea	Debt
472	" " "	"	Benjamin Johnston	Petition
	" " "	"	Benjamin Posey	"
473	Elwick's Executors	"	James Irwin	"
	" "	"	Benjamin Hinson	Debt
	William Johnston	"	Daniel Smith	"
474	Thomas Anderson	"	Thomas Flynn	Petition
	Jane Albred	"	William Carlisle	"
	Francis Nash, Assignee	"	Alexander Mahone	"
475	John Meherg	"	Wm. Mebane & Al.	Sc. Facias
	James Young & Co.	"	Daniel Oakes	Petition
476	James Alley	"	Gabriel White	"
	Peter Copeland	"	Samuel Farlee & Al.	Case
	George Felton	"	James Alley	"
477	William Few	"	Barnaby Cabe	"
	John Williams, Esq	"	Thomas Brooks	"
	Nash & McNair	"	Hosea Tapley, Sr.	"
	James Young & Co.	"	Nathaniel Gammage	Petition
478	Jacob Chavis	"	Chas. & Wm. Humphries	Debt
	John Dowell	"	John Woods	Petition
	" "	"	John Dennice	Case
479	" "	"	Samuel Ricketts	"
	Nathaniel Hart	"	Wm. McLean & Al.	Debt
	James Dobbins	"	James Fulkerson & Al.	"
	Cunningham Sample	"	David Ray	Petition
480	" "	"	Joseph Polk	"
	John Dowell	"	Hugh Smith	Case
481	" "	"	Niel McCallister	"
	John Hannah	"	David Frames	Or Attch
	James Powell	"	Zachariah Martin	" "
	Benjamin Nicholson	"	James Minnis	Case

(Joseph Maddock & James Riley were arbitrators in the above case - "assessed the Plaintiff Judgement of £ 2-10- & his costs £ 2-14-8.")

482	John Patterson, Esq	vs	Abraham Childers	Petition
	Hugh Smith	"	James Herbinson	"
	James Herbinson	"	Hugh Smith	
483	Weldon's Administrators	"	John Dowell	"
	Bibby (?) Brooks	"	" "	T.A.B.
	John Campbell	"	William Barton	Case
	Richard Parker, Adm.	"	Richard Hill & Al...	Debt
484	" " "	"	Absolom Tyler & Al.	"
	John Meherg	"	Nicholas Robinson	Case
	Hugh Smith	"	James Herbinson	T.A.B.

Court of August 1766 continued -

485	James Herbinson	vs	Hugh Smith	Case
	John Kelly	"	Barnaby Cabe	"
	Elwick's Executors	"	John Grimes & Al.	Debt
486	" "	"	Hugh Smith & Al.	"
	Nash & McNair	"	" "	Petition
	William Alrid	"	William Todd	Or. Attch.
	Augustine Bate Adm's	"	Thomas Copestick	Debt
487	John Williams, Jr. Esq	"	Andrew Shankland	"
	John Dowell	"	John Davis	"
488	John Patterson, Esq	"	John Booth	"
	William Nunn, Esq	"	Samuel Watt	"
	" " "	"	Patrick Porter	"
489	" " "	"	Joseph Avent	"
	" " "	"	Thomas Shiels	"
490	" " "	"	William Ursury	"
	Nash & McNair	"	William Davenport & Joseph Reed	"
	" "		William Ballard & Zackariah Stanley	"

491 "Court adjourned till Court in Course."

Finis

The volume dated August 1762 through August 1766 closes with the entry on page 491 "Court adjourned till Court in Course." The Minutes of the Courts covering the years from this date to May, 1777, are missing.

INDEX

ARMSTRONG, James 46-230', 52-242, 53-243', 64-265', 58, 410;
John 10-158', 18-174, 59-255', 63-263, 69-276', 27, 30, 150, 157, 223, 230,
" 239, 249, 350, 385, 403, 468; Joseph 16-169, 230; Lancelot 25-189, 263;
William 13-26, 21-41, 37-73, 43-85, 48-96', 49-97', 55-109, 60-120', 16-170,
Wm. 59-256', 7, 123, 177, 194, 253, 385
ARRINGTON, John 332
ASHLEY, William 363
ASHMORE, James 62, Waller or Walter 53-207, 62, 144, 189, 314, 340
ASPEY, James 60-120, 5-148', 61-259 see ESPEY
ASTIN, Nathaniel see AUSTEN & OSTEEN
ATKINS, Joseph 46-229'
AUSTIN, Nathaniel 90, 237, 240, 241, 261, 272, 319, 338, 370, 373, 464;
William 240 see ASTIN & OSTEEN
AVEN, AVENT, Joseph 363, 489
AWTREE, Alex 42-83, 42-84'
AXUM, Mathew 332
AYCOCK, James 25-188', 39-216, 43-223, 55, 160, 356, 405, 450;
William 356, 405, 450
AYLIOT, James 239 see ALLIOT & ELLIOTT

BAGBEY, BAGBY, BAGLEY, George 37-211', 57-252, 239;
BAILEY, Andrew 73; Edmund 54; Edward 47-232; William 243
BAILIFF, Thomas 300
BAIN, John 147
BAKER, Andrew 34-68', 14-165; Barnaby 350;
Blake 27-54, 32-63', 40-79, 43-86, 44-88, 55-110', 68-135', 17-172;
Robert 104, 301; William 217; William Sr 52-241, 348
BALDWIN, John 39-77, 53-243; William 31-62, 39-77 see BAULDIN
BALL, Edward 1-1; James 27-192, 359, 443; James Jr 224
BALLARD, James 30; Plunkett 49-98', 50-100, 14-166', 35-207', 24, 40, 86, 111,
BANCSON, BANCSTON, BANKSON, Alexander 46-91; Andrew 16-32', 40-80, 164, 435;
Lawrence Jr 435; Lawrence 1-1, 1-2', 4-7', 17-33, 19-37, 32-63, 35-70, 37-73,
Lawrence 37-74, 38-75' 39-78', 48-96', 49-97', 55-109, 56-112', 64-127';
" 5-148, 435; Addenda; Peter 54-108', 364
BANKS, Nathaniel William 208; William 217, 462
BARBE, Lawrence 15-30'
BARBEE, Betty 98; Christopher 15-168', 25-188', 43-223, 55; Francis 5-148;
John Sr 30-198'; John Jr 57-251';
John 5-148, 15-168', 25-188', 43-223, 31, 58, 98;
Joseph 26-52', 31-61, 36-71, 49-98', 54-108, 55-109, 69-138', 25-188', 30-198
" 39-216', 43-223, 55, 98, 148, 156, 164, 307, 441; Manning 98;
Micajah 98; Raichel 69-138', 5-148', 12-162';
William 15-30', 19-38, 20-39, 36-71, 37-74, 51-101, 69-138', 5-148, 12-162',
" 15-168, 15-168', 20-178, 21-180, 31-200, 98
BARGEL ? BRIDGET ? Andrew 35-70
BARKER, John 30; Nicholas 104; Samuel 69-276', 450
BARKOR, ... 33-64'
BARKLEY, Thomas 26-52', 32-64, 62-123', 66-132'
BARNES, Brumley 29; Thomas 57; William 39-216'
BARNETT, Hugh 36-71, 2-142, 57-252, 221, 248; Humphrey 33, 176; Joseph 9-18', 3
Robert 2-142, 87, 88, 90, 180, 191, 227, 230, 248, 249;
Samuel 22-182', 191, 221; Thomas 29, 33, 248;
William 21-42, 36-71, 36-72', 37-73', 37-74', 38-75', 48-96', 49-97', 55-109,
" 69-138, 57-252, 248

BARNEY, Richard 163;
William 30, 58, 149, 203, 241, 268, 272, 373, 468 see BURNEY
BARNHILL, James 60-120', 35-207, 58-254
BARTIN ? Thomas 38-75
BARTON, John 407, 445; Lewis 450; Samuel 167;
William 55-247', 65-268, 182, 483 see BURTON
BASINGDINE, Charles 55-248'
BASKETT, William 19-176
BATE, Augustine 486
BATOWN ?, John 158
BATTEN, Henry 156
BAZELL, Henry 37-74
BAULDIN, James 221; Thomas 199; see BALDWIN
BEAL, Thomas 98, 364, 406
BEASLEY, Henry 30-198', 55; James 407, 430 (BEAZLEY)
BEAVER, Michael 398
BECK?, BEEK?, Jeffrey 53-243', 104, 223
BEDFORD, Thomas 2, 461
BEDINGFIELD, Henry 1-1, 3-5', 5-9, 12-23, 35-70, 35-70', 36-71
BELL, James 57-252; John 446; Robert 57-252; Samuel 37-211', 57-252
BENGERMAN, ... 453
BENNETT, Dred 55
BENTON, Epaphroditus 172, 333; James 63-263, 6, 17, 213; Joseph 45-228;
Lazarus, Titus 29-196'; Samuel 6-12, 8-15, 42-83, 43-86, 60
BERRY, Richard 302; Robert 47-94', 52-104' 19-176; Thomas 61, 221A;
William 18-173'
BERT, John 50-100' see BURT
BEST, ... 18-35
BEVERLEY, Elijah 405; Isaac 300; Hannah, Jesse 302;
John 40-79, 40-80', 48-96, 245, 251, 308, 302, 405
BICKERSTAFF, John 32-202, 48-233', 205, 367
BIDINGS, Henry 4-7
BIRD, James 59-255, 30, 226
BIRK, William 36-210' see BURKS
BLACK, David 37-73; Frederick Albert 456; George 311, 456; Jacob 87, 365;
Peter 147; William 30
BLACKLEY, James 99, 147
BLACKWELL, Joel 74
BLACKWOOD, John 161; William 2-4, 26-52, 27-54, 34-67', 49-97, 54-108, 69-137',
William 4-145, 31-199, 158
BLAIR, Samuel 302, 457
BLAKE, Benjamin 39-216, 55, 356; Thomas 151
BLALOCK, Mullington 358
BLEDSOE, Jacob 30-198'
BOBBIT, William 32-64, 39-77', 62-123', 3-143', 4-145, 29-196; Wm Jr 16-31'
BOGGANS ADMINISTRATORS 66-132
BOGGAN, Jane 49-98', 57-114'; Margaret 16-169, 55-247;
Patrick 6-12, 11-22', 13-26, 21-43;
William 21-41', 46-92', 49-98', 57-114', 59-118', 2-142, 6-150
BOGG'S ADMINISTRATORS 110
BOGGS, Ester 52-242; Captain 51-102, 54-108;
Joseph 1-1, 4-7, 4-8', 15-30', 19-37, 35-70, 35-70', 37-73, 37-74, 41-81',
" 48-96', 49-97', 49-98, 55-109, 56-112', 60-119', 65-129', 22-181,
" 34-205', 52-242, Addenda

BOHANNON & CO, 8
BOHANNON, Ann 5-147', 13-163, 23-183; Archibald 469;
Benjamin 58-252', 260, 339, 368; Duncan 31-61, 46-91', 5-147', 13-163, 20-178
Duncan 23-183, 57-252'; Duncan Jr 27-53; James 18, 138;
John 9-156', 39-216', 47-231', 57-251', 25, 393, 452;
Joseph 65-130, 69-138', 23-183; Patty 65-130, 69-138', 23-183; Richard 58-253
Susannah 58-253
BOID see BOYD
BOLING, BOLLING, BOWLING, Archibald 151, 244, 311, 409, 443;
Benjamin 5-11, 50-237'; Charles 222A; John 3; James 54
BONDS for Sheriff & other County Officers 279-300 not abstracted.
BOOKER, Patience 164, 231
BOON, Jacob 65-129', 158, 355; Mary, Peter (or Pastor?) 159 see SEBOON
BOOTH, Daniel 456; Gilly 55; John 59-255', 55 (2), 158, 488; Joseph 55
BORAN, Robert see BORING 8-153'
BORDEN, John 61-259', 106
BORING, BOWRING, Joseph 8-15, 147
BOWIE, James 19-38, 29-57, 60-120, 69-138', 5-147', 5-148', 16-169', 38-213',
James, 39-215', 40-219, 53-243, 57-251, 9, 12, 28, 63, 69, 74, 85, 89, 99,
" 118, 122, 124, 127, 129, 132, 135, 147, 150, 163, 192, 257, 265, 266,
" 273, 329, 419; Samuel 23-45'
BOWLING see BOLING
BOWMAN'S ADMINISTRATORS 69-276
BOWMAN SPIERS & CO 121, 320
BOWMAN, Thomas 43-225, 50-237'
BOYD, George 313;
James 16-31, 14-166, 40-219', 54-246, 59-255, 111, 171, 408;
John 2-3', 13-25, 17-33, 35-69, 37-73, 44-87', 18-174', 47-232, 64-127
Exec's of, 4-145', 53-244', 58-254, 35, 38, 54, 166, 232, 398, 452;
John Jr 22-43, 48-233'; John Sr 21-41', 63-124';Michael 47-232;
Robert 26-189', 64-265; William 60-120, 250; BOYD'S ROAD 54-108'
BOYLE, Michael 45-227, 45-228, 62-262, 63-264, 389; Nicholas 7
BRACEY, John 30
BRACKETT, William 177
BRADFORD, David 15-30, 38-75', 45-228, 63-264; David Jr 54-108';
Thomas 51-101, 57-113
BRADLEY, Enoch 300, 461; Hugh 37-73, 40-217'
BRANSON, Thomas 38-75
BRANTLEY, George 32-201; James 225; Joseph 40-217, 57-252', 393;
John 43-86, 68-135', 17-171', 40-217, 46-230, 35, 53, 156, 225, 246, 454(2);
Lewis 46-230; Mary 46-230; William 394
BRASFIELD, John 380
BRASHEARS, Basil or Braswel 8-15, 14-28', 17-33, 21-41', 24-77', 40-80, 43-85',
Basil or Braswel 44-88, 45-89, 62-123, 68-135, 10-158', 40-238', 39, 60, 80,
" " " 188, 207, 310, 458;
Jesse 47-93, 46-229', 53-243, 53-244, 69-275;
Middleton 53-244, 100, 125, 126, 127, 133, 134, 231, 260, 270, 322, 330;
Othar 30-59';
Robert 29-58, 34-67', 36-71, 66-131, 4-145, 11-159, 32-203, 51-240', 11,
" 126, 166, 369, 410, 431, 463; Robert Samuel 100

BRASWELL, Benjamin 225; Henry 46-230, 47-231, 47-231', 57-252', 363, 403;
Richard 4-146', 40-217, 47-231, 47-231', 57-252';
Valentine 47-231', 24, 345, 363, 373, 385;
William 47-232, 92, 151, 351, 363, 416
BRATCHER, John 364
BRAXTON, William 301
BRAZIER, William 16-169 see BREZZER
BREEZE, Thomas 359, 443
BRENT, Joshua 14-166
BREWER, Henry 4-146, 52-242', 53-245, 58-253, 361;
Howell 16-170', 28-193', 350, 361; Oliver 361; Sackfield 359
BREWITT ?, Henry 28-194' see PREWITT & FRUIT
BREZZER, William 53-243 see BRAZIER
BRIAN, McCorgan or Morgan 35-70'; Thomas 20-39
BRIDGER, BRIDGES, BRIDGET, Andrew 30-198'; John 53, 147, 150;
Josiah 5-10; Thomas 150; William 212, 251, 419
BRITTAIN, Joseph 149, 221, 231, 414
BROMFIELD, Empson or Epson 429, 469, Watson 25-188'
BROOKER, John 47-231' see BOOKER
BROOKS, Bibby ? 483;
Jacob 12-23, 35=70, 36-71, 37-73, 37-74, 48-96', 49-97', 56-112', 24-185';
Joel 25-189, 246, 302, 357; Joab 56-112', 12-161;
John 39-215', 59-256, 205, 386, 390, 396, 429; John Jr 57-113;
Thomas 49-97, 49-97', 55-109, 25-189, 49-236', 68-274, 124, 213, 273, 316,
" 418, 477; William 58; William Sr. 451
BROWN, ... 65-130'; Daniel 104, 407; Frederick 63; Jacob 52; James 163;
John 24-47, 27-54, 46-91, 128, 196, 389; Joseph 1-140', 20-177, 32-202;
Joshua 36-209; Mathew 235, 309, 334; Sackfield 37-212';
Thomas 61-260, 363; William King 456; William 32-201', 55-247, 166, 222, 246
BROWNING, Elizabeth, Thomas 57-251; William 259, 277, 339, 431
BRUM, Charles 47-231'
BRUNT, David 30-59
BRYANT, John 53-244, 222A; Needham 15
BUCHANNON & CO 79, 170, 200, 230, 241
BUCHANNON SPIERS & CO, 120, 319
BUCKNER, John 224
BULL, Captain (an Indian) 1-140; Edward 81, 201
BULLARD, Richard 191
BUMPASS, John 34-68', 39-77, 53, 147, 150, 416; Robert 53, 147, 150;
Samuel 1-140, 53, 147, 359
BUNCH, Batholemew 306; Gideon 43-86
BUNDRAKE, BURNDRAKE, Nicholas 195, 196, 209 see PUNDRICK
BURCH, William 406
BURCHFIELD, John 211; Joseph 211, 217; Thomas 19-38'
BURFORD, William 28, 355
BURGESS, William 60-258, 68-273
BURKS, John 39-215 see BIRK
BURNEY, John 28; William 5-148', 53, 270 see BARNEY
BURNS, Charles 66-270
BURNSIDE, Robert 59-256
BURT, John 45-89' see BERT

BURTON, Beer or Bur 25-49, 54-107'; James 25-187; see BARTON
Richard 31-62', 6-149, 25-187, 25-188', 27-192', 55-248, 68-273', 14, 122,
" 312, 314, 417; Robert 100, 309;
Samuel 2-142; 6-149, 23-183', 25-188', 32-201, 40-220, 41-220', 56-250',
" 69-276, 21, 32, 38, 63, 75, 84, 108, 142, 168, 178, 383
BUSTARD, William 33
BUTLER, John 30, 460; Walter 248
BUTNER, Adam 63-264'
BUTTS, Elinor 303, 406, 455; Mary 5-147; Nicholas 157, 303, 406
BYARS, BYASS, James 248; John 9-155', 68-135', 53; William 148, 150
BYNUM, John 117, 198, 462; Luke 51-101, 39-216', 40-220, 41-221', 362, 409;
William 53-243, 30

CABE, Barnaby 16-170, 42, 48, 250, 300, 409, 418, 451, 460, 461, 477, 485
CADDELL see CALDWELL
CADDLE, Zachariah 50-238'
CADE, Benjamin 26-52'; Zachariah Jr 26-52'
CAINE, CANE, Benjamin 242, 336;
Daniel 51-102, 60-120', 61-121', 69-137', 15-168, 38-213, 40-217, 40-218,
" 45-227, 48-234, 62-262; Elijah 30, 35, 61, 336, 403, 452
CALBURTON, James 29 see CULBERTSON
CALDWELL, Andrew 53-243', 51, 356, 498, 443, 445, 454, 460; Elizabeth 460;
Jannett 356, 445; Margaret 454, 460; Simon, William 460
CALLAHAN, William 93, 317
CALTO? CATTO?, George 307
CALWILL, John 198 see CALDWELL
CAMMER, Henry 61-259'
CAMP, Edward 151, 424;
John 31, 54, 90, 192, 212, 268, 337, 345, 371, 384, 386; Richard 405;
Thomas 342; Thomas Sr 375; William 192
CAMPBELL, Adam 103; Andrew 73, 91, 119, 121, 255, 318, 365; Henry 461;
James 25-189; John 56-112', 37-211', 57-252, 58-253', 446, 483;
Laughlin 46-229, 29, 159, 245, 408; Mary 446; Moses 47-93;
Thomas, William 461
CANADY, ... 58-115'; William 46-93'
CANE see CAINE
CANTRIL, Benjamin 30-198'; Isaac 221, 224; James 47-232;
John 18-174', 30-198, 40-217, 58, 359, 405, 409, 446;
Joseph 30-198, 40-217, 409; Stephen 209
CAPPER, Thomas 2-141', 31-200', 42-222, 43-223, 45-227, 47-231, 62-262', 55,
Thomas 206, 307, 324
CARGDEL, John 4-7
CARLISLE, William 170, 247, 250, 474
CARMICHAEL, ROBERT & CO 401
CARNEY, Francis 57-252, 342
CARR, Thomas 269 see KARR
CARRAGAN, James 449; John 58-116', 119
CARRINGTON, George 15-167; John 147, 151
CARSON, John 172, 360; Robert 300
CARTER, Benjamin 46-229', 31; Edward 38-75; John 160; Lurania 13-163';
Nathan 64, 337
CARUTH, Adam 14-28', 20-40' see CRETHERS
CARVER, Robert 14-165'

CARY, ... 68-136; James 41-82', 45-89, 64-128, 42-222, 64-265;
James Jr 68-136, 3-144', 9-156', 10-157, 15-167, 15-168', 18-173', 18-174',
" " 19-175, 34-206, 36-210, 7, 72; Mathew 50-99;
Nathaniel 16-170', 22-181, 29-195', 36-209', 51-240, 56-250, 60-258', 64-265
CASTELBERRY, David 159, 215, 259, 277, 339, 431; Richard 303; William 98, 362
CASTON, Glass 45-90, 51-102; John 45-89
CASWELL, Richard 3-5'
CATCHAM, Israel 37-73 see GATHAM
CATE, Benjamin 51-240; Benj Sr 84; John 30-198', 27, 29,
John 36-72', 44-87, 53-106', John Jr 53-244, 237; John Sr 35-69', 328;
Joseph 37-73', 49-97; Margery 53-106'; Richard 37-73, 445;
Robert 7-13, 17-34', 36-72, 37-73', 38-75, 48-96', 49-97, 55-109, 58-253,
" 26, 149, 224; Robert Jr 49-97, 52; Robert Sr 56-111, 25;
Thomas 15-29', 26-51', 51-102, 31-199, 53-244', 149, 159, 221, 224, 359;
Thomas Jr 38-75, 49-97, 149; Thomas Sr 37-73', 49-97, 70-277', 238, 259, 339,359
CAULEY, George 150
CAVANAUGH, James 33, 248, 409
CAVEN, ? John 206
CELLARS, George 305; James 306, 356, 409; Phillip 305; Robert 409 see SELLERS
CHAMBERS, David 57-252; Edward 20-177', 57-252, 248; Henry 33-65;
William 1-1, 19-38, 47-94', 52-242', 248; William Jr 57-252, 248;
William Sr 16-170, 33
CHAMNESS, CHAMNEY, Anthony 1-1, 9-18', 37-211, 39-215; Sarah 9-18'
CHANCE, Ezekiel 222A; Mary 221; John 221, 221A, 302; Ruth 302
CHANEY, Francis 224 see CHENEY
CHAPEL, NEW HOPE 409
CHAPMAN, David 363; George 218;
Giles 5-147, 9-155', 17-171, 38-213', 53-243', 67, 165, 251; John 2-4';
Moses 45-89'; Samuel 38-213', 129
CHAPPLE, Edward 128, 196, 197
CHAVIS, Charles, Hannah 31; Jacob 478; Thomas 18-35'
CHEEK, James 149; Richard 19-175', 47-231', 363; Randall 47-231'
CHENEY, James 28-194 see CHANEY
CHILDERS, Abraham 482; Creed 461; William 236, 369; William Cannon 262, 433
CHILDSBURG, the county seat, formerly called Corbintown and lastly,
Hillsborough, see "Town laid out ..." 43-223, 53-244', 57-251, 30, 52, 146,
249, etc.
CHILTON, Joseph 232
Church Wardens 52-103
CHURTON, William 2-3, 4-8', 9-18', 27-53, 31-61', 56-112', 57-114' 58-116,
Wm. 7-152', 8-154', 12-161, 34-206', 35-207', 39-216', 52-242, 63
CIMBRO, John 222A see CUMBO & KIMBROUGH
CLANTON, Benjamin 59-256, 397; Charles 40-217, 59-256
CLAPP, Barnard or Barney 158, 356, 390, 451, 460; John 30-59;
John Phillip 426; Lodowick 3-5', 5-9, 11-22', 26-52', 49-97, 51-101, 59-117',
Lodowick 69-138, 25-169, 52-242, 53-243', 52, 59, 159; Tobias 164
CLARK(E), Alexander 124, 403; James 38-75' 46-229, 151, 304, 444;
John 55-247, 43, 139, 323; Thomas 19-176, 57, 162;
Vachel 149, 181, 361, 409 (2), 451
CLAYBORN, CLAYBOURNE, Leonard 43-226, 62-261'.
CLAYTON, Stephen 67-271, 66

CLEMENS, CLEMENTS, Benjamin 30; Richard 38, 311, 357
Clerks of Court for Orange County;
Richard Caswell 3-5', 4-8; Francis Nash 25, 251;
James Watson 27-53, 244; deputy clerk William Reed 3-5'
COATES, Judith 5-9; Thomas 5-10'
COBB, Henry 58; Samuel 53-106', 40-217
COBLE, George 63; John 63
COCHRANE, ANDREW & CO 81, 118, 193, 265, 316; COCHRANE & CO 88, 147, 148
COCK, Benjamin 407
COCKBURNE, Michael 248
COLEMAN, Benjamin 303; John 469
COLLEY, George 147; Robert 59-256
COLLINS, ... 59-118'; Hezekiah 56-111, 47-232, 52-242', 59-253, 54;
Isaac 20-39, 53-243, 57-251', 61, 361;
James 5-9', 17-34', 36-72, 40-79', 41-81, 41-82', 48-96', 49-97', 52-242',
" 55-109, 58-116, 224, 302, 352, 451; James Jr 30-197';
John 46-93', 68-136, 22-181, 25-187, 53-243, 63-264, 25, 402;
Joseph 66-131', 67-134', 464; Paul 27-192';
Samuel 46-92', 52-103, 59-118', 10-157'; Stephen 65; Thomas 402;
Thomas Jr 51-102; William 48-96', 315
COMB, William 50-99, 54-108', 57-114', 32-201, 32-201', 62
COMBAST, Thomas 3-5
COMBER, Joseph 224
CONALLY, Charles 68-136
CONE, William 47-231'
CONN'S ADMINISTRATORS 5, 69; Mary's Adm's 83
CONNELL, Hugh 68-274'
CONNER, Elizabeth & Peggy 57; John 221
Constables, appointed 1-2', 2-4, 3-6, 3-6', 4-7', 5-9', 15-29, 15-29', 15-30,
" 19-38, 21-42, 26-52, 27-54, 30-60, 45-90, 50-100', 51-101', 51-102,
" 59-117, 69-137, 69-137', 1-140, 1-140', 2-142, 6-150, 8-153, 12-161,
" 12-161', 16-169, 20-177', 37-212', 38-213, 39-215, 39-215', 40-217',
" 42-222, 46-229, 53-243', 28, 29, 30, 33, 34, 35, 36, 38, 51, 104, 149,
" 158, 159, 161, 165, 229, 355, 356, 357, 358, 359, 360, 408, 409, 443,
" 444, 445, 448, 452, 460; staffs for 58-253'
COOK(E), Arthur 25-188', 39-216', 43-223; James 32-63; John 20-178;
Nicholas 368, 420; Richard 26
COOKER, Joseph 340
COOPER, Isaac 47-231', 22, 41, 142, 226
Copeland's Island 225
COPELAND, COUPLING, James 69-137', 47-231'; John 50-100; Joseph 30;
Nicholas 40-217, 356; Peter 242, 370, 388, 437, 476; Richard 17-172, 361;
William 1-1, 2-3, 17-34', 23-45', 36-72, 49-97', 50-100', 55-109, 60-120',
" 8-154, 157, 451; William Sr 30; COPELAND & CO 42-83'
COPESTICK, Thomas 33-204, 487
CORBIN, Colonel 26-52; Francis 249
*Corbintown, "laid out" 24-47; references to 65-129, 69-137', 21-179',
30-198, 42-222; name changed to Childsburg 97, 146, 156, 220, etc;
deeds to lots in, 51-102, 57-114'(6), 58-116, 59-118', 60-120'(4), 61-122',
65-129, 7-152', 15-168', 21-179(2), 35-207 see CHILDSBURG & HILLSBOROUGH
CORTNER, ? John 397

COUCH, James 60-120', 65-129, 67-133', 49-236, 52-241, 65-268, 246, 272:
John 188; Mathew 11-22, 100; Thomas 50-99'; William 12-161, 362
Counterfiet Money 37, 226, 227, 439
Courthouse of Orange County, first site chosen 1-2; new site 38-75;
Roads from 25-188' (2); called Corbintown 54-108, 25, etc; Childsburg 43-223;
called Hillsborough 11
COWAN, Andrew 454; Edward 221
COWLEY, William 448
COX, Francis 2-142', 36-209, 93, 104; Harmon, Herman 104, 221; James 17;
John 62-262', 89, 104, 206, 215, 234, 271, 317, 324; John Jr 224;
Samuel 224; Solomon 224; Thomas 104, 224;
William 5-11', 43-86, 22-182', 36-210', 43-223, 31, 131, 142, 450; *25-188'
William Jr & Sr 104;
COZART, Francis 400
CRAIG, David 30, 225, 247, 355, 361; James 30, 53, 157, 362, 443;
John 26-51', 60-119, 36, 104, 311, 358; Margaret 47-231;
William 9-18, 12-24, 15-29', 37-73, 51-101, 54-108, 60-120, 69-137',
" 31-200, 38-213, 47-231 see CRUGS
CRAVEN, Peter 68, 187
CRAWFORD, Andrew 18-173, 22-182; Charles 55, 103;
James 60-119', 40-217, 68-273, 52, 245; John 49-97', 60-258; Samuel 27
CREEL, Ruth 3-5
CRESAP, Thomas 225, 256, 305, 307
CRETHERS ?, Sarah 57-252' see CARUTH
CROCKETT, Gabriel 14-27'; Grace 15-29; William 74
CROFT, Ralph 25-189, 46-229
CROKER, Benjamin 130, 322, 381; COKER & CO 216, 259, 269, 339
CROKER & NASH 132
CRONK, Richard 2-8, 4-7
CROSS CREEK (near Fayetteville, N. C.) 223
CROW, James 20-39, 409, 410; John 59-256, 58; Crow's Ford 224
CRUGS ?, John 58-253 see CRIAG
CULBERTSON, Andrew 30-198'; Nicholas 27-53, 27
CUMBO, Drury see CIMBRO & KIMBROUGH
CUMMINGS, James 57-251', 53, 59, 278, 305, 455; Mary 455;
William 4-146', 39-215, 45-228, 63-264', 66-270, 69-275', 64, 69
CUNNINGHAM, James 246; John 36-209
CUPPLE, Charles 3, 461
CURRIE, CURRY, James 5-9', 19-38, 37-211', 58, 221; John 414; Maryann 37-211'
CURTIS, Rice 4-145'
CYPART, CYPRUS, Francis 29-196', 305

DAILEY, DALEY, John 207, 325
DANIEL, James 39-215', 42-222, 50-238'; John 81, 82; William 58-254
DARK, Samuel 37-212, 450; Thomas 24-185'
DAVENPORT, Henry 4-7; William 490
DAVEY, Gabriel 19-176, 53; Gilbert 53
DAVIS'S ADMINISTRATORS, 60-258, 67-272'
DAVIS, Benjamin 30-197'; Charles 37-211, 37-212, 220; Edward or Edmund 49-97;
Elnathan 30-197', 59-256; Gabriel 19-38, 46-230, 147; James 275;
John 60-120', 20, 98, 487; Joseph 11-21, 12-24', 26-52;
Robert 37-211', 52-242'; Thomas 16-31'; William 137

DAVIDSON, John 17-172'
DAWSON, John 16-31', 52-242
DAY, Francis 14-27', 21-43, 23-46, 24-48', 36-71', 36-72, 68-135', 9-155, 9-156,
Francis 14-166', 22-181', 26-190, 27-192', 48-233, 438, 461; Henry 363;
John 150, 320
DEAN, Daniel 52-241
DEAR, Peter 361 see DERBE
DEBOW, Solomon 23-45', 46-91, 30-197, 37-211', 57-252, 27, 33, 151, 160
DELISHMENT ?, John 36-209
DENNEY, DENNY, Edmund 30-198', 40-217; Edward 30-198; James 12-24, 12-24'
DENNICE, DENNIS, John 26-52', 38-75, 49-97, 2-141', 10-157', 38-213, 129, 215,
John 220, 242, 300, 349, 402, 404, 422, 478; DENNIS, Abraham 402, 404
DERBE, Solomon 54-108' see DEBOW
DESERN, Francis 88
DEWIT, Joseph & William 18-35'
DICKEY, James 1-1, 2-3, 3-5', 4-7', 4-8', 7-14, 14-27, 15-29, 15-30', 19-37,
James 21-41', 26-51, 32-63', 33-66, 35-70, 35-70', 36-72, 37-73', 38-75',
" 43-85, 48-96', 51-102, 60-120, 61-122, 13-163, 18-174, Addenda -
DILLIARD, James 56
DINKINS, James 19-176, 39-216'
Dividing Line for Orange County, those who ran it 4-8, 9-18'
DIXON, A. 43-226'; Adam 62-261', 64-266, 67-272', 14, 125, 236, 369, 402, 422;
Elizabeth 16-169;
Josias 1-1, 1-2', 4-7', 6-12, 7-14, 9-18', 19-37, 20-39, 24-47, 35-70, 37-73,
" 37-74(2), 38-75', 39-78', 54-107', 55-110', 56-112', 4-146, 16-169,
" 41-221, 46-230, 51-239', 129, Addenda;
Michael 3-5', 11-22', 54-107, 61-122', 69-137', 3-143, 16-170,221
DOBBINS, Hugh 5-9', 23-45' (2), 30-60, 41-82', 51-101, 19-175, 26-189',
Hugh 63-263, 221, 311, 374, 446; James 479; John 30-197';
Thomas 26-189', 29-195, 37-211', 57-252, 259, 275, 466
DOBBS, Solomon 60-119'
DOCH OR DOCK, John 33-65', 39-77'
DOCHESTER, DOCHERTY, DORCHESTER, James 42-83, 43-85, 49-98', 8-153, 37-211',
James 47-231', 53-224'
DODSON, Charles 7-13
DOGESTER see DOCHESTER
DOHO?, James 460
DOLITTLE, Joseph 7-14', 30-60, 35-69', 8-154', 36-209, 52-242', 5, 29, 65, 72,
Joseph 83, 89, 110, 151, 222A, 313, 342; 8-15, 47-232
DOLLAHIDE, Ezekiel 61-121'
DONALDSON, DONALSON, Robert 19-176, 46-230, 57-252, 27, 51; Samuel 26-52';
Thomas 52-241, 60-257
DOROM?, William 55, 407 see DURHAM
DOSSETT, Francis 26; Moses 63-263', 227; Phillip 369; Phillip Sr 432, 458
DOUGLAS, Elizabeth 4-7; George 1-1; Jeremiah 20-39, 54-107';
Joseph 20-39; Mary 20-39, 54-107', 39-215';
John 1-1, 9-18', 54-107', 35-207, 57-251', 58-254, 248;
Thomas 57-252, 27, 248, 249
DOVER, John 34-67, 67-133, 18-174
DOWDIE, DOWDY, Thomas 98; William 98

DOWELL, John 21-179, 30-198, 35-208, 38-213', 41-221', 47-232, 51-240, 55-248,
John 65-267', 68-274, 70-278, 5, 6, 34, 38, 49, 62, 67, 88, 119, 125, 164, 168,
" 176, 185, 189, 194, 201, 219, 230, 235, 236, 238, 256, 300, 307, 315, 318,
" 321, 334, 338, 342, 346, 363, 371, 372, 383, 384, 391, 393, 403, 405, 412,
" 444, 445, 458, 466, 478, 479, 480, 483, 487
DOWNING, James 51-101', 69-137, 21-179
DOWTHET, George 10-158'
DOYLE, Henry 405; Isabella 101; Martin 31-199, 100
DRAPER, Solomon 362; William 51-239'
DRUMMOND, Benjamin 385
DUDGEN, Richard 40-79, 40-80'
DUCKWORTH, Jeremiah 179, 181, 255
DUGGER, William 64-266
DUNCAN, Daniel 33, 311; John 21-42; Joseph 9-18, 69-137; Jos Sr 373
DUNCANSON, Joseph 5-9'
DUNLAP, Robert 313
DUNLOP, Thomas 13
DUNMAN?, William 211
DUNNAGAN, ... 58-115;
John 5-9, 19-38, 20-39, 23-45', 36-71', 38-75', 39-78, 41-81', 42-84, 44-87,
" 63-125', 32-202, 151, 176, 219, 241,360, 373; Joseph 100, 147;
Thomas 29-57, 14-165', 28-193; William 46-230, 63, 147, 231, 406
DURHAM, Isaac 41-221'; Mathew 1-140'; Thomas 1-140', 53-243, 362, 409
DURNING, Nicholas 457

EASKIN?, Thomas 60-120' see ERSKINE
EASON, Joshua 157, 204, 214
EASTWOOD, Elihah 54, 401, 424, 451; Elisha 272; Israel 25-187, 26-190', 32-202
EATON, William 7-13, 32-64, 39-77', 44-87', 55-109', 43-85'
EDWARDS, Isaac 451;
John 4-146, 1-140', 53-243, 30, 53, 224, 349, 361, 362;
Nathaniel 350; Philemon 4-146
EDMUNDS & CO 40-79
EGLETON, Thomas 44-88
ELLIMAN, Enos 25, 361 see ELMORE
ELLIOTT, James 55-110, 31-199, 66, 335, 393, 403, 443 see ALLIOT & AYLIOT
ELLIS, William 35-70'
ELMORE, Enos 46-230'; George 90 see ELLIMAN
ELWICK, Derwin 60, 384, Derwin's Exec's 398;
ELWICK'S EXEC'S, 406, 410, 431, 460, 473, 485, 486
EMBREE, EMBRY, David 248, 331, 335, 400, 420 see AMBREE
EMSLEY, Alex 15-168', 29-196'
ENGLAND, James 162, 363; Josiah 69-275' see INGLE
Entry Taker for Orange County 34-206'
ERSKINE, Thomas 69-138, 68, 72, 170, 416, 432 see EASKIN
ERWIN, ... 16-169'; George 49-97, 54-108;
Robert 14-27', 36-71', 36-72, 48-96', 49-97', 55-109, 60-119, 30 see IRWIN
ESDALE, John 22, 167
ESPAY, ESPEY, ... 16, 148;
James 2-142, 18-173, 21-180, 28-194', 35-208, 36-209, 13, 94, 103, 106, 132,
" 140, 141, 147, 230, 323, 380; Samuel 20-177' see ASPEY
EUSEN?, Robert 2-4
EUSTIN, Christopher 245; see HOUSTON

EVANS, Amos 453; Andrew 57-252; Henry 27-192'; Joseph 47-231'
EVERAND, Gabriel 3-143', 4-145', 26-189'; Gilbert 39-78

FAGAN, George 42-84'
FALCONER, John 10-158
FANNING, Edmund 53-243, 67-271, 25, 46, 71, 151, 152, 163, 219, 225, 233, 240,
Edmund 245, 250, 310, 342, 343, 345, 426, 434, 444, 455(2), 460;
Thomas 68-273', 6, 109
FARLEE, Samuel 476 see FURLEY
FARMER, 27, 160, 161, 334, 369, *Samuel
FARRAL, John 43-86'
FARROW, Thomas 439
FAUCETT see FOSSETT
FEAR?, Samuel 352
FELTON, George 476
FERGUSON see FOGERSON
FERRIES, 2-4, 58-115', 4-146', 30-198', 31-199, 36-209, 37-212', 41-221',
47-231, 58-254, 163
FERRIS, James 453
FEW, James 33, 160, 364;
William 1-140, 28, 42, 62, 132, 244, 323, 380, 384, 418, 451, 460(2), 477
FIELD, Jeremiah 408; John 408; Nathaniel 153
FINCH, Richard 91, 193
FIKE?, John 361; Micajah 361 see PIKE
FINCHER, Jane 69-138';
Jonathan 51-101, 64-127, 65-130, 69-138', 20-178, 151;
Joshua 16-170, 18-173, 43-225', 62-261'
FINDLEY, FINLEY, Andrew 147;
George 30-59', 30-60, 54-108', 32-201, 35-297, 182, 362, 444
FISH, John 186
FISHER, Naomi 220
FITZGARRAND, Frederick 184, 365
FITZWOOD?, Isaac 311
FLATT, Margaret 21-43', 27-54, 63-124'
FLATT & HENDERSON 34-67
FLETCHER, James 409; William 39-215
FLYNN, George 9-155', 51, 53, 143, 147, 206, 425; Thomas 54, 70, 474
FOGERSON, Alexander 30-197', 58-253', 464; Andrew 57-252; Charles 5-10', 37-73'
James 302; John 37-211', 57-252; Robert 394
FOGLEMAN, Malachi 249
FOOSHE, Charles 49-98, 5-147', 11-159', 31-200, 35-208, 52-242', 58-253', 222;
(Mrs) Christian & Hannah 58-253';
Joseph 5-147', 31-200, 52-242', 53-243', 58-253', 59-256, 471;
Simon 59-256, 118, 428;
Susannah 5-147', 11-159', 31-200', 35-208, 52-242', 58-253', 105
FORBIS, FORBUS, William 147, 362
FORD, Henry 54
FORREST, FORRESTER, FORRIST, Benjamin 37-212, 244, 362, 458;
James 2-3, 27-53, 37-212, 39-216; James Sr 11-22; John 249; Thomas 37-212, 3
William 37-212, 39-216, 362
FORSYTH, Gilly 453; James 455
FOSSETT, David 246; James 246

FOSTER, Hugh 68-136', 56-249
FOUNTAIN, Paul Jr & Sr 69-137
FOUTZ, George 59, 310, 361; John 413
FOWLER, Elisha 5-11'
FRAMES, David 481
FRANCIS, Charles 443
FRAZIER, Joseph 12-23; Frazier's Road 223
FREELAND, James 356, 443, 451, 460
FREEMAN, George 34-67
FRESHWATER, Reuben 49-97'
FROHAWK, John 2-141'
FRUIT, Francis 69-137;
James 38-75, 49-97, 60-120', 2-142, 20-177', 25-189, 52-241', 196;
John 302 see PREWITT
FRY, William 204, 328, 419
FUCANNON, Peter 223
FULKERSON, Abraham 30; James 469
FULLER, Alexander 236, 334; Henry 151, 160, 201, 300, 311, 324;
John 26-52, 49-97, 40-217', 158; Joseph 232; Mary 34-205'; Thomas 60
FULTON, Samuel 63-263', 2, 54, 147, 376, 392
FURLEY, Peter 60-257' see FARLEE
FUSSELL, Thomas 53-244'

GADDIS, Isaac 65-129', 20; John 30-198', 38-213
GALLOWAY & CO 211
GAMBLIN, William 225
GAMMAGE, Nathaniel 477
GARDENOR, John 25-189
GARNER, John 223
GARNETT, Jacob 54
GARRARD, Jacob 97
GARRETT, William 190, 470
GARROT, Benjamin 152
GATHAM?, Benjamin 37-73; William 37-73 see CATCHAM
GATTREN?, William 60-119
GATTIS see GADDIS
GEE, Phillip 13-164', 36, 52, 123, 161; William 28
GEORGE, Jesse 471; Joseph 222
Geographical Information - boundaries, creeks, rivers, etc. see last page of index
GEST see GUESS
GIBBONS, Arthur 14-165; Charles 66-131'; William 90, 332, 415, 427
GIBSON, Charles 44-87; John 26-189'; Thomas 18-34, 63-264;
William 63-124', 67-133, 301, 448
GILBERT, William 341
GILCHRIST, James 49-58'; GILCHRIST & CO 331
GINN, Moses 40-217 see GWINN
GLADDEN, William 3, 40
GLASS, Powell 407
GLASSON, Joseph 454
GLENN, Warham 20-177', 25-188', 228, 409
GLOVER, George 137; John Jr 229
GODE, William 66-270'

GOFORTH, Giles 214; Miles 58, 163, 164; Thomas 163
GOING, Alexander 11-21, 46-229', 91, 123, 190, 193, 231, 232, 321, 374, 389, 468;
John 184, 383; William 116, 232
GOLD, Ephraim 46-229', 53-244', 33, 151; George 57-252;
Henry 54-107, 54-108, 53-243', 53-244, 54; Jane 5; Joseph 54-108', 53;
Peter 12-23; William 53-105'
GOODRUM, Joice or Joie ? 408; Thomas 408
GORDON, Catherine 4-146', 6-150; David 21-180; Elizabeth, James 4-146';
.... 16-169'; James & Co 425;
John 4-7', 4-8', 11-22', 19-37, 21-41', 4-146', John Addenda; William 64-127
GOSS, Thomas 65-129, 69-138; William 34-68, 58-116, 65-129 see GROSS
GOUGE, George, orphans of 20-177; John 39-215', 42-222, 55, 58
GOULD, Epaphroditus 441
GOWN?, John 103
GRACE, John 38-213; William 5-147, 37-212, 48-234, 52-242' see GRAW
GRADEN, William 445
GRAHAM see GRAYHAM
GRANT, John 59-255; William 34-68
GRANVILLE, Earl of, 39-215; deeds from proved 47-94', 26-189', 31-199, 42-223,
deeds 43-224', 12-162, 23-183', 24-186, 26-189'
GRAVES, James 28-194, 34-306, 49-236, 161, 223, 308;
John 4-145', 16-170, 20-177', 46-229, 53-243', 29, 96, 104, 112, 148, 161,
" 209, 222A, 245, 311, 355, 360, 441, 453(2); John Jr 271;
Robert 308, 443; William 360
GRAW, Haner & William 52-242', 58-254' see GRACE
GRAY, Isaac 76, 180, 424, 434;
John 1-1, 4-7', 4-8', 11-22', 15-30', 19-37, 23-46, 31-61', 37-73', 38-75,
" 48-96', 49-97', 55-109, 56-112', 62-123, 5-147', 8-154, 53-243', 103,
" 221, 249, 457
GRAYHAM, ... 33-66'; William 222A, 425
GREEN, Jacob 329; John 65-129, 22-182, 160; Lewis 250; Thomas 86, 186, 189, 306
GREENAL, GREENELS, Jonathan 21-179', 28-194'
GREGG, Jacob 444; Joshua (a Quaker) 19-176'; William 444 see GRIGGS
GREGORY, James 460
GRESHAM, GRISHAM, Edward 53, 362; Phillemon 151 see GRISAM
GRIFFIN, James 429; Joseph 307; Joshua 58-254'; William 53-243, 30, 409
GRIGGS, John 56-250' see GREGG
GRIMES, John 485; Thomas 45-90';
William 63-125, 30-198, 41-220', 41-221', 53-243', 61-259, 29, 247, 253, 307
GRISAM, Isaac 53-243' see GRESHAM
GRIST, John 69-137' see GUESS
GRIST MILLS 3-5', 26-52, 69-138, 13-164', 16-170, 22-182(2), 24-185', 30-197',
30-198', 32-201, 37-211', 39-215', 46-229', 47-231, 57-251', 25, 28(2),
52, 59, 63, 149, 150(2), 245, 246, 248, 250(2), 300(2), 305, 310, 311(2),
355, 356, 358, 452, 455
GROSS, Solomon 234; William 36-72 see GOSS
GROVE, Richard 350
GRUBBS, John 447
GUESS, Benjamin 47-231, 29, 357
GUNTER, Charles 358; John 409
GUTTERIE, Garett 248; William 39-78'
GWINN, Mordecai 19-175, 38-213, 53-244, 55-248, 24, 111

HADLEY, James 52; Jeremiah 26, 29; John 49-97, 34-205; see HEADLE
Joseph 450; Joshua 54-108, 37-212, 41-221, 42-222, 52, 300, 406, 430;
Josiah 49-97, 57-252, 300; Patience 41-221; Simon 29; Thomas 30-198, 31-199
HAGAN, James 390 see HOGAN
HAGGES, James 38
HAGGINS, Jacob 19-175 see HUGINS
HALCOMBE, ... 52-103; William 66-131, 66-132
HALES?, Abraham 334; Sarah 41
HALL, James 60, 229, 256, 303, 308; Thomas 26-189'
HALLADAY, Jeremiah 158
HALLUM, HELLUMS, HULLAMS, John 33-203, 57-251', 69-275;
William 19-38, 27, 51, 104, 122, 149
HALLEY, Sherrod 10-158
HALLEYBURTON, David 359
HALLIDAY, Henry 54
HALTHAM?, William 35-70'
HAMBRE, David 68 see AMBREE, EMBRIE
HAM, Paul 248
HAMER, John 34-67
HAMILTON, Wm & Co 260, 396, 401, 407, 425, 428, 430, 467, 471;
Hamilton's store 363
HAMLET, John 150; HAMMET, HAMLET, Robert 10-158, 38-194'; William 47-93
HAMPTON, Andrew 50-238'; Anthony 183, 383; James 35-70'; Nathan 105
HANDLEY, Daniel 194, 201, 338, 371; Darbey 114; John 414, 469
HANNAH, John 408, 481
HANNAN, Adam Sr 10-158'
HANSON, Dorman 69-276'; Richard 74, 213, 327 see HENSON, HINSON
HARDIN, Edward 104; Jonathan 431; Joseph 19-38'
HARGAS, HARGIS, William 160, 360
HARLAN, Aaron 19-37', 21-42, 58-254', 246, 311; Elizabeth 19-38, 21-42;
Samuel 19-37', 19-38, 21-42, 23-46
HARLEY, J. 248; John 36-72'
HARLIN, George 452; Robert 439; Zachariah 53-244'
HARMON, Paul 30, 99, 453; Paul Jr, Peter 453
HARPER, Robert 2-3, 4-8', 17-33
HARRELSON, Burgess 248; Paul 248; Robert 248 see HARRISON
HARRINGTON, John
HARRIS' ADM'S 108, 168; Charles 56-250; Ebenezer 408;
Elizabeth 53-243, 70-277', Eliz. (Webb) 20-177, 63;
Nathaniel 162, 217, 462; Nathaniel Jr 63-263', 150, 441; Robert 3-5', 6-149;
Thomas 20-177', 39-215', 40-219, 41-221, 42-222, 53-243; Thompson 38-75;
Tyrie 20-177', 32-201, 28, 36, 53, 56, 58, 97, 146, 156, 158, 166, 220,
" 221, 227, 229, 244, 247, 251, 301, 307, 309, 363, 405, 406, 412, 414,
" 439, 441, 445, 449, 457, 458
HARRISON, Burgess 160; Charles 154; Thomas 106, 115, 139, 379
HART, Benjamin 9, 56, 98, 387;
David 30-198, 32-201, 40-217, 41-220', 46-230, 36, 56, 156, 161, 223, 227(3),
" 363, 441, 445, 455; James 38-75', 69-137', 57-251', 58-253', 100;
Nathaniel 30-198, 40-217, 41-221', 56-216, 310, 328, 329, 479;
Thomas 2-141, 25-188', 70-277, 3, 9, 28, 40, 47, 56, 59, 69, 94, 96, 98, 99,
" 105, 112, 119, 129, 131, 133, 141, 156, 164, 182, 207, 209, 218, 237,
" 243, 244, 249, 250, 251, 258, 263, 276, 278, 305, 306, 307, 309, 310,
" 346, 349, 358, 360, 363, 378, 390, 405, 409, 412(2), 422, 439, 441,
" 445(2), 448, 449, 455(2), 458, 460, 461(2); William 39-215', 363;
Hart's Road 29

HARTSO, Phillip 356
HARVEY, Joseph 400
HASELL?, Richard 3-6'
HASTIE BUCHANNON & CO, 114, 416; HASTLE & CO 410
HASTIE, Robert 49-236', 59-256', 23, 73, 112, 174, 177, 193, 318
HASTINGS, Henry 26-51', 38-75, 347, 378; John 37-73'
HATLEY, see HADLEY
HATTERLEY, Evens, George, Samuel 103
HAUGHTON, Joshua 259, 276, 338
HAWKINS, Drury 330, 463; John 49-235'; Joseph 337, 425;
Joshua 274, 330, 331, 425, 463; Robert 91, 213; William 214, 248
HAWLEY, Amy 18-35'
HAYES, Henry 29, 355; John 221
HAYGOOD, George 64-128; James 30
HAYLES, Sarah 254
HAYS see HAYES
HEADLE, Jacob 41-81'; Zach. Sr 2-6, 21-42, 36-72, 38-75 see HADLEY
HEIR?, David 103; William 103
HELLEMS see HALLAM
HEL(ES)VESTON, HILVISTON, Phillip 86, 188
HEMBRIE, David 238 see AMBREE, EMBREE, HAMBRE
HENCOCK, Joseph 101
HENDERSON, Argulus 59-256; Hercules 40-217; James 41-221; Joseph 46-230, 361;
Richard 26, 157, 427, 453; William 56-111'
HENDRICKS, HENDRIX, James 1-1, 5-9, 21-42, 35-70, 36-72, 37-73, 37-74', 54-108';
John 11-22', 37-73', 31; Thomas 42-222
HENLEN, Daniel 5-147
HENSON, Benjamin 358, 473; Mary 358; see HINSON
HERBINSON, James 482(2), 484, 485
HERNDON, HER(RE)NDON, George 2-142, 25-188', 43-223, 36, 55;
Jacob 232, 347; James 380, 427; Lucy 408; Stephen 408
HERREN, HERRING, Edward 40-219, 55; John 50-238'
HICKS, David 55; Samuel 400
HIDE, Thomas 57-113
HIGDEN, HIGDON, Daniel 92, 317
HIGHETT, John 47-231 see HYATT
HIGHTOWER, Augustine 360; Austin 444; Oldham 61; William 444
HILBREATH?, Andrew 448
HILL, Richard 200, 267, 483; Samuel 350
Hillsborough, first reference to 11, roads in 230. see CHILDSBURG & CORBINTOWN
& "town laid out" ...
HILTON, Abraham 356; Hannah 61-122;
Peter 5-9', 36-71, 36-72, 48-96', 49-97', 61-122, 21-179;
Peter Sr 12-23, 51-102
HINCHEY, HINCHIE, ... 16, John 33-204', 66-269
HINES, James 101; Thomas 55, 58, 101, 156, 301, 303, 305, 307, 387, 410, 456,
Thomas 457, 461 see HYNES
HINSON, Dorman 58-254, 98, 452 see HENSON
HINWALT, Ralph 223
HOBSON, George Jr 27, 261 see HOPKINS, HOPSON
HODGE, Thomas 15-30'; HODGES, William 48-95; HODGE'S Ford 225
HODGINS, John 224; Robert 224 see HUGINGS
HOFF, HUFF, Leonard 53-244', 33
HOGAN, John 338, 410, 461 see HAGAN

HOGWOOD, James 409
HOLDEN, Isaac 392; James 225; Richard 200, 225, 267;
Thomas 30-59, 46-93', 48-96', 49-97', 55-109, 69-137', 69-138', 1-140,
" 39-216, 63-264, 205, 225, 367
HOLEMAN see HOLMAN
HOLLIFIELD, Daniel 27-54, 51-102
HOLLINGSWORTH, Elizabeth 452; Jesse 19-176', 307; Valentine 19-37, 5-147, 452
HOLLIS, Moses 15-29, 46-229', 141, 190, 383; Notley 45-228'
HOLLOWAY, Robert 31-199, 459
HOLMAN, Richard 41-220', 48-233, 53, 244
HO(L)MES, William 221
HOLT, David 61-122'; George 451; Jacob 59-255, 100;
John 25-187, 303, 311, 449, 455, 460;
Michael 21-179, 59, 104, 148, 300; Michael Sr 311;
Michael Jr 53-244, 56-249', 59-255, 56, 59, 97, 103, 107, 223, 249;
Nicholas 223; HOLT'S Mill 38-75'
HOOPER, Thomas 9-156
HOPKINS, Aaron, David, George 31-199
James 37-73, 30-197', 31-199, 38-213'; John 37-73, 30-197, 31-199, 30;
Mary 31-199; William 37-73, 30-197'
HOPSON, Edward 407; George 37-74', 48-96', 49-97, 55-109, 221;
Leonard 57-252; Richard 55 see HOBSON
HORNADAY, HORNEDY, HORNIDAY, John 29, 157
HORNER, George 25-189, 39-216'; William 156
HORTON, Aaron 361; James 41-220', 406, 451; Sarah 355;
William 15-30', 19-38, 34-67', 8-153, 12-161, 46, 229, 355, 408
HOUSTON see EUSEN & HUSTEN
HOWARD, Nathan 69-276, 147; Phillip 62-123; Stephen 20-177
HOWE, Peter 332
HOWELL, John 364; Lewis 24-47', 228; Robert 231
HOWLETT, John 104;
William 56-111, 58-116, 61-121', 63-126, 68-136, 28-194', 29-195', 36-209',
" 50-237, 60-258, 67-272'
HUBBARD, Charles 14; Mathew 99, 163, 328
HUCKER, William 51-239'
HUFF see HOFF
HUGGINS, Jacob 49-236 see HAGGINS
HUGHES, HUGHS, Thomas 30-198, 36-210, 40-217
HUGHSTUFF, Solomon 246
HUGHLETT, John, John Jr 160
HUGINGS, Phillip 15-167
HUMPHRIES, Charles 478; Mary 426; Thomas 48, 185; Wm. 29-196, 258, 372, 477
HUNTER, Ann 57-112; Henry 37-73'; James 27, 29, 81, 226, 357, 408, 445;
John 4-8', 38-75, 54-107, 54-108, 46-229', 58-253, 53, 444; Moses 22-181';
Robert 31, 101; Widow 54-107
HURLEY, HURTLEY, John 1-1, 23-45', 57-252, 248
HUSAY, HUSSEY, Christopher 413; Stephen 224 see HUSTEN
HUSBAND, Harmon or Herman 19-176', 32-201, 111, 146, 245, 251, 302, 304, 307,
Harmon or Herman 362, 407
HUSTEN, Christopher 29, 52, 222A, 224 see EUSEN & HUSAY
HUT?, George 3-6'
HYATT, John 246 see HIGHETT
HYNES, (Mrs) Christian 101 see HINES

KELLEY, KELLY, Hugh 24;
John 43-225', 45-228, 61-259, 61-259', 62-261', 63-263, 66-269, 16, 17, 378,
" 459, 485; Lawrence 53-105'
KEMP, Richard 9-18'
KENADY, KENNEDY, David 412; William 162
KERLOCK, Frederick 57-252
KETOR?, William 388
KEY, KEYS, Francis 307; Charles 246; Joseph 423
KILGORE, KILGOW, Robert 26-52'; Robert Sr 164, 361, 364; Thomas 158; Wm. 8-15
KILLINGER, Michael 384
KILPATRICK, Joseph 60-120, 13-163; Mrs. 54-107'; Mrs. Mary 60-120, 13-163;
William 54-107', 61-122
KIMBROUGH, Marmaduke 1-1, 2-3, 2-4, 4-7', 12-23, 12-24, 19-37, 35-70,
Marmaduke 35-70', Addenda; Nathaniel 25-188', 30-198' see CIMBRO & CUMBO
KINDRAKE, James 98
KING GEORGE III, Foreword, 6-149
KING, Benjamin 21-41, 37-73, 38-75, 48-96', 49-97', 55-109, 30-198, 40-217,
Benjamin 152, 408; Elizabeth 447; George 259, 467; Henry Jr 32-63;
John 26-52', 35-70', 38-75, 50-99', 9-155', 28-194', 53-243, 58-253, 29,
" 34, 148, 156, 364, 444; Joseph 53-243', 53-244, 22, 29, 54, 245, 437;
Peter 54-108', 35-207; Samuel 447;
Thomas 15-29', 25-189, 35-207', 39-215', 39-216', 41-221, 41-221', 42-222,
" 53 -243, 63, 99, 124, 136, 208, 209, 246, 315, 321, 325, 388
KIRBY, James 453; William 65-267
KIRK, John 151; Joseph 40-217, 30, 158, 244, 260, 339, 361, 406; Richard 225
KIRKBEY?, William 49-235
KIRKSEY, Christian 58-253, 6; Christopher 52-243, 30, 53, 109;
Edward 68-273', 239; Gideon 53-243, 53-243', 58-253, 300; Isaac 409;
John 114; John Jr 270
KIRNES?, Isaac 221
KNIGHT, David 6-150, 63-263', 2, 36, 54, 84, 134, 143; Richard 7-13, 35-69

LACEY, William 17-172
LACKEY, Adam 33; Alexander 69-137', 1-140, 37-212'
LAMBERT, John 33-65', 67-134, 52-242, 205, 211, 358, 390
LAMBISS?, Thomas 17
LANCKSTON, James 452
LANDROP, Thomas 45-228, 63-264
LANDRUM, Benjamin 45-90; Charles 361; John 49-98, 30-198'; Joseph 189;
Reuben 246, 429
LANE, Edward 51-102; John Fuller 29, 31, 222A, 266, 361, 451;
Richard 29, 222A; Samuel 51-102; Tydence 221
LANGDON, Thomas 348
LANGLEY, Robert 266; Thomas 45-89; Thomas Sr 25
LANIER, Robert 49-97'
LANCFORD, LANKFORD, James 7-13'; William 114
LAPSLEY, LAPSEY, LAPSLIE, Thomas 29-57', 62-122', 10-158', 47-232, 60, 149, 410
LASPIE, John 26-52
LARD? or LAW?, Mathew 163
LASSLIE, LESSLIE, William 147, 221A
LATTA, James 21-41', 45-90, 304

LONG, Benjamin 59-255, 58, 161, 248, 300, 370, 409; John 26-52, 248;
Mary 103, 147; William 58-253, 5, 23, 30, 225, 247, 361
LOONEY?, Absolom 49-236
LOVELATTA, LOVELATTY, John 133, 186; Marshal 36-209, 70-277, 134;
Moses 47-93;
Thomas 1-2', 16-31, 32-63, 38-76', 43-85', 45-89', 60-119, 63-126', 36-209,
" 125; Thomas Jr 59-117', 1-140'
LOVING, Adam 45
LOWE, Conrod 12-162', 21-180', 45-228, 69-275';
David 12-162', 47-231', 59; George 39-216'; Isaac 429, 469;
Thomas 49-97, 26-189', 39-215', 52-242', 61-259', 121, 252, 365, 445;
Lowe's Road 410
LOWTHER, William & Co 27-191
LOYE, Martin 157, 455
LUMPKIN, George 9, 46, 58, 82, 88, 115, 116, 120, 142, 152, 153, 154, 173,
George 179, 184, 191, 197, 199, 200, 207, 229, 230, 319, 325, 379;
Robert 404, 421
LUSK, John 248
LUTEN, William 31; Wm. Sr 28, 103, 172, 221, 243, 259, 276, 338, 410, 457
LYLES see LILES
LYNCH, Thomas 47-232, 449 see LINCH
LYON, John 40-79'; Richard 201, 385
LYTLE, LYTTLE, Robert 69-137', 17-171, 70-277', 58, 148, 156, 159, 225, 231,
Robert 301, 406, 441; William 37

MABRY, Francis 45-89', 50-100' see MOOBRY
MADDOCK, MADDOX, Joseph 38-75', 48-96', 49-98, 50-99, 55-109, 8-153, 24-186,
Joseph 37-211, 47-232, 52-241, 364, 481
MAGISTRATES, their districts described 35, 363, 446; see Justices of the Peace
MAHEN?, Patrick 69-137'
MAHONE, MEHONE, Alexander 377, 474; Patrick 4-146'
MAINES, William 30 see MEANS
MANGUM, Arthur 360
MANEN, John 458
MANNING, Derrick 381; Derring 179
MARET, MARITT, Grace 445 see MERRITT
MAROON, John 427
MARR, Gideon 28, 86, 93, 315, 317
Marriages of widows which are proved in these MINUTES:
Christian Alston to James Hines 101 (James Alston's will names his wife Christian);
Janet Caldwell to Archibald McAllister 445;
Elizabeth Douglas to William Reed 4-7;
Mary Kilpatrick to James Dickey 60-120;
Winifred Gouge to Micajah Pickett 20-177, 23-183;
Jane Wade to William Mebane 41-220', 58-253'
MARSH, John 160; Robert 57-251', 118, 396; Samuel 59-256;
William 52-242', 53-243', 83, 160, 193, 361; William Jr 59, 256, 393
MARSHAL, John 49-97, 54-108, 37-211, 39-215, 37-251, 214
MARTIAL, John 245

MARTIN, Benjamin 3-5', 19-38'; Captain 356; Cary 428; James 29, 221, 255;
John 24-48, 68-135'; Roger 59-256; William 15-30', 70-277', 3, 89, 192;
Zachariah 3-5', 4-8', 17-34', 18-35', 19-38, 25-49', 42-83, 48-96', 55-109',
" 24-185', 25-189, 34-206, 38-213, 1, 225, 274, 362, 374, 481;
Zachariah Jr 11-22', 25-49 , 44-87', 59-118, 3-143', 59-256, 26;
" Sr 37-73, 49-97'
MASHBURN, David 458
MASON, James 412;
Jacob 51-101, 56-111', 59-118', 60-120', 62-122', 4-146', 9-156, 10-157',
" 10-158', 11-159', 14-165', 16-169', 17-172', 18-173, 21-179, 22-181',
" 27-191', 32-201', 32-202', 40-217, 40-220, 47-232', 52-241, 52-242',
" 57-251, 57-251', 65-268', 67-272, 19, 40, 48, 56, 83, 120, 121, 124,
" 169, 172, 184, 418, 463
MASSEY, William 447, 458
MATHEWS, ... 14-28; Phillip 161; Thomas 3-5', 5-9, 8-15, 10-19'
MATTOCK see MADDOCK
MAULDIN, Richard 108, 150, 252
MAXWELL, David 57-252; Robert & Co 391; William 57-252
MAY, James 27-54; John 2-8, 53-243', 159, 451; John Jr 67-271
MAYNER, Ann, Betty, Jane 39-215; Henry 37-211, 39-215; John 3-144'
MAYO, ... 248
MEANS, Samuel 63-264, 362; William 2-4, 164 see MAINES
MEBANE, Alexander 3-5', 4-7', 14-27', 19-37', 21-42, 24-47, 33-65, 36-71',
Alexander 37-73, 38-75, 48-96', 49-97', 36-71', 36-72', 51-102, 55-109,
" 56-112', 64-128', 69-138, 2-141, 7-152', 16-169', 25-189, 29-195',
" 31-199, 53-243', 30, 36, 53, 56, 103, 146, 148, 150, 209, 222, 250,
" 326, 450, 460, 461, Addenda; Jane 58-253';"Major" 38-75;
William 2-4, 25-189, 31-199, 58-253', 61-260, 31, 124, 151, 163, 222, 227,
" 228, 235, 242, 265, 370, 411, 421, 475; William Jr 244
Meeting House 364; Quaker Meeting 25-189; New Hope Chapel 409
MEHAFFY, Adam 103, Martin 124, 160, 265; Mathew 103
MEHERG, James 75; John 43-226' 55-248, 56-250', 62-261', 64-266, 67-272',
John 68-273', 70-277, 101, 108, 122, 131, 163, 167, 169, 212, 235, 307,
" 314, 346, 368, 385, 389, 404, 411, 421, 432, 475, 484
MELTON, MILTON, Anson 409; Mourning 52; Nathan 23-183, 37-212', 30, 451;
Nathaniel 409; Robert 23-183, 34-206', 37-212', 52
MERRETT, MERRITT, Benjamin 7-14', 459;
Stephen 12-23', 29-58, 28, 41, 47, 89, 183, 246, 247, 445, 459;
William 90 see MARITT
METCALF, Anthony 7-13
MIANS? William 54-108 see MEANS & MIERS
MIDDLEBROOKS, Isaac 55, 103, 115, 389
MIER, MIERS, David 1-1, 4-7, 15-30, 32-63, 35-70, 39-77, 80; Grace 32-202;
William 1-1, 3-5', 4-7, 5-9, 5-10, 6-12', 13-26', 23-45, 33-65, 35-70,
" 37-73, 38-75'
MILBURN, Jesse 28-55
MILES, Abraham 90, 99, 100, 307, 360, 451; John 300; William 54, 221 248
see MILLS
MILICAN, Charles 224 see MILLIGAN
Military Officers, commissions to 4-8', 62
MILLER, Benjamin 19; George 5-147, 410, 434, 444; John 420;
William 68-136', 250, 448

MILLIGAN, MILLIKEN, Charles 57-252', 443 see MILICAN
Mills, see Grist Mills
MILLS, Charles 27-192; George 27-191'; John 47-232, 146, 330;
Robert 47-232; Thomas 450; William 47-232; William Sr. 38-75, 58-254
MILLWEE?, William 355
MILTON see MELTON
MIMS, MIMMS, David 33-204, 34-206', 47-232'; Drury 363; Henry 133;
Joseph 47-231'
MINNIS, James 45, 100, 120, 319, 348, 392, 409(2), 454, 481
MINOR, George, James 33
MINTER, Cary 225, 428
MISHELLY?, Andrew 246
MITCHEL, Andrew 1-1, 2-3, 4-7', 19-37, 56-112', 35, 36, 53, 54, 156, 406, Addenda;
David 2-3, 19-38, 69-137', 225, 229; Jacob 40-80;
John 25-188', 41-220', 56-250', 68-273', 70-277; Josiah 186, 364;
Judith 40-218; Winnifred 40-218;
MOFFITT, Adam 56, 107, 221; William 104, 302
MONDAY, Christopher 223
MONEY, John 3-143'; Joseph 57-112, 54-107, 63-125', 5-148, 39-216';
Samuel 35-207', 58-254, 104, 303
MONTFORT, Joseph 16-34, 25-49
MONTOGOMERY, Alexander 55, 103; Alex Sr 55; Hugh 60, 229, 256, 303;
Mary 50-237 see McGOMERY
MOOBRY?, Joseph 27-192' see MABRY
MOOLER?, John 47-93
MOON, James 220, 405
MOORE, ... 29-58; Edward 14-166', 37-211, 61-259, 54, 69, 114, 384, 454;
Jesse 426; John 357, 359, 444; Samuel 31-199, 50-237, 212, 419;
Thomas 185, 383, 457;
William 29-58', 44-88, 17-171, 25-188', 29-196, 49-235'
MORGAN, Ann 57-251, 57-251', David 407; Henry 41-81', 57-251; John 20-178;
Joseph 47-231';
Mark 1-1, 4-7', 4-8', 15-29, 15-30', 17-34', 19-37, 21-41', 35-70, 36-72,
" 37-74, 51-101, 61-122', 9-156', 18-173', 30-198', 32-201, 43-223,
" 59-255', 103, 221, 457, Addenda; Solomon 223; William 171
MORRIS, Christian 41-82', 255; Ellinor 56; George 4, 43, 141;
Henry 60-120', 52-242', 58-253, 128, 129, 328, 366, 419; John 42;
Mary 373; Patrick 4, 169; Phillip 6; Shadrick 358, 405
MORROW, Benjamin, Ann 20-178', 22-182', 37-212'; James 36-71, 358;
John 359, 405; William 3-6, 37-212, 46-229, 46-230' see MURRAH
MORROWMORE, John 26-52; William 19-37
MOSELEY, Edward 13
MOSS, James 27-54, 37-73', 67-133', 47-233
MOTHEREL, Robert 163, 164, 214
MOUAT?, William 42-83, 42-84'
MULDIN see MAULDIN
MULHOLLAND, Charles 37-211'
MULKEY, James 227
MULLEN, MULLIN, Henry 399; John 165, 363; Patrick 58; Thomas 248
MULLIS, John 59-256
MURAHIN?, Alexander 57-251'
MURDOCK, James 50-99, 37-211'
MURPHY, Timothy 359, 446
MURRAH, MURROW, William 51-101', 232, 446 see MORROW

MURRAY, MURRY, James 21-179, 29; John 67-133'; Michael 15-167', 47-231, 54-246';
Walter 30; William 25-189
MUSE, John Jr & John Sr 11-21
McADOW John 3-6', 24-48', 60-119
McALLISTER, James 1-1, 3-5', 21-41', 30-60, 38-75', 41-81', 48-96', 49-97',
James 55-109, 57-114', 61-121', 69-137', 6-149, 32-201, 46-229, 53-244,
" 222A, 244, 405, 443 see McCALLISTER
McBRIDGE, Bryant 61
McBROOM, Andrew 19-176, 37-211', 37-212', 378
McCALL, James 41-221, 46-230
McCALLISTER, Archibald 445, 454; Jannet (Caldwell) 445;
Neal or Neil 200, 481; Neal Sr 267
McCARVER, James 60-120; John 22
McCAWL, LYTLE & CO 114, 117, 190
McCEAR, William 355
McCLAYLAND, McCLELLAND, Daniel 31-61; Hannah 27-53, 31-61
McCOMB(S), John 37-73, 63-263, 30,52
McCONNELL, Adam 61-259, 16; Hugh 16-169', 22-182, 60-257', 37; Robert 387
McCORGAN?, David 222A
McCORMACK, John 65-268
McCOY, Henry 36, 51; Neil 57-251', 364; MCOY'S MILL 37-211', 57-251', 57-252
McCRACKEN, Alexander 69-137', 26-190, 58-254
McCRAW, James 270
McCULLOCH, Alexander 57-113, 26-189'; Daniel 30-198;
Henry 57-113, 23-183'; Henry Eustace 59, 249
McCULLOM, Daniel 2-141', 21-179, 39-216', 40-217, 227, 249, 408; John 68-136'
McDANIEL, Absolom 12-161'; Eli 26-190;
Daniel 5-9', 49-97, 12-161', 67, 100, 151, 251, 300, 303, 455; James 29, 244;
John 2-4, 47-93, 18-174, 33, 165; John Jr 65-129'; Michael 56-111;
William 59-256, 213, 327
McDONALD, Absolom 80; James 222A
McDOWEL, Michael 17-172' see DOWELL
McDUFF, Samuel 49-97'
McFARLAND, James 57-252; John 2-3, 3-5', 21-179, 57-252, 33; Robert 57-252;
Robert Jr & Sr 248
McGARROCK, Hugh 182
McGEE, Captain 62; James 3-6';
John 4-7', 9-18, 12-23, 13-26, 15-29, 27-53, 32-63', 37-73, 39-77, 49-97',
" 51-101, 56-112', 55-109, 21-179, 53-244', 10, 24, 36, 53, 56, 148,
" 156, 278, 301, 307, 409, 439, 449, 457(2), 458
McGOING see McGOWAN
McGOMERY, Hugh 54-246 see MONTGOMERY
McGOAN, McGOWAN, McGOWEN, James 2-4, 30-59, 35-70, 36-72', 37-73, 2-141',
James 19-176, 27, 149, 164, 247, 412, 418, 450; James Jr 1-140
McGOWN, McGOWAN, Jane 426; John 19, 48, 183
McKNIGHT, David 61-259
McLEAN, William 479
McLEROY, John 258
McLESTER, Joseph 160, 453
McMAITH, John 165, 174
McMATH, William 12-161', 358
McMILLEN, Mathew 9-18'
McMILLION, Andrew 103, 259; John 55, 103, 261, 372, 385; Stephen 46-92;
William 115

McMULLIN, Terrance 68-274'
McMURRY, Samuel 248
McNAIR, Ralph 99, 135, 161
McNEEL, Hector 17-171'
McPHERSON, William 26
McQUERY, John 399
McVEY, Edward 34; John 391

NALL, NATT?, Frederick 15-167', 105, 348
NASH, Abner 52, 80, 95, 137, 138, 139, 140, 144, 248, 264, 308, 345, 389,
Abner 406, 425, 470; Edward 37-211', 248;
Francis 25, 52, 53, 56, 57, 62, 63, 74, 93, 123, 143, 144, 156, 194, 223,
" 225, 247, 248, 249, 251, 303, 306, 342, 343, 345, 364, 370, 375,
" 406, 412, 424, 435, 448, 459, 460, 470, 474
NASH & McNAIR, 217, 310, 345, 346, 348, 377, 387, 422, 426, 435, 437, 439,
477, 486, 490
NEAL, NEIL, William 34, 357
NEALEY, William 61-259, 331, 357
NEATHERLY, NETHERY, George 421; James 103, 107, 147, 148
NEBLET, Elizabeth 64-128'; Mary, Tilman 451
NEEDHAM, John 223
NELSON, Abraham 37-212, 305; Alexander 57-251';
David 13-163', 31-199, 355, 407; Henry 378; Margaret 355, 407;
Robert 2-3; Samuel 2-4, 7-14, 15-30, 18-35; Thomas 213, 305, 378, 379;
William 2-4, 21-42, 195
NELSON & KNIGHT 10-157
NEW HOPE CHAPEL 409
NICHOLS, James 27-54, 36-72', 29
NICHOLSON, Benjamin 481; James 36, 377, 422, 439
NOBLES, Thomas 48-95
NOE, NOEY, NOWEY, Caleb 226;
Peter 51-102, 55-109, 5-147, 22-181', 35-207, 40-217', 53-244, 4, 30,
" 52, 169, 223, 300, 311, 357, 407
NORRIS, Daniel 27-53', 30-60', 38-75', 25-189, 58-254, 98, 374, 406;
John 68-274'; Martha 406; Samuel 37-212
NORTH, Thomas 59-256
NORTON, William 221
NORWOOD, Andrew 120, 176, 350
NUGENT, Robert 59
NUNN, William 26-52, 48-96', 51-102, 54-108', 13-164', 32-201, 51-240',
Wm 57-251', 53-244', 60-258', 52, 161, 218, 222A, 224, 249, 258, 261, 274,
" 347, 355, 357, 372, 387, 406, 434, 488, 489

OAKES, Daniel 475; John 33
O'DANIEL, John 47-232; William 47-232
ODEAN, Lewis 47-232
ODENEAL, John 451(2)
OFFIL?, OSSIL?, John 55-110'
OGLE, Hercules 24-185', 50-237', 224
OLDAY, Josias 248
OLDHAM, Jesse 223, 250, 362
OLIVER, John 30, 52, 60, 156, 159, 357, 361, 405, 406, 449, 453, 456, 458,

Orange County boundary line 4-8, 9-18'
Orange County Charter registered 69-137
Orange County Clerks of Court see Clerks
Orange County Courthouse see Courthouse
Orange County "Goal" or Prison 49-98', 50-99, 54-107', 57-114', 58-115, 21-179, 25-187, 26-190, 53-244', 59-255, 60-256, 53, 105, 224, 229, 230, 309, 364, 413, 414, 443, 460
Orange County, Public Registers for, William Churton 2-3, 4-8'; William Reed (Churton's Deputy) 2-3; Edmund Fanning 25
Orange County Standard of Weights & Measures 13-164, bought 42-222, mentioned 53, 305
Orange County Sheriffs see Sheriffs
Orange County to be divided into districts 24-47
Ordinaries see Taverns
OSTEEN, Thomas 35-69 see ASTIN & AUSTIN
OWEN, James 3-5; OWENS, Nathaniel 32-64'; OWINS, Richard 38-75

PAGE, Thomas 48, 184, 200, 267
PAINE, Arthur 39; James 9-18', 38-76'; Joseph 250
PANKEY?, JOHN & CO 380
PARISH, Joseph 203, 366
PARKER, Jonas 53, 148, 150; Joseph Preston 75, 389, Mr. 12-24', 19-38; Miles 2-3, 11-22', 37-74, 50-100; Patrick 216; Peter 50-100;
Richard 5-9', 56-112', 69-138, 23-183, 58-254', 62, 146, 156, 164, 166,
" 225, 227, 229, 231, 247, 248, 251, 305, 323, 410, 441(2), 454,
" 456, 457, 459, 483, 484; Samuel 54, 150; Thomas 33-66, 59-255
PARKS, John 53; Samuel 47-231', 55-247', 59-255, 60-257, 8, 55
PARMOR, George 352
PARR, Arthur 147, 309, 362
PATTERSON, Gilbert 49-97, 49-97', 55-109, 58-115', 37-211; James 128, 366;
John 1-1, 3-5', 4-7, 15-29, 17-34', 19-37, 20-39, 23-45', 23-46, 24-47,
" 27-54, 29-58', 30-60', 35-69, 35-70, 37-73, 46-91, 47-93, 51-101,
" 51-102, 54-107, 55-109, 56-112', 69-138', 12-162, 25-188', 29-196,
" 43-223, 52-241, 31, 35, 36, 53, 54, 101, 156, 220, 227, 357, 364, 410,
" 439, 456, 458, 482, 488, Addenda; Jones ? 430; Joseph 450;
Robert 3-5', 5-9, 21-41', 29-58', 51-101, 63-124, 19-176, 20-177', 29-196',
" 40-217, 49-235, 53-243, 57-251, 57-251', 27, 30, 62, 87, 92, 362,
" 409(2)
PATTON, John 302
PAUL, James 447; Samuel 52-242', 55, 103, 244
PAYNE, John 53; William 358 see PAINE
PEARPONT see PIERPONT
PEARSON, Jacob 447; John 53-244, 56-249', 59-255; Thomas 147
PENDERGRASS, Robert 53-243, 362
PENDRAKE, Nicholas 60, 91, 384 see BUNDRAKE & PUNDRAKE
PENN, Abraham 56; Gabriel 232; William 56
PERKINS, Bathena 187, 197; Nicholas 36-209;
Peter 46-229', 237, 247, 370, 464; Robert 94
PERSONS, William 63-126'
PERVICE?, Thomas 402
PETTY, William 43-226, 62-261', 220; Wm Sr 40-217, 47-231', 59-256, 241
PEVEY, Dyall 37-211'; Joseph 6-150, 12-161 see POVEY

PHILLIPS, Benjamin 25-187, 53-244, 59-255, 60-257', 66-270', 7, 47, 71, 92,
Benj. 170, 183, 215, 314, 317, 383, 408, 409; Charles 54, 247;
David 42-83, 49-97', 6-150, 20, 311, 374; James 54, 423; Jesse 59-255;
John 35-69, 398; Phillip 311; Wm 30-59', 30-197', 243, 311, 352
PHIPPS, Isaiah 1-140
PICKETT, Benjamin 37-212; Micajah 69-138', 7-151', 20-177, 23-183, 25-187,
Micajah 25-188', 85, 98, 122, 179, 271, 381, 417;
William 25-188',43-223, 66-269, 68-273', 14, 166, 243, 264;
Winnifred 20-177, 23-183
PIERCE, John 168; Windsor 223, 360
PIERPONT, Larkin 197, 198, 348
PIGGOTT, Benjamin 47-231; Jeremiah 357, 385, 468
PIKE, John 1-1, 37-211
PILES see PYLE
PILKIN(G)TON, John 203, 366; Richard 218
PINKERTON, David 69-137'
PINSON, Aaron 25-189; Pinson's Ferry 36-209; Pinson's Path 364;
Joseph 2-3', 8-15, 26-52', 35-70', 38-75; Pinson's Settlement 38-213
PITTMAN, James 223;
John 1-2, 2-3, 4-7', 12-24, 19-37, 35-70, 36-71, 37-73, 37-74, 38-75,
" 48-96', 49-97', Addenda; William 93
PITTS, John 61, 100; Young 328
PLEDGER, Thomas 186
POE, James 59-256; Simon Jr 59-256; Stephen 59-256, 220, 408
POLK, Jacob 221; Joseph 480
POMFREY, POMPEY, James 122, 265; John 92 (this is actually POMPHRETT)
POPLEN?, George 150
PORTER, Henry 60-257;
Hugh 29-58, 49-97', 49-98', 55-109, 56-112', 32-202, 46-229', 57-251',
" 223, 250, 362, 378;
Patrick 29, 55, 160, 216, 222, 266, 275, 328, 466, 489;
Susannah 222; William 29-58, 30-59', 52-242', 250, 362
POSEY, Benjamin 45-228, 63-264, 18, 472; Francis 333
POSTEN, Charles 358
POVEY, Benjamin 33-204 see PEVEY
POWELL, Elias 52, 97, 221, 223, 247, 311, 355; James 481;
John 49-97', 21-179, 48-233, 53-244, 59-255, 20, 33, 36, 52, 56, 104, 158,
" 159, 160, 221, 223, 311, 379;
Joseph 50-100, 54-108, 62-122', 2-141', 7-151'
PRATT, Jacob 2-8, 4-7; James 409
PRATOR, PREATHER, Phillip 46-229', 250
PRESTWOOD, ... 52-103;
Thomas 5-9', 7-13, 9-18, 12-23, 17-33', 19-38, 31-61', 37-74, 46-90'
PREWITT, Richard Sr 416 see BREWITT & FRUIT
PRICE, John 157, 361,409(2)
PRIESTHOOD see PRESTWOOD
PRITCHETT, James 106, 250, 263; Joseph 250
PROE?, Paul 49-97
PRYOR, John 4-7', 11-22', 19-37, 21-41', 23-45', 36-61', 37-74, 56-112',
John 61-122', 69-138, 30-198, 57-252, 36, 53, 57, 148, 156, 158, 247(2), 248,
" 409, 441, 454, 457, 459, 460, Addenda; Phillip 39-78', 229;
Robert 37, 148
PUGH, Even 156; Jessee 408; John 156; Thomas 37-212', 408
PULLIAM, Mary, William 161
PUNDRICK, Nicholas 60 see PENDRAKE

PURSLEY, John 223
PYKE see PIKE
PYLE, John 49-98, 5-147, 26, 303, 311

Quakers, persons named as: BROWN, William 246; CHANMESS, Anthony 39-215;
COX, Wm. 9-18'; DAVIS, Charles 37-211; DENNIS, John 2-141';
GREGG, Joshua 19-176'; HOLLINGSWORTH, Valentine 19-38; KEMP, Richard 9-18';
KEYS, Charles 246; LINLEY, James 21-179; MARSHAL, John 39-215;
PYKE, John 37-211; STOUT, Charles 246; TAYLOR, James 23-46, Robert 65-129;
WELLS, Joseph 3-5'. Quaker. Cain Creek Meeting House 25-189
QUINN, QUYNN, Hugh 81, 84, 87, 130, 257, 264, 266, 365

RABORN, RAIBURNE, Thomas 340, 410, 452
RAILEY, RILEY, Jacob 47-232, 443; James 37-73', 38-75, 49-98', 244, 481;
John 51, 58, 419; Rachel 63; William 2-141'.
RAINEY, RANEY, Isaac 179; Ann 447; James 15-30', 447;
John 56-112', 19-175, 20-178'; Robert 56-112', 57-113, 31-199;
Thomas 2-141', 30-198', 31-199, 78, 178;
William 59-255, 158, 355, 460
RAMAGE, James 93
RAMBO, Lawrence 1-1, 3-5', 19-38, 21-41', 19-176, 32-201, 232, 248, 274,
Lawrence 414, 450; Lawrence Jr 414; Ruth 414
RAMSEY, Isaac 255; John 103, 450
RAN, Phebe 53-105'
RANKIN, William 31, 54
RAY, REA, Christmas 209, 246; Christopher 325; David 479;
James 21-41', 69-137', 25-188', 32-201, 39-216'; Robert 166, 222;
William 222A, 360
REAM, Mary, Peter 249
REAVES, George 47-231';
William 2-3, 5-9, 19-38, 27-53, 31-62, 20-177, 25-188', 39-215', 41-220',
" 88, 101; William Jr 39-216
REDMAN, REDMOND, Lawrence 54-108', 39-216'; Mary 330, 341, 343
REED, Andrew Corbin 60-120', 460; Clement 41-82, 141;
Elizabeth 4-7, 9-18', 20-39, 25-50; Joseph 456, 490; Nathaniel 35-69, 49-97;
Owen 158, 186, 273, 326, 364; Robert 15-30, 132, 310;
William 2-3, 3-5', 4-7, 18-34, 24-47, 25-50, 35-70', 36-72, 43-85, 50-99,
" 51-102, 56-112', 57-113, 57-114', 59-117, 64-127', 66-131, 15-168,
" 16-169', 21-179, 26-190, 34-306, 35-207, 38-213, 39-215, 39-215',
" 53-244, 57-252, 59-255, 59-256, 146, 225, 250, 305, 340, 454, 456,
" 460; William Jr 59-255'
Registers for Orange County; William Churton 2-3, 27-53;
Edmund Fanning 25; William Reed, deputy 2-3
REVES see REAVES
REYNARD, Albright 224
REYNOLDS, Dudley 17-33', 29;
Henry 7-14, 21-41, 33-65, 37-73, 38-75, 48-96', 49-97', 55-109, 46-229',
" 29, 133, 244, 426; Henry Jr 56-250; Nathaniel 46-229', 222A;
Sherrod 39-215', 40-219, 55-247, 436; William 3-6', 127 see RUNNOLDS

SIMMON?, Henry 86 see LEMON
SIMPSON, Richard 41-82', 59-118', 61-122, 61-122', 2-141', 46-229, 66-271, 43,
Richard 100, 156, 223, 250, 301, 362, 363, 406, 441, 457(2), 458
SIMS, John 57-114'
SINCLER?, SINKLIN, Ann, Charles 453
SISSON, William 98
SITTON, John 399
SIZEMORE, Ephriam 10-20
SLATER, Henry 46-229';
John 34-68', 51-102, 57-114', 66-121, 3-143', 5-148', 8-154', 33-204',
" 34-206, 36-209', 41-220', 57-251', 58-254, 104, 238
SLOSS, Hugh 56; Joseph 223, 372, 410, 466
SMITH, ... 59-118'; Ambrose 25-189; Ann 414; Christopher 162, 407, 453;
Daniel 33, 244, 446, 473; Edward 53-244, 53-244', 221, 245;
George 38-75, 45-90, 69-137, 28-173, 37-212', 28, 392; Henry 223;
Hugh 26-51', 36-71, 38-75, 50-100', 51-101, 56-111, 6-119, 62-122',
" 67-134, 69-137, 69-137', 3-144', 15-168', 19-176, 25-189, 33-204,
" 39-216', 43-225', 46-229', 50-237, 54-246', 55-248', 59-256', 62-261',
" 27, 64, 119, 149, 174, 204, 337, 340, 371, 385, 386, 417, 460,
" 480, 482(2), 484, 485, 486; Jacob 25-189;
John 57-112, 36-209, 8, 52, 138, 175, 163, 376; Joshua Ambrose 38-254',
Joshua Ambrose 39-216, 42-222; Luke 11; Richard 29, 157, Robert 433;
Samuel 157, 203; Thomas 5-10; William 55
SNOW, "Captain", a Catawba Indian 50-100
SOOTEN?, Joseph 16-31' see SUTTON
SORRELL, SOWELL, Edward 55, 394; Samuel 5-9', 20-39' see TOWEL
SOUTHERLAND, Mordecai 172, 303, 333
SOUTHWEL, Edward 24-47', 59-118'
SOWELL, John 150
SPANN, John 39-216, 69-276'
SPRATT, James 16-170', 21-179, 58-253
SPENCE, SPENCER, Alex 40-219, 59-256; William 40-219, 59-256
SPINKS, Enoch 156, 159, 166, 227, 229, 360, 454
SPOON, Peter 63
SPRADLING, John 74, 153; Thomas 82
SPRINGER, John 432; John Jr 221
SPRUCE, William 28-193'
SPRUGG, Richard 110
STABLER, John 2-142
STAFFORD, Mary 58-254
STAGG, Mrs. Judy 26;
Thomas 6-150', 23-183', 32-201, 39-215', 39-216', 40-220, 41-220', 41-221,
" 41-221', 46-229', 53-243, 56-250, 57
Standard Keepers; William Reed, 4-8, 39-215; James Cummings 53
Standards, set of, purchased, 13-164, 42-222
STANFIELD, Hannah 37-211; John 24-86, 37-211
STANDFORD, Anthony 37-73, 58-254
STANLEY, George 444; Zachariah 490
STANTON, Thomas 453
STAPTOE?, STAPLER?, David 1-1', 3-5'; Edward 352
STARRAT, James 250, 362
STATES, Abraham 369
STATON?, John 410

STEEL, Anthony 238; Charles 11-21;
David 2-4, 8-15, 37-73, 62-122', 63-125', 32-201, 213, 300, 309;
John 55-110', 64-127'
STEPHENS, STEVENS, Charles 46-230, 160, 213, 327;
David 54-107, 29, 117, 462; William 61-259, 112, 117, 253, 462
STEWART, STUART, James 37-74, 38-75', 49-97', 69-137, 32-201;
John 39-216', 40-217, 59-256, 452; Joseph 274, 376, 410, 452
STEWART'S Road 245;
Samuel 69-137', 9-155', 16-169', 20-177', 38-213, 51-240, 53-253', 85, 95,
" 150, 451
STILWEL, Danel 8-15
STING, Michael 413
Stocks, Pillory & Whipping post to be built, 54-107'
STOKES, Silvester, Silvester Jr 248; William 142, 275, 424, 432
STOKES & WADE 433
STONE, Edward 25-49, 36-72, 65-129, 25-188', 39-216', 43-223, 57-251', 31;
Prichett 69-275'
STOUT, Charles 246
STOVAL, George 56
STRADER, Conrod 195
STRAHAN, STRAYHAM, Bendal 16-170', 34-205'
STRANGE, Charles 223
STRATTON, Mary 23-183
STRAYHORN, Richard 123
STREAN, STRAYHORN, Gilbert 37-73, 54-108', 62-122', 2-141, 31-199, 38-213,
Gilbert 46-230, 46-230', 56-249, 59-255', 27, 37, 53, 244, 305, 409;
Thomas 37-73, 48-234
STREET, Anthony 335
STRINGFIELD, James 47-231'
STRIPLAND, STRIPLEN, Thomas 53, 229; Stripland's Path 148, 150, 229
STROTHER, Anthony 63-124
STROUD, David 61; Elizabeth 65-130'; James 58-253;
John 52-242', 11, 48, 56, 183, 210, 244, 300, 306; John Jr 327;
John Sr 59-255', 60-258', 151; Joshua 38-75, 56-249', 69-276, 19-358;
Justice 65-130'; Oliver 4-146', 26-190;
William 51-103, 58-116', 65-130', 36-210, 224, 464;
Wm Jr 58-253, 161, 360,; Wm Sr 2, 32
STUART see STEWART
STUBBLEFIELD, Bynum 323; John 2-142'; Mary 100;
Robert 69-138, 76; Syth 117; Wyatt 116, 198, 271
STUBBS, John 57-114', 61-259, 1, 11, 230; Thomas 5-148', 245, 446
SULLIVANT, SWILLIVANT, Daniel 47-232, 238; Dennis 14-166;
John 201, 219, 324; Michael 372, 466; Thomas 49-97'
SUMMERS, Jacob 60-119
SUTHERLAND see SOUTHERLAND
SUTTON, Joseph 43-225, 50-237', 61-260, 58; Phillip, Thomas 50-238
SWAFFER, SWAFORD, SWAFORT, James 2-3, 5-9, 36-72', 38-75'
SWEETEN, Edward 136
SWIFT, Flower 249, 450
SYNNOT, ... 52-103; Captain 25-189,
Michael 4-8', 5-10, 11-22', 16-32', 18-34, 27-54, 29-57, 30-59, 36-71',
" 46-92', 46-93', 50-100, 54-107', 54-108, 67-134', 14-165, 34, 348,
" 350, 461; SYNNOT'S Road 364

TABB, Thomas 76; William 90, 415
TABOR, John 53, 91, 161, 248, 415; John Sr. 10-57, 74
TALBERT, James 446; John 51
TALLY, John 363
TAPLEY, Hosea 2-3, 3-5, 5-9, 11-22', 17-33', 42-83', 42-84, 47-94,
Hosea 52-104, 53-105, 54-107, 58-116, 63-124', 67-133, 9-156'', 15-167,
" 53-244, 56-250', 42, 54, 120, 163, 215, 230, 269, 319, 432;
Hosea Jr 477; Sarah 3-5
TATE, George 300; James 452;
Joseph 1-1, 2-3, 3-5', 31-61', 35-70', 452, Addenda;
Robert 2-3', 2-4, 8-15, 69-137', 58-254, 452 (2), 459
Taverns & Ordinaries 2-3'(3), 2-4, 3-6, 11-22(2), 13-25', 14-27, 14-28',
15-29((2), 18-35, 19-38, 20-39'(2), 21-42, 21-43, 24-47, 26-52(3),
27-53', 30-60, 45-90, 46-91(2), 47-94', 48-95, 57-113, 59-117', 59-118,
59-118'(2), 61-121', 61-122', 64-128', 65-129(3), 66-131, 69-137'(3),
5-147, 7-152', 11-159', 13-164', 15-168, 15-168', 16-169', 20-177', 21-179',
30-198(3), 32-201, 32-201', 35-207, 37-212, 38-213(2), 40-217(2),
41-221, 41-221', 42-222, 46-229', 46-230', 25, 27(2), 31(2), 34, 52, 56(4),
57, 63(2), 99, 101(2), 103, 104, 149, 150, 151, 161(2), 163, 164, 222, 223,
247(3), 249, 251, 278, 300, rates listed 304, 357(3), 359, 444, 445, 447,
448, 449, 452, 453, 458, 461(4)
TAYLOR, Hope 340; Hugh 53-106'; Isaac 234;
James 5-9, 9-18', 23-46, 30-60, 54-107, 61-121', 62-122', 62-123, 65-129',
" 1-140, 10-157', 158, 446, 461; John 5-9, 57-251', 36; Phillip 333;
Robert 1-1, 65-129', 69-138', 53-243, 57-251', 58-254, 46, 160, 273;
William 3-5, 34-205'; TAYLOR'S Road 38-75', 49-97', 40-217, 47-232
TEAGUE, Edward 25; Elisha 15; Moses 27; William 450
TEMPLE, Henry 40-218; TEMPLES, Samuel 61-122, 41-200', 98, 246
TERRELL, James 240, 335, 340; Judith 210, 326, 327; Mary 303, 453;
Solomon 451;
Timothy 1-1, 4-7, 7-14, 15-30, 18-35, 26-52', 35-70, 3-144, 18-174, 24-185',
" 44, 303, 353 see TYRRELL
TERRY, Garland 31; James 2, 3, 156, 160, 253, 306, 449, 461;
Peter 173, 216, 269; Stephen 46-230, 30, 244
TETSWORTH, Thomas 46-229'
THARP(E), Allen 54; Benjamin 54; Benjamin Allen 347, 429; John Allen 441
THETFORD, Isaah 54; Walter 54
THOMAS, James 450; John 103, 147, 261, 360, 372; John Jr 360;
John Giles 4, 84, 264; William 157
THOMPSON, Baswell 204, 268, 275, 467; Benjamin 341; Edward 13-26;
James 20-177, 60-257; John 53, 147, 175, 381, 406;
Lawrence 4-7', 4-8', 12-24, 15-29', 15-30', 19-37, 20-39, 21-41', 24-47,
" 49-97', 51-102, 54-107, 54-107', 56-112', 4-146', 28, 36, 55, 156,
" 158, 163, 220, 245, 406, 439, 449(2), 458, Addenda;
Robert 2-3, 41, 97, 239, 254, 360, 432;
Thomas 36-72', 38-75', 69-137', 19-176, 30-188, 27, 53, 202;
William 30-59, 46-230', 98, 146, 262, 336, 409, 416, 451
THRASHER, John 40-217, 8, 100, 312; Joseph 36-209, 309
THROWER, William 229
TILLEFEARRS?, John 139
TILLETT, Giles 8-15, 11-21, 13-26, 16-32, 26-52, 35-70'
TINDEN?, Thomas 65-130

TINNEN, TINNING, Cairnes 1-1, 2-3, 14-27, 21-41', 51-101, 58-116, 68-135,
Cairnes 69-137', 1-140, 30-198, 37-212, 53-243, 60, 149, 163; Hugh 451;
James 37-73, 57-252', 100, 159, 224;
John 1-1, 2-3, 21-41, 61-121', 1-140', 2-141, 2-142, 32-201', 57-251',
" 158, 160; Robert 32, 149, 210, 224, 326
TINSLEY, James 55, 103
TODD, William 486
TOLLOCK, Vincent 457
TOMLIN, John 247, 260
TOMLINSON, John 38-75', 50-99', 37-212
TONY?, Timothy 248
TORINGTINE (TURPENTINE), Alexander 40-219, 59-256, 221; Samuel 149
TORRINGTON, Mary, Sarah 10-20
TOWER HILL 25-188'
"Town laid out on the Enoe", Commissioners for, 24-47; road in 230;
Trustees for 24-47; see Childsburg, Corbintown & Hillsborough.
TRAMMEL, John 224
TRAP, John 147, 150
TRAVIS, William 14-28', 20-40', 27-54
TRICE, Edward 30-198', 55;
James 30-198', 41-220', 43-223, 55, 63, 127, 244, 254, 394;
John 30-198', 55, 58; Thomas 305 see PRICE
TIRCKEY?, TUCKEY?, Giles 248
TRIP, Nicholas 407
TROCKS, Barnett 355 see TROXLER
TROLLINGER, Adam 54-108', 62-122', 59-255, 358; Edward 451;
Henry 27-192, 59-255, 372, 455; Michael 37-121'; TROLLINGER'S Ferry 58-254,
Ferry 59-255
TROTTER, Joseph 63-264', 64, 437
TROUSDALE, Barnett 46-229'; John 452
TROXLER, Barnett 52 see TROCKS
TUCKER, Thomas 40-217, 47-231'; William 59-256; TUCKER'S Road 53-243
TUMBLESTON, Rachel 100
TURNBULL, Charles 8-153
TURNER, Venerius 138, 222A
TURRENTIBE see TORRINGTINE
TYASS, Rich'd 85; TYERS, Richard 218, 262 see BYASS
TYLER, Absolom 484
TYRIE, Christian 67-133'; Edward 42-222
TYRRELL see TERRELL
"Tythables", (1113 in 1752-1753) 24-47; (list of 27) 37-73

UNDERHILL, Elizabeth 18-174; Mr 2-3, 3-5
UNDERWOOD, Alexander 246
URSURY, William 87, 92, 161, 213, 249, 327, 331, 420, 490
UTLEY, Thomas 5-9

VANAL?, William 5-10
VANDERGRAFT, Christopher 118, 135, 163
VANHOOK, ...37-74, Aaron 30-60, 38-75', 18-173', 19-176, 39-215', 41-221',
Aaron 47-231; Catherine 39-215', 41-221'; David 42-222, 53, 54;
Executors 170;
Lawrence 2-241, 21-180, 21-180, 27-191', 47-231, 58, 409; Lucy 39-215', 39-21
Samuel 206, 408, 449

WEBB, Con't. James 16-32', 60-258, 66-270', 68-273, 64, 79, 108; John 23-183';
Richard 22-43, 243; Thomas 20-177', 59, 63, 85, 101, 131, 253, 312, 410;
Wentworth 23-183'; William 70-277'
WEBSTER, Charles 59-256; John 59-256, 347, 434, 386; Thomas 101; Wm 70-277', 3
WELDON, ... 35-70, 53-105', 69-136;
Daniel 12-23, 24-48', 45-90, 60-120, 10-157, 10-157', 57-251';
David 451; Martha, Mary 451; Adm's 483
WELLS, Joseph 1-1, 3-5', 119, 302, 417; Joseph Jr 246;
Robert 40-217, 53-243', 56, 223, 247, 362
WELSH, Henry 407, 453; Jamey 34-205'
WEST, Alexander 8-15, 223; Hugh 26-52; Jacob 19-175';
John 4-7', 8-15, 21-42, 25-188', 100, 362; John Jr 47-232, 52-242';
John Sr 3-5', 35-70, 36-71, 51-101, 55-109', 54,
Solomon 47-232, 52-242', 54, 100, 362, 452
WHALER?, WHEALER, John 58, 220
WHEELER, Dennis 52-241'
Whipping post 54-107', 228, 457, 459, 461, etc
WHITE, Ann 51-102; Gabriel 393, 476;
John 5-9, 11-22', 21-41', 23-45', 36-72, 38-75', 45-90, 49-97', 51-102,
" 54-108, 10-158, 14-166, 28-194, 43-225, 50-237', 54-246', 61-260',
" 188, 227; Michael 427; William 64-128', 226, 228
WHITEHEAD, Amos 6, 47, 128, 183, 379; Benjamin 230, Jacob 58;
Reason 186, 226; Thomas 19-176, 38-213'; 47; Thomas Jr 131
WHITFILLS?, Henry 30-197
WHITHERSWORTH see WHITWORTH
WHITMAN, John 30
WHITSETTS, Henry 48-233'
WHITTER?, Isaac 66-269'
WHITTON, George 116, 451; Nathan 400; Robert 76; Thomas 33, 385, 414
WHITWORTH, Abraham 3-5', 5-9, 13-26'
WHORTON, William 176, 241 see HORTON
WIERMAN see WIREMAN
WILBOURN, Edward 20-177', 221; William 160, 414; William Jr 221
WILESTON, James 388
WILEY, ... 16; John 147, 221A; Robert 37-73', 38-75', 49-97, 2-142, 162;
Thomas 48-95, 51-102, 7-152, 53-244', 46, 67, 94, 122, 168, 456;
William 49-98, 51-102, 54-108, 55-109, 60-120, 68-136', 41-220', 51-239,
" 30, 52, 147, 181, 207, 352, 357, 362, 456; William Sr 51-102
WILKERSON, James 15-30', 8-153; Thomas 41-81
WILKINSON, Francis 47-232, 57-251', 58-254, 59-255, 149;
James 15-30', 32-201, 53, 451;
Thomas 14-27, 26-52, 30-60, 38-75, 38-75', 40-79
WILLIAMS, ... 356; Benjamin 12-23, 19-176, 67-271; Burwell 363, 430;
Edward 37-74, 19-176, 30-197, 48-234; Elizabeth 47-94; George 98;
James 5-9', 12-23, 19-37, 25-189, 37-212, 67-271;
John 1-2', 15-29', 46-93', 58-116', 16-170', 208, 218, 232, 250, 262,
" 340, 342, 351, 367, 374, 403, 455, 468, 477; John Jr 260, 487;
Jonathan 38-75'; Mary 38-75', 46-93', 48-96', 49-98, 58-116';
Mathew 221A; Phillip 260; Ralph 53, 359, 444; Robert 199;
Sampson 33-204, 40-218, 47-231', 47-232'; Samuel 35-69, 221A;
Thomas 23-45', 46-92, 62-123', 66-132, 4-145, 19-176, 197; Webster 79;
William 5-10, orphans of 46-93', 47-94, 48-95, 49-98', 58-116', 67-133,
" 13-163, 19-176, 30-198, 43-223, 179, 206, 207

WILLIAMSON, John 223
WILLIARD, John 240, 309, 340, 349
WILLICE, Henry 248, 275, 432; Price 358
WILLICE or WILLIS, William 66-269, 160, 358, 405
WILLIS, John 147
WILLOCK, Joseph 57-113
WILSON, Henry 149; Michael 272, 424; Peter 7-13', 13-26',
Thomas 37-211', 46-229, 57-252, 408; Thomas Jr 57-252, 86, 118;
Thomas Sr 51, 58, 408; Wm 8-15, 16-32, 3-143, 10-157', 46-229', 27
WIMBUSH, JOHN & CO, 118, 365, 383, 470
WINBERRY, Thomas 352
WINCHESTER, Thomas 21-180'
WINFIELD, Lawrence 53-105', 56-111'
WINTER, Daniel 407; Moses 28-193
WIREMAN, William 39-216, 224
WITHER & CO. 383
WITHROW, Jacob 100
WITTIE, WITTY, Joshua 224; Robert 9, 175, 409, 418
WOLF, Edward 63
WOMACK, Abraham 57-252; Jacob 57-252, 27, 151, 221, 248, 401, 403;
Richard 57-252, 23, 44, 113
WOOD, WOODS, Elizabeth 159, 408;
Hugh 11-22', 12-24, 19-38, 61-122', 19-176, 39-216, 39-216', 46-229, 55;
James 63-125, 9-156', 159, 408;
John 13-25, 24-48, 49-98, 53-105', 60-120', 21-179, 25-188', 33-203',
" 35-208, 41-220', 60-257', 67-272, 101, 103, 160, 167, 229, 244,
" 253, 363, 444, 447, 457; John Sr 309;
Mathew 49-97, 65-129, 30-198;
Richard 16-169', 31-199, 36, 360, 409; Zachariah 40-79', 41-81, 21, 79
WOODIE, WOODY, John 30-198', 31-199, 98, 160, 164, 221A;
Robert 25, 26, 27, 98, 160, 164
WOOTER?, George 225
WRIGHT, Francis 57-252, 33; James 13-163';
John 27-53, 30-60', 37-74', 48-96', 55-109, 22-181, 25-189, 33-204', 49-97',
" 52-242', 55-248, 56-249', 57-252, 21, 226; Micajah 60-257';
Richard 408
WRIGHTSMAN, John 59-255'
WYATT, John 323

YANCEY, James 110
YARBOROUGH, Samuel 148, 150; William 47-231', 23, 44
YORK, Henry 221; James 29, 470; John 445; Joseph 408;
Semore 39-215', 52-242', 27, 45, 221
YOUNG, Alex 11-21, 41-221, 46-229'; Edward 306; see GOING
James & Co. 207, 215, 242, 324, 336, 349, 376, 386, 396, 400, 402,
" " " 438, 475, 477; William 21-42
YOUNGBLOOD, Peter 12-23, 25-189, 53-243', 53-245;
Magdelene 53-245; Sarah 12-23

GEOGRAPHICAL INFORMATION

Boundaries Mentioned:

Cumberland County line 98, 146, 224;
Granville County line 57-252, 97, 248, 359;
Johnston County line 43-223, 47-231', 55;
Rowan County line 35, 221, 224, 244; Virginia line 49-97

Localities Mentioned:

Bush Camp 29; Hawfields 3-5', 15-29, 18-34', 54-108', 65-129, 69-137';
Old fields 149; Pinson's Settlement 38-213; Red fields 58-253, 163, 362, 409;
Runnolds Cabins 29, 360; Stinking Quarter 37-212, 29

Roads Mentioned:

ALLISON'S 362; BOYD'S 54-108'; BUFFALO 12-162';COLLIN'S 104; COX'S 450;
CAPE FEAR ROAD 31-102, 54-107, 54-108, 31-290, 37-212, 26, 29, 31, 35,
" " " 55, 221, 224, 362, 407; JOHN CUNNINGHAM'S 36-209;
FINLEY'S 362; FRAZIER'S 223; GREAT 37-211', 57-251'; HARMON HUSBAND'S
146, 407, 408, 453; HART'S 29, 223; LINDLEY'S 223; LOWE'S 410;
LOWER TOWN ROAD 58; OLD (CAPE FEAR?) 150; ORANGE NEW 21-41;
PINSON'S PATH 364; STRIPLAND'S PATH 53, 147, 150, 229; SYNNOT'S ROAD 364;
TARBOROUGH ROAD 97, 360; TAYLOR'S 49-97', 40-217, 47-232;
TRADING PATH 1-2', 3-5', 14-27', 21-41, 36-71', 38-75', 25-189, 363, 410;
TUCKER'S ROAD 53-243; WESTERN PATH 1-2', 4-7, 26-52, 49-98, 60-119, 31-199;
WOODY'S ROAD 35, 224

Watercourses:

Creeks: ARON'S 35; ADAM'S 36-72'; ALAMANCE 358; GREAT ALAMANCE 54-108',
40-217', 355; ALAMANCHY "RIVER" 300; BEAR 37-212, 98, 146, 452, 453;
BEAVER 35; BOLING'S 98; BUSH 35; CAIN 25-189, 37-212, 35, 357;
CAMP 37-73', 37-74; COUNTY LINE 21-41, 27-54, 37-73', 60-119', 2-142',
C. LINE, Cont. 22-182', 41-221', 47-232, 53-244', 54, 58, 147, 150, 229, 450;
CRABTREE 363; CROSS 223, 224; DEEP 54, 359; FLAT 146; GIBSON'S 97;
GREAT 54-244'; HENDERSON'S 35-207;
HICO 1-2', 19-38, 36-71, 49-98, 54-108', 53-244', 30, 54, 244, 248;
HOGAN'S 47-32, 60-199', 69-138, 30-198, 41-221', 47-232, 55, 249;
HOSLEY'S ? 310; LICK 37-212; LITTLE 52; LITTLE BARTON'S 39-215'
LITTLE TROUBLESOME 36-72'; LOWE'S 146, 453; MABRY FORK of CAIN 35;
MARLOW'S 36-71, 16-170; MORGAN'S 53-243, 53; NAPPER REEDS 54;
NEW HOPE 1-2', 36-71, 37-74, 2-142, 31-290', 35, 58, 61, 157, 305, 311;
RICH 28; RICHLAND (or RICHARD?) 224; ROBINSON'S 452;
SANDY 22-182, 47-231, 146, 220, 244, 450; SLATER'S BRANCH 410; STAGG'S 59-255;
TERRELL'S 37-212, 26; WHITE OAK 57-251', 59-255'; WOLF ISLAND 245, 249;

Rivers:

CAPE FEAR 18-34', 36-71, 36-71', 36-72, 49-97, 49-98, 4-146', 40-217, 47-231,
" " 57-251, 362, 450; DAN 15-29, 27-54, 36-209, 52, 249, 250;
DEEP 2-4, 27-54, 32-201, 37-313, 40-217, 35, 146, 224, 452;
ENOE 19-38, 26-52, 36-71', 36-72, 49-97', 2-142, 25-189, 53-244', 63, 405, 450;
FLATT 15-30, 36-72, 6-150', 29, 54, 452;
HAW 1-2, 1-2', 2-4, 3-5', 4-7, 12-27', 26-52, 36-71, 38-75, 48-96', 49-97, 49-9
" 54-108, 69-137', 16-169, 25-189, 25-189', 26-190, 30-197', 31-199, 32-201,
" 37-212, 40-217, 40-217', 47-231', 53-243, 58-253', 58-254, 59-255, 31, 35,
" 61, 149, 150, 163, 223, 225, 250, 300, 361, 363, 409,

Rivers continued -
(FORDS ON HAW RIVER: BREWER'S 361; ISLAND 29; PINE (Y) 1-2, 35-207, 37-212', 58-255; TRADING PATH 58; TROLLINGER'S 250;)
REEDY FORK OF HAW 311; LITTLE 11-22', 15-30, 54-108,361, 362;
NEUSE 1-2', 2-142; PEEDEE, warehouse on 25-189;
ROCKY 2-4, 27-54, 48-96', 49-98, 37-212, 26, 246, 356, 363;
YADKIN RIVER 35-70'

www.ingramcontent.com/pod-product-compliance
Lightning Source LLC
Chambersburg PA
CBHW021906020426
42334CB00013B/508
9780893084561